D1116678

THE NEW CLARENDON BIBLE
(NEW TESTAMENT)

General Editor; THE REVD. H. F. D. SPARKS, D.D., F.B.A.

———

THE GOSPEL ACCORDING TO
MATTHEW

THE GOSPEL ACCORDING TO
MATTHEW

IN THE
REVISED STANDARD VERSION

Introduction and commentary

by

H. BENEDICT GREEN, C.R., M.A.

PRINCIPAL,
COLLEGE OF THE RESURRECTION, MIRFIELD
AND ASSOCIATE LECTURER IN THEOLOGY
UNIVERSITY OF LEEDS

OXFORD
UNIVERSITY
PRESS
1975

Oxford University Press, Ely House, London W.1

GLASGOW NEW YORK TORONTO MELBOURNE WELLINGTON
CAPE TOWN IBADAN NAIROBI DAR ES SALAAM LUSAKA ADDIS ABABA
DELHI BOMBAY CALCUTTA MADRAS KARACHIE LAHORE DACCA
KUALA LUMPUR SINGAPORE HONG KONG TOKYO

PRINTED IN GREAT BRITAIN BY OFFSET LITHOGRAPHY BY
BILLING & SONS LIMITED,
GUILDFORD AND LONDON

GENERAL EDITOR'S PREFACE

THIS volume replaces the old Clarendon Bible *Saint Matthew*, based on the Revised Version, which was edited by the late Canon F. W. Green (my tutor while reading the Hanover School of Theology at Oxford) and first published in 1936. It has set out to embody the developments in scholarship which have taken place since then. In level and purpose this volume follows its predecessor, but in common with the present general policy of the series it is based on the Revised Standard Version.

The design of the new volume follows that of the old, except that it has been decided to omit the biblical text, partly in the interests of economy, and partly in order to tie the notes less closely to the RSV and facilitate cross-reference to other versions. Subjects requiring more comprehensive treatment than the scope of the notes allows will be found as before in the Introduction and in appendixes at the end of the volume.

H. F. D. S.

AUTHOR'S NOTE

THERE is a special continuity between this commentary and its predecessor in the original *Clarendon Bible*, in that the authors were father and son. Frederick Wastie Green (1884–1953) was my earliest theological mentor, and his *St Matthew* (1936) my first introduction to gospel studies. That the progress of these since he wrote has made it necessary not simply to revise but to replace his work would have come as no surprise to him. To rewrite it for the new series has been nevertheless, in the fullest sense, a labour of love.

I am grateful to the General Editor of the series, the Rev. Dr H. F. D. Sparks, and to the staff of the Oxford University Press both for their patience over the long delay in the preparation of the book and for their critical comments on the original draft; Dr Sparks in particular saved me from a number of follies. Fr Denys Lloyd, C.R., and the Rev. Michael Pratt also read sections of the typescript and made useful suggestions. The responsibility for any remaining errors is of course my own. Mrs Ruth McCurry has relieved me of the onerous task of making the index. All this assistance is gratefully acknowledged. Finally I would thank my own community for the leave of absence without which the first draft of the book could not have been finished, and the Dominicans of Blackfriars, Oxford, whose hospitality was at once a support and a stimulus to its completion.

H. B. G.

CONTENTS

ABBREVIATIONS

BIBLICAL

AV	Authorized (King James) Version
RV	Revised Version
RSV	Revised Standard Version
RSVCE	RSV, Catholic Edition
NEB	New English Bible
mg	margin
NT	New Testament
OT	Old Testament
LXX	Septuagint (the ancient Greek version of the OT)
Gk	Greek
Heb.	Hebrew
Mt Mk Lk Jn	Matthew Mark Luke John (used of the gospels and their authors indiscriminately)

ANCIENT AUTHORITIES (ET=English translation)

Danby	H. DANBY (ed.), *The Mishnah* (Oxford, 1933).
Did.	*Didache* (*Teaching of the Twelve Apostles*); ET in *Early Christian Writings*, Penguin Classics (Harmondsworth, 1968).
DSS	Dead Sea Scrolls
CD	The Damascus Rule
1 QM	The War Rule
1 QpHab	The Habakkuk Commentary
1 QS	The Community Rule
V	G. VERMES, *The Dead Sea Scrolls in English*, Pelican Books (Harmondsworth, 1968).

Jos.	Josephus; complete edition and ET by H. St. J. Thackeray and others, Loeb Classics (London, 1956–65)
Ant.	*Antiquities*
BJ	*The Jewish War*; ET also in Penguin Classics (Harmondsworth, 1970)
NTAp i	E. HENNECKE, W. SCHNEEMELCHER, R. McL. WILSON (eds.), *New Testament Apocrypha*, vol. i (ET London, 1963).
Thomas	*The Gospel of Thomas*; ib., pp. 178ff.

MODERN AUTHORITIES

Black, *AA*	M. BLACK, *An Aramaic Approach to the Synoptic Gospels and Acts*³ (Oxford, 1967).
Bultmann, *HST*	R. BULTMANN, *History of the Synoptic Tradition* (ET Oxford, 1963).
Daube, *NTRJ*	D. DAUBE, *The New Testament and Rabbinic Judaism* (London, 1956)
Davies, *COJ*	W. D. DAVIES, *Christian Origins and Judaism* (London, 1962)
SSM	*The Setting of the Sermon on the Mount* (Cambridge, 1963)
Derrett, *LNT*	J. D. M. DERRETT, *Law in the New Testament* (London, 1970)
Gerhardsson, *Testing*	B. GERHARDSSON, *The Testing of God's Son* (Lund, 1966)
Gundry, *Use*	R. H. GUNDRY, *The Use of the Old Testament in St. Matthew's Gospel* (Leiden, 1967)
Hare, *JPC*	*D. R. A. HARE, *The Theme of Jewish Persecution of Christians in the Gospel according to St. Matthew*, SNTS Monographs Series, no. 6 (Cambridge, 1967)

Jeremias, *EWJ*	J. JEREMIAS, *The Eucharistic Words of Jesus* (ET² London, 1966).
PJ	*The Parables of Jesus* (ET² London, 1963)
PrJ	*The Prayers of Jesus* (ET London, 1967)
Kilpatrick, *Origins*	*G. D. KILPATRICK, *The Origins of the Gospel according to Saint Matthew* (Oxford, 1947)
Lindars, *NTA*	B. LINDARS, *New Testament Apologetic* (London, 1961)
Linnemann, *Parables*	E. LINNEMANN, *Parables of Jesus* (ET London, 1966)
Manson, *SJ*	T. W. MANSON, *The Sayings of Jesus* (London, 1949)
Nineham, *Mark*	D. E. NINEHAM, *The Gospel of St. Mark*, Pelican Gospel Commentaries (Harmondsworth, 1962)
NTS	*New Testament Studies*
SNT	K. STENDAHL (ed.), *The Scrolls and the New Testament* (London, 1958)
Stendahl, *School*	*K. STENDAHL, *The School of St. Matthew*² (Philadelphia, 1968)
TDNT	G. KITTEL (ed.), *Theological Dictionary of the New Testament*; ET by G. W. Bromiley (Grand Rapids, Michigan, 1963–74
TIM	*G. BORNKAMM, G. BARTH, H. J. HELD, *Tradition and Interpretation in Matthew* (ET London, 1963)

LITERATURE ON THE GOSPEL OF MATTHEW

(A) COMMENTARIES

On the Greek Text:

A. H. McNeile, *The Gospel according to St. Matthew* (London, 1915)

On the English Text:

S. E. Johnson, *The Gospel according to St. Matthew*, Interpreter's Bible (New York, 1951)

F. V. Filson, *The Gospel according to St. Matthew*, Black's NT Commentaries (London, 1960)

J. C. Fenton, *The Gospel of St. Matthew*, Pelican Gospel Commentaries (Harmondsworth, 1963)

D. Hill, *The Gospel of Matthew*, New Century Bible (London, 1971)

See also the shorter commentaries of K. Stendahl in *Peake's Commentary on the Bible* (London, 1962) and J. L. McKenzie in *The Jerome Bible Commentary* (New York, 1970)

In French:

P. Bonnard, *L'évangile selon saint Matthieu* (Neuchâtel, 1963)

B. Rigaux, *Témoignage de l'évangile de Matthieu* (Bruges–Paris, 1967)

In German:

J. Schniewind, *Das Evangelium nach Matthäus* (Göttingen, ⁷1956)

E. Lohmeyer and W. Schmauch, *Das Evangelium des Matthäus* (Göttingen, 1956)

W. Grundmann, *Das Evangelium nach Matthäus* (Berlin, 9168)

(b) OTHER STUDIES

The major works on Mt current in English are those marked with an asterisk * in the list of Abbreviations (pp. xi–xii).

Those who read German may also consult:

W. TRILLING, *Das wahre Israel* (Munich, 1964)
G. STRECKER, *Der Weg der Gerechtigkeit* (Göttingen, 1962)
R. HUMMEL, *Die Auseinandersetzung zwischen Kirche und Judentum im Matthäusevangelium* (Munich, 1963)

Summaries of these books will be found in J. ROHDE, *Rediscovering the Teaching of the Evangelists* (ET London, 1968).

The important book by M. D. Goulder, *Midrash and Lection in Matthew* (London, 1974) appeared too late for account to be taken of it in this commentary.

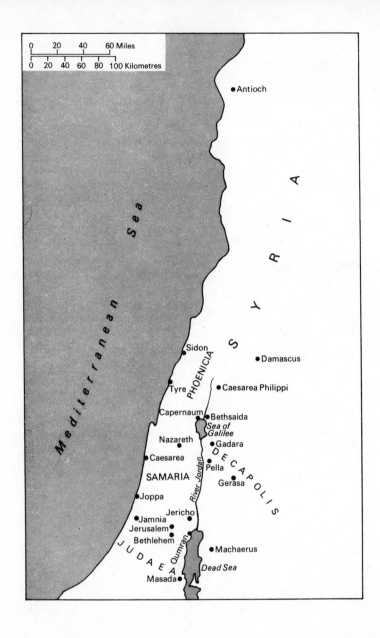

INTRODUCTION

THE GOSPEL OF MATTHEW AND ITS SOURCES

1. *The first gospel*

Though the order in which the four canonical gospels are arranged in ancient lists[1] varies considerably, the gospel of Matthew stands, and with insignificant exceptions has always stood, at the head of the list, and thus of the writings that go to make up the canon of the New Testament. This position represents a priority of esteem and not of dating. In the century following its publication, Mt is quoted by Christian writers not only more than any other gospel, but more than any other NT book.[2] The earliest direct references to it, in the letters of St. Ignatius of Antioch (martyred c. A.D. 115), speak of it as 'the' gospel[3]—not necessarily implying that he knew of no other, but certainly that he regarded no other as comparable. The reasons for this immediate popularity will be considered in due course. But it is to be regarded as a response to the positive qualities of the book rather than as reflecting any knowledge of its prehistory.

An objector to this conclusion could point to the fragment of Papias, bishop of Hierapolis in Asia Minor, (written probably in the period A.D. 130–50) quoted by the historian Eusebius:[4] 'Matthew compiled the *logia* in the Hebrew language, and everyone translated them according to his ability'. This on the

[1]Details of these will be found in J. Moffatt, *Introduction to the Literature of the NT* (London, 1911), p. 14.
[2]This is the conclusion of E. Massaux, *Influence de l'évangile de saint Matthieu sur la littérature chrétienne avant saint Irénée* (Louvain, 1950).
[3]Ignatius, *To the Smyrnaeans*, 5, 7; *To the Philadelphians*, 5, 8, 9; cp. *To the Ephesians*, 19.
[4]*History of the Church* (usually cited as *H.E.*), III, xxxix. 6.

face of it means that behind our present Mt there lies a collection of the sayings of the Lord (the most likely meaning of *logia*, but with the implication that the sayings are treated as the word of God) in the original Aramaic. If it could be established that Papias really meant this and that he had reliable authority for such a statement (i.e. that he had seen the document in question or could appeal to somebody who had), we should then have external evidence for at any rate one stage in the gospel's development. But this is just what is missing. It must be emphasized that Papias is writing well into the second century and with its special preoccupations in mind; he is an early and humble representative of the tradition that culminated, at a vastly higher level, in the work of St. Irenaeus of Lyons (himself a native of Asia Minor, d. A.D. 202), which opposed the innovations of the Gnostic heretics with an emphasis on the original gospel and the apostolic witness to it. His purpose is thus apologetic, not antiquarian; he is not concerned to satisfy the curiosity of his readers, but to assure them that the tradition they have received is authentic. And since he makes a parallel statement about Mark, he is obviously speaking about gospels and has before him one going by the name of Matthew; the date at which he is writing and what we already know of the early circulation of our Mt make it extremely unlikely that his starting-point is another gospel ascribed to the same apostle. Now a striking feature of our Mt and one which would commend it to Papias is the prominence it gives to the sayings of the Lord; an apologist whose primary concern was for these could quite naturally have used 'the sayings' as a shorthand title for the whole gospel. If that is what Papias has done, he is simply saying that the gospel of Mt—our Mt—was composed by its apostolic author in Aramaic and then translated. And this statement, in the absence of his reasons for making it and of any external confirmation, can only be tested by the internal evidence of the NT writings themselves.[5]

[5]The reasons for this conclusion are given in more detail in the Additional Note, p. 44.

2. *Internal evidence: Mark and Matthew*

We are therefore thrown back on the contents of the gospels, and this confronts the reader with a factor which Papias in his preoccupation with the sayings of the Lord either missed or passed over as unimportant, but which modern critical study puts in the centre of the picture: the close documentary relationship of the first three (called for this reason 'synoptic') gospels. The facts, as summarized by Streeter,[6] are as follows:

(a) Mt reproduces 90% of the subject-matter of Mk in language largely identical with that of Mk; Lk does the same for rather more than half of Mk.

(b) In any average section which occurs in all three gospels, the majority of the actual words used by Mk are reproduced by Mt and Lk either alternately or both together.

(c) The relative order of incidents and sections in Mk is in general supported by both Mt and Lk; where either of them deserts Mk the other is usually found supporting him.

To argue from the facts as so far stated that the only possible explanation of them is that Mk was a source for both Mt and Lk is, as Bishop Butler[7] has shown, logically fallacious; the proper conclusion is that Mk is (in the material common to all three) the *middle term* between Mt and Lk. But while it is therefore equally possible, logically speaking, that Mk depends on Mt and Lk on Mk (or Mk on Lk and Mt on Mk, though this latter solution has not been seriously canvassed), there remain what may be called strong reasons of common-sense for still thinking that what has become the accepted modern solution, the priority of Mk,[8] is in fact the right one:

(a) Mk's Greek is relatively unpolished and not free from grammatical solecisms, and his narrative style, though vivid, is sprawling and wordy; while his gospel includes only half the

[6] B. H. Streeter, *The Four Gospels* (London, 1924), p. 151.
[7] B. C. Butler, *The Originality of St Matthew* (Cambridge, 1951), pp. 62ff.
[8] For a restatement of this in the light of Butler's book see the Excursus by G. M. Styler in C. F. D. Moule, *The Birth of the NT* (London, 1962), pp. 223ff.

material found in Mt, the narrative sections almost always appear in a more expanded form. A progression from the polished and compact to the rough and sprawling is on literary grounds improbable.

(b) Mt is altogether more reverential in his treatment of the person of Jesus (cp. especially $19^{16f.}$ with Mk $10^{17f.}$, which would really be impossible to understand as Mk's correction of Mt; also 8^{25} with Mk 4^{38}, and 13^{58} with Mk $6^{5f.}$, etc.). We should expect on general grounds a progression in devotional attitudes from the less developed to the more developed; the priority of Mt to Mk would imply the reverse.

The validity of this line of argument has been confirmed by a more intensive application of it in recent years. Systematic study of the ways in which Mt (and Lk) can be shown to have altered Mk (known technically as redaction-criticism)[9] has greatly increased our understanding of the theological outlook of the later evangelists, and the coherence of the findings arrived at by this method amounts to a strong corroborative argument for the priority of Mk which it assumes.

(c) Though St. Augustine and other ancient writers could hold the view that Mk abbreviated Mt, its inadequacy to account for the complexities of the evidence is borne out by the fact that virtually no modern scholar goes all the way with it. Of the closest recent approximations to it, Butler[10] interposes between Mt and Mk the oral preaching of St. Peter based on his recollection of Mt, while W. R. Farmer[11] makes Mk dependent on Lk as well as on Mt. Most other scholars of this tendency have preferred to postulate the dependence of Mk on an Aramaic proto-Mt rather than on our Greek Mt.[12] Among the reasons for this have been:

[9] See N. Perrin, *What is Redaction-Criticism?* (London, 1970); Rohde, *Rediscovering the Teaching of the Evangelists.*
[10] Op. cit., pp. 165ff.
[11] *The Synoptic Problem* (London, 1967), pp. 199ff.
[12] Among German scholars, A. Schlatter and E. Lohmeyer; among French-speaking R.C. scholars, L. Cerfaux, L. Vaganay, X. Leon-Dufour, A. Gaboury. The ablest statement of this position in English is that of P. Parker, *The Gospel before Mark* (Chicago, 1953).

(i) Those who have regarded Papias as a witness to authentic tradition have felt a need to confirm what he says from internal evidence. Certainly Papias' statement needs to be checked against the NT, but without prior commitment to his reliability.

(ii) Mt is in some sense a more Jewish book than Mk, and the hypothesis of a Jewish–Christian gospel behind both was one way of explaining this. But the extent and derivation of Mt's Jewishness is too complex a question to be disposed of on this theory alone (see pp. 20 ff.).

(iii) Some individual passages, of which 15²¹⁻⁸ (par. Mk 7²⁴⁻³⁰) is the most striking, have suggested to some scholars that our Mt was following an older and more reliable form of the tradition than appears in Mk. But the application of the redaction-critical method to these passages has very largely eliminated the need to resort to this kind of explanation (see, e.g., commentary on 15²¹⁻⁸).

3. *Other written sources?*

We are therefore justified in concluding that Mk is a principal source for Mt. Had he others?

(a) A substantial part of the non-Marcan material in Mt (consisting mainly of sayings) is found also in Lk. For this the following explanations have been offered:

(i) Mt and Lk are both drawing on a lost source, known to scholars as Q (German *Quelle*, source).[13]

(ii) The material found its way by independent oral transmission into the separate traditions from which the two evangelists drew.[14]

(iii) Lk derived the material from Mt.[15]

Each of these explanations can be plausibly advanced in respect of some of the material. But if a single solution to cover

[13]So Streeter and the majority of scholars.
[14]Proposed for some of the material by J. Jeremias, C. K. Barrett, H. T. Wrege.
[15]Maintained for all the material by J. H. Ropes, B. C. Butler, A. M. Farrer, W. R. Farmer. The logical alternative that Mt derived it from Lk has, not, so far as I know, been discussed at length.

all of it is demanded, (i) is the only one possible, since (ii) hardly does justice to the cases of word-for-word correspondence in the material, and (iii) cannot make room for the instances in which Lk's version seems to be more original (see, e.g., commentary on 6^{25-33}, $10^{9-15, \; 26-33, \; 37f.}$). For these reasons (i) has remained the majority view among scholars. But it is not without serious difficulties of its own. The closeness of the correspondences between the parallel passages in the two gospels varies very greatly, from verbal near-identity at one end of the scale to a mere general similarity of theme at the other. The former call for a documentary explanation; the latter are hardly compatible with it, even on the theory that Mt and Lk were working from separate recensions of the document. Yet if Q was anything less than a document it can hardly be regarded as a distinct source, since in that case the symbol represents no more than the overlap between the unwritten traditions available to the two evangelists, and this is insufficient to justify an absolute distinction of the material covered by it from other gospel material. The proper conclusion would seem to be that the parallels between Mt and Lk are of multiple origin and not susceptible of a single explanation; and within the framework of this working hypothesis the suggestion that Lk copied Mt acquires a plausibility for some of the material, particularly where the verbal agreement between the two gospels is very close, which it could not have for the whole of it, as an overall alternative to Q. Detailed consideration of this solution belongs to a commentary on Lk rather than to one on Mt; its interest for the student of Mt lies in the fact that signs of Mt's characteristic literary and exegetical methods can be detected in some of the passages in question, notably in the temptation narrative (4^{1-11}), in 8^{5-13}, and throughout Chap. 11.

(b) Those who accept the Q-hypothesis mostly distinguish Mt's other non-Marcan material from it by the symbol M. M has no significance of its own apart from Q, and the material which it is supposed to have contained is even less homogeneous than that which has been usually assigned to Q.

There may perhaps be shorter written sources behind, e.g., parts of the Sermon on the Mount, but a continuous source for the gospel as a whole is not so far justified by the evidence.

As far as written sources are concerned, then, we cannot confidently add much to Streeter's statement that Mt is 'an enlarged version of Mk'.[16] But we can point to two distinct, though overlapping, kinds of material with which he can be shown to have enlarged it.

(a) *Sayings of Jesus orally transmitted*

It is striking that whereas Mt only adds one miracle-story (8^{5-13}) to those before him in Mk, he clearly has access to a far more comprehensive tradition of the sayings of Jesus,[17] which he uses not only to supplement the fragmentariness with which they are often reproduced in Mk (See, e.g., 10^{9-15}, 12^{25-8}), but for a systematic presentation of Jesus as the true teacher of Israel. The bulk of this material consists of collections of sayings which the evangelist (undoubtedly continuing the work of earlier Christian scribes) has knitted together with great skill; but there are also single sayings with short introductory narratives ('pronouncement stories'[18]; e.g. 8^{18-22}), and a much larger collection of parables than in Mk (see especially 13, 18^{23-35}, $19^{30}-20^{16}$, $21^{28}-22^{14}$, $24^{32}-25^{30}$).

It may be assumed that what the tradition of his church transmitted to Mt as genuine sayings of Jesus he accepted as such. But the converse, that what he offers as sayings of Jesus had in all cases come down to him through the tradition, does not follow. Apart from those sayings which appear to have been constructed out of OT texts interpreted along contem-

[16]Streeter himself, as the originator of the symbol M, was prepared to add a great deal.

[17]Some indirect light is thrown on the transmission of this by B. Gerhardsson, *Memory and Manuscript* (Lund, 1961); *Tradition and Transmission in Early Christianity* (Lund, 1964).

[18]The expression coined by V. Taylor, *The Formation of the Gospel Tradition* (London, 1933); Bultmann, *HST*, prefers 'apothegm', M. Dibelius, *From Tradition to Gospel* (ET London, 1934), 'paradigm'. These books remain the best introduction to the study of 'form-criticism', i.e. the pre-literary history of the gospel material.

porary Jewish lines (see next section), there are extended passages whose style and vocabulary betray their Matthaean authorship (e.g. the interpretation of the parable of the tares, 13^{36-43}, and, in whole or part, the great assize, 25^{31-46}). We have reason moreover to believe that the early Church, assisted of course by the activity of Christian prophets speaking to it 'in the name of the Lord',[19] was not incapable of creating and transmitting 'dominical' sayings, especially for controversial purposes; and though it is hard to arrive at a criterion which is free both from subjectivity and from unwarranted scepticism[20] for distinguishing these, it is not difficult to recognize in Mt those sayings which reflect the situation of the post-resurrection Church (e.g. 7^{21}, 18^{20}), let alone those which derive from the particularist standpoint of early Palestinian Christianity, demanding strict observance of the OT law and opposed to any mission to Gentiles (e.g. $5^{18f \cdot}$, 7^6, $10^{5,23}$, 18^{15-7}, $23^{2f \cdot}$). Mt faithfully reproduces these latter sayings which reflect a position very different from his own; but in order to neutralize their original force he brings to bear on them, as we shall see, an ingenuity learned from long practice in reconciling discrepant passages of the OT.

(b) *Reflection on the scriptures of the OT*

The most immediate indication of this activity and its influence on the text of Mt is the series of 'fulfilment' quotations at 1^{23}, (2^6), $2^{15,18,23}$, 4^{15}, 8^{17}, 12^{18-21}, 13^{35}, 21^5, $27^{9f \cdot}$. These are all found in narrative contexts and (with one exception)[21] introduced as comments of the evangelist; they

---

[19] Cp. Bultmann, *HST*, p. 163.

[20] The criteria offered by N. Perrin, *Rediscovering the Teaching of Jesus* (London, 1967), which admit only those sayings which distinguish Jesus both from his Jewish background and from later Christian attitudes, are unrealistically stringent; at the other end of the scale, those of J. Jeremias, *NT Theology i* (ET London, 1971), too readily assume that to establish a Palestinian and Aramaic-speaking background is sufficient.

[21] 2^6 is introduced as the reply of the scribes to Herod, but its composite character in language and derivation is entirely in line with the rest of the list.

are all prophetic citations prefaced by some variant of the formula 'that it might be fulfilled which was spoken by the prophet . . .', and all differ from the other OT citations taken over from Mk or introduced by Mt himself (which follow the LXX) in that the form of the biblical text which they represent diverges more or less sharply both from the LXX and from the Massoretic text of the Hebrew represented by our English versions.

Rendel Harris[22] suggested many years ago that the character of these quotations could be explained on the hypothesis that Mt was working with a 'testimony book' or catena of OT texts assembled for apologetic purposes, on the lines of those known to have existed in patristic times. It is beyond question that Christians from a very early date 'searched the scriptures' for confirmation of the Messiahship of Jesus and other items in the gospel message, and there is no *a priori* improbability in the theory that they made collections of texts which provided this; comparable collections have come to light in Cave IV at Qumran.[23] But C. H. Dodd[24] has shown conclusively that these collections, if they existed, were a by-product rather than the starting-point of Christian apologetic, and examination of the Qumran anthologies in the light of the scripture study practised there tends to support this. It may be assumed that the texts in Mt generally had a history of previous use; the outstanding question is whether the exegetical process which produced their peculiar wording was complete before they came into Mt's hands,[25] or was actively continued by the evangelist himself.[26] The fact that a number of these quotations, though they do not fully conform to the LXX, nevertheless

[22]J. Rendel Harris, *Testimonia* (Cambridge, i, 1916, ii, 1920).
[23]See J. A. Fitzmyer, *Essays on the Semitic Background of the NT* (London, 1971), pp. 59ff.
[24]*According to the Scriptures* (London, 1952), pp. 28ff. and especially 57–60.
[25]The position of Lindars, *NTA*, and of scholars who hold that Mt was written by a Gentile.
[26]An intermediate view is that of Stendahl, *School*, pp. 31ff., who sees behind Mt the work of a 'school' of biblical exegetes.

betray its influence in some of their wording (e.g. 1^{23}, 2^6, 4^{15}, 12^{21}, 13^{35a}, 21^5) suggests that the process of reflection on them in the light of textual variants had continued in a Greek-speaking *milieu;* while the probable conclusion that the wording has in some cases been influenced by their context in Mt or by significant themes in the gospel as a whole (see on 2^{23}, 4^{15}, 12^{18-21}, 13^{35}, 21^5) makes it difficult to exclude the evangelist himself from a share in their formation.

Now if Mt was not only in a position to draw on a living tradition of scripture exegesis but practised it himself, it is unlikely that its influence on the content of his gospel was limited to a series of isolated quotations. In order to discover what else it could have included, it is necessary to take a longer look at the contemporary Jewish approach to the interpretation of the Bible.[27] The methods known collectively as *midrash* ('study') have little in common with those of modern historical criticism, which concentrates on the original meaning of the text as intended by its author, but considerably more (and indeed some historical continuity)[28] with the earlier tradition of 'pulpit exposition' in various parts of the Christian Church. Like the latter, *midrash* was essentially oral exposition which accompanied the public reading of the text. If the reading took place in the synagogue, as it commonly did, it was usually followed by a free vernacular (originally Aramaic) version of each passage, known as a *targum*, and this might play its part in the exegesis that followed.

The underlying purpose of *midrash* was a constructive one: to enable the word of God to contemporary Israel, which the scripture was assumed to contain, to be heard and understood better; and this must not be forgotten when its more pedantic aspects are being considered. But in practice not a little of it

---

[27]On this see P. R. Ackroyd and C. F. Evans (eds.), *Cambridge History of the Bible*, i (1970), especially pp. 199ff. (G. Vermes), 377ff. (C. K. Barrett), 412ff. (R. P. C. Hanson); G. Vermes, *Scripture and Tradition in Judaism* (Leiden, 1961); J. W. Bowker, *The Targums and Rabbinic Literature* (Cambridge, 1969), pp. 40ff.
[28]See Hanson, loc. cit.

had to be devoted to clearing up difficulties: elucidating legal precepts (*halakah*: see below), explaining the meaning of unfamiliar words, harmonizing discrepancies between texts, supplying gaps in the narratives or dealing with questions they left unanswered, and eliminating offensiveness in the material.

Its method (and this is where it is most remote from our ways of thinking) was predominantly verbal; to read a passage in the light of its immediate context was not difficult, but cross-referencing would have depended on the expositor's recollection of other passages, and these were in fact mostly memorized on the basis of single words which they had in common. Word-play was thus prominent in Jewish exegesis, and comparison with other versions of the text (facilitated by the *targum*) enlarged the scope of this[29].

The results were traditionally classified by their subject-matter as *halakah* and *haggadah*. *Halakah* was essentially case-law (some of it actually arrived at by way of judgements in court), the application of the legal parts of the Pentateuch to specific contemporary cases. *Haggadah* (from a Hebrew root meaning to 'tell') means 'what scripture tells in addition to its obvious meaning'. Although in theory this could include *halakah*, in practice it was confined to non-halakic material, and more particularly to the narrative parts of the Pentateuch, its object being to make these come alive for the contemporary hearer by appealing to his imagination. It brought to its task not only close study of the actual text but illustrative material from other sources, and the result could amount to a free imaginative re-telling of the original story. The process is already at work within the OT (e.g., the P source in the Pentateuch, the priestly revision of Samuel–Kings which produced the Books of Chronicles, the narrative parts of Daniel, and the praise of OT worthies in Sir. 45–50). It continued within Judaism long beyond Mt's day (see the remarkable *haggadah* on the life of Abraham reproduced by

[29]For a summary of the *middot* or principles of Pharisaic exegesis see Barrett, loc. cit., p. 383.

Vermes,[30] which in its final revision dates only from the eleventh century, but in an earlier form may well have contributed something to the portents related in Mt 2; cp. commentary on 2²).

The methods outlined so far took the sacred text itself as their starting-point; they were thus broadly common ground between the different parties in Judaism. By the first century A.D., however, they had come to be supplemented by another approach (which Vermes[31] calls 'applied', as opposed to 'pure', exegesis), which started from the contemporary situation that the scripture was expected to illuminate, and on this the parties differed sharply. The underlying assumption of this approach was that the present situation of Israel (or of a privileged group within it) must have been anticipated and provided for in scripture, if only the requisite hermeneutical key could be discovered. The quest for this involved taking isolated passages out of context and straining the primary meaning of the text, and was thus responsible for the major extravagances of Jewish exegesis, as well as for the wide divergences in interpretation between the contending groups. Of these, the two of most interest to the student of Mt are the Pharisaic *halakah* designed to weld together written Torah and 'oral' law (see p. 23), and the special characteristics of the exegesis practised at Qumran.[32]

It is the Covenanters of Qumran (see p. 24) who come nearest to the Christians in certain of their exegetical assumptions, notably in their sense of an imminent eschatological fulfilment and in their attachment to a figure in the recent historical past (the 'Teacher of Righteousness') whose ministry in some sense pointed forward to the end (though they lacked the Christians' conviction that in *their* founder the fulfilment had already been inaugurated). The freedom with which they

[30]See *Scripture and Tradition in Judaism*, pp. 68ff.
[31]*Cambridge History of the Bible*, i. 202, 221ff.
[32]For this see Barrett, loc. cit., p. 386; F. F. Bruce, *Biblical Interpretation in the Qumran Texts* (London, 1960); Fitzmyer, op. cit., pp. 3f.

handle the OT reflects this. Their anthologies of scriptural passages have already been mentioned; biblical narratives re-told and compositions of their own based on books of the OT have also been found among their writings. A feature that calls for special notice, since the term has been much used by commentators on the NT, is the *pesher* method of commentary. The word *pesher* means 'interpretation', and its use implies that the words of scripture (especially prophecy) have, over and above their original sense, a special meaning for the present time (understood as the end; St. Paul in 1 Cor. 10[11] comes very close to this: 'these things happened to them as a warning, but they are written down for our instruction, upon whom the end of the ages has come'; cp. also Rom. 15[4]), but that it remains opaque to the reader until some inspired figure supplies the key. So at Qumran God was understood to have revealed his purpose (concerning the end-time, which was now at hand) in advance to the prophets, but their words contained it in cryptic form and could not be understood until the interpretation had been imparted to the Teacher of Righteousness.

In what ways have these exegetical methods contributed to the content of Mt?

(a) Of *halakah*, in the strict sense of casuistry in the interpretation of OT law, the only example which Mt does not originally owe to Mk seems to be the question about the temple tax (17[24-7]), and this clearly came to him by way of Christian oral tradition. On the other hand the first main section of the Sermon on the Mount (5[21-48]), where Mt has enlarged a previously existing (probably written) source, can be taken as a Christian rejoinder to the Pharisaic *halakah* which interpreted the Torah by the 'unwritten' law.

(b) The infancy narratives (Chaps. 1–2) and the end of Judas (27[3-10]) are generally recognized as Christian narrative *haggadah*, and I follow B. Gerhardsson[33] in adding the temptation (4[1-11]) to the list (though not in assigning it to an early

[33] *Testing.*

'floating' source). Many of Mt's shorter additions to Mk seem also to fall into the general category of *haggadah* (e.g. 3^{13-5}, 21^{14-6}).

(c) In addition to the apocalypse, based on Daniel, which Mt already had before him in Mk, the genealogy of 1^{1-17} has been composed in imitation of parts of 1 Chr. 1–3, the hymn of jubilation of 11^{25-30} in imitation of Sir. 51, and the final commission (28^{18-20}) (probably) of 2 Chr. 36^{23}.

(d) The 'fulfilment' quotations discussed above are sometimes referred to as *pesher*;[34] but though they share with the latter method the characteristic of referring the meaning of prophecies to near-contemporary events, they differ from it in seeing them as already fulfilled in the figure of Christ. In addition the *pesher* method as it is found in the Qumran commentary on Habakkuk (1 QpHab) provides running commentary on a consecutive text (like Rom. 10^{5-10}, Heb. 10^{5-10} in the NT)[35]; the quotations in Mt do not conform to this pattern. Sayings such as 16^{18-9} actually come much nearer to it (see Note C, p. 242).

(e) Not only do some of these quotations reveal extensive cross-referencing of OT texts (e.g. 2^{23}, 27^{9-10}), but this factor can be seen operating elsewhere in the gospel material; cp. 2^{1-12}, 9^{36}, 11^{25-30}, etc.
But further, no hard and fast line can be drawn between Mt's treatment of OT material and his treatment of the sayings of Jesus. Jesus has come to fulfil the law and the prophets (5^{17}); his words will survive the end, whereas the older scriptures will not (24^{35}; cp. 5^{18}) and they are accordingly taken as the equivalent of scripture and handled in the same way. We may therefore add:

(f) It is not difficult to see in Mt's arrangement of the sayings, especially where joined by link-words (e.g. 'brother', 5^{21-4}; 'eye', 5^{28-30}; 'scandal', 18^{6-9} (already in Mk)) the

[34]Notably by Stendahl and Lindars.
[35]See Fitzmyer, op. cit., pp. 54f.

influence of the Jewish method of collecting and comparing texts, and in his habit of neutralizing the force of particularist sayings ascribed to Jesus by arranging them in context with other sayings, the type of *midrash* which is intended to resolve discrepancies between individual passages. The parables of Jesus are not only collected but, with the aid of allegorization, applied to the altered situation of the Church of Mt's own day (cp. 13^{36-50}, 22^{1-14}, $25^{1-13,14-30}$, etc.). And at some points he seems to combine OT texts and themes with sayings attributed to Jesus in a single piece of Christian *midrash* (e.g. 11^{25-30}, $16^{18f.}$).

(g) There are clear parallels between the way in which the later strands of the OT reshape their predecessors (see above) and Mt's rewriting of Mk. The concentration on particular themes which is readily recognizable in, e.g., the priestly compiler of Chronicles is present, *mutatis mutandis*, in Mt also. In the field of *halakah*, for example, he modifies the controversial judgements on sabbath observance ($12^{1ff.}$), handwashing before food ($15^{1ff.}$), and divorce ($19^{1ff.}$) to present the teaching of Jesus as consistently opposed not to the written Torah but to the oral tradition to which Pharisaism gave all but equal weight. H. J. Held[36] has drawn attention to the way Mt has modified Mk's miracle stories so as to transfer the emphasis from Jesus as a figure in the past to the glorified Christ at work in his Church, and this tendency can be observed in other narrative passages also. A great many of Mt's briefer additions to Mk (e.g. 14^{26-33}, and the legendary additions to the passion narrative ($27^{19,24f.,52f.}$)), cannot have existed independently of Mk; their relationship to the gospel has been compared with that of the mistletoe to the oak. Mt's larger additions all arise out of Marcan contexts, and in many cases can be explained as midrashic elaborations of them; thus the starting-point of the genealogy and birth narrative seems to be the word *beginning* in Mk 1^1; the temptation story is a haggadic expansion of the brief outline in Mk $1^{12f.}$, and

[36] *TIM*, pp. 246ff.

the Sermon on the Mount spells out in detail the implications of Mk 1^{22} ('he taught them as one who had authority and not as their scribes').

G. D. Kilpatrick[37] has suggested that Mt's gospel took shape as a result of the regular reading and exposition of Mk and Mt's other sources in the liturgical assemblies of the Church. The features of it that we have been examining suggest that there may well be truth in this, though the hypothesis must not be pressed to the point of excluding either the work of a 'school' of exegetes such as that postulated by Stendahl, or the creative impress of Mt as the author of the book. His influence is to be discerned especially in its overall structure.

STRUCTURE OF THE GOSPEL

1. *Matthew's treatment of Mark*

If Mt is viewed as a whole, it is not hard to detect that he uses Mk in two quite different ways. His second half follows Mk very closely, retaining the main narrative sequence; his first half uses mainly Marcan material in its narrative sections, but, apart from such obvious fixed points as the preaching of the Baptist, the baptism of Jesus and the inauguration of his ministry, selects and drastically redistributes it. Mk is here treated as a general source rather than as a continuous chain of events. The reason for this is that these chapters are not intended to be taken as consecutive narrative. They are an answer to the question 'Who is this?', a comprehensive but essentially static presentation of Jesus as the Christ in five clearly defined phases: his origins (cc. 1–2), the circumstances of his first public appearance in Israel (3^1–4^{16}), his definitive interpretation of the Torah (4^{17}–7^{27}), his Messianic acts of power (7^{28}–9^{34}), and his inauguration of the continuing mission of his disciples (9^{35}–10^{42}). Only at Chap. 12 (not Chap. 14, as is often stated) does the narrative begin to get moving, and then it is, more obviously than in Mk, a narrative of the rejection of the Christ by his own people. This is introduced by Chap. 11, which is a recapitulation of what has been revealed

[37]*Origins*, pp. 59ff.

about Jesus in the first part, and this indicates that the real
break in the gospel comes between Chaps. 10 and 11. An OT
precedent can be offered for this. It has already been noted
that Mt both begins and ends on a note suggested by the
Books of Chronicles, and these books contain a similar division.
1 Chr., after the lengthy genealogies with which it opens,
concentrates entirely on the figure of David; 2 Chr. is concerned with the subsequent history (which involves the decline
and fall) of the royal house of David, beginning with Solomon,
his son. One of Mt's special aims is to present Jesus as the 'Son
of David', the Messiah of the house of David (see 1^{1-17}, 12^{23},
$20^{30f.}$, 21^9, 15, $22^{41ff.}$, etc.). The structure of his gospel may
well give this formal expression.

2. *The five discourses*

Of Mt's major insertions into Mk, five stand apart from the
rest. These are the five 'discourses' compiled from sayings of
Jesus:

5^3–7^{27}	The Sermon on the Mount
10^{5-42}	The Mission Discourse
13^{1-52}	The Parables of the Kingdom
18	Pastoral Care and Forgiveness in the Church
23–5	The Judgement[38]

These are not the only extended passages in the gospel built
up from the sayings of Jesus; cp., e.g., 11, 12^{25-45}, 19^1–20^{16}.
But they are clearly distinguished from the others, in particular
by the formula with which at the end of each the reader is
recalled to the narrative context: 'When Jesus had finished ...'
(see 7^{28}, 11^1, 13^{53}, 19^1, 26^1); and together they comprise Mt's
systematic arrangement of the teaching of Jesus. This fact did
not go unobserved in ancient times; a fragment of a prologue
to Mt dated not later than the third century A.D., and very
possibly earlier than this, begins:

'Matthew curbs the rash error of the Jews,
    Having muzzled it with the bridle of five discourses.'[39]

---

[38]For the reasons for including Chap. 23, see commentary.
[39]See Rendel Harris, *Testimonia*, i. 109, ii. 110.

and the fact that Papias' 'Exposition of the Lord's *logia*' (see Additional Note, p. 44) was written in five books may conceivably be connected with it.

B. W. Bacon,[40] writing in 1930, put forward the suggestion that each of these five discourses is to be taken with the narrative section that precedes it, so that the whole gospel (exclusive of the infancy and passion-resurrection narratives) consists of five 'books'. He went on to argue that this fivefold arrangement was designed to correspond with the five books of the Pentateuch and thus to present Jesus as the new Moses. Influential as this suggestion has been, there are serious objections to it:

(a) The structural features that it sets out to explain are less even than the theory demands; the last three discourses do seem to serve as conclusions for the narrative which precedes them, but it is less clear that the first two do the same. An account of the overall structure of the gospel that relegates the infancy chapters and the passion-resurrection narratives to the positions of prologue and epilogue hardly does justice to the emphasis laid by Mt on the opening and conclusion of his book.

(b) The 'typological' function suggested for the five discourses clashes with the unfolding of Pentateuchal themes which is undoubtedly present in the early chapters.[41] Chap. 1 is dominated by the word *genesis* (see on $1^{1,18}$), Chap. 2 carries reminiscences of the patriarchs, there are Exodus themes in the baptism and temptation narratives (Chaps. 3–4), leading up to the echo of Sinai in the setting of the Sermon on the Mount (5^1), and the correspondence may run on even beyond this.

Some scholars deny that there is any Moses-typology (i.e. any use of the figure of Moses as a 'type' foreshadowing and interpreting that of Christ) in Mt. This is hardly convincing if it be allowed that typology can include contrast as well as comparison; clearly there is, for this evangelist, some relation

[40]*Studies in Matthew* (London, 1930), pp. 80ff.
[41]See Davies, *SSM*, pp. 14ff.; A. Farrer, *St Matthew and St Mark* (London, 1954), pp. 177ff.

between what Moses did for the law and what Jesus does, even if it is not one of simple repetition (see introduction to the Sermon on the Mount, p. 70). But it is by no means the dominant typology in this gospel. Mt's Christ alternates between the new Moses (or the prophet 'like' Moses of Dt. 18^{15}; see commentary on 11^3), the Son of David, and the true Israel; and the OT echoes and allusions vary accordingly.

The five discourses have nevertheless their own special character and function in the gospel. It has often been suggested that they are really addressed, as it were, over the shoulders of their ostensible audience, the disciples of Jesus, to the Christians of Mt's own day. But it seems that the truth may be more subtle than this. Each of these discourses can be shown to fall into two distinct halves, of which the first speaks, on the face of it, to the disciples of Jesus in their original situation, while the second applies the message to the changed situation of Mt's contemporary Christians, facing the imminent prospect of final judgement. Thus:

A

5^3–7^{12}: The new and definitive interpretation of the law of God.

10$^{5-23}$: The mission of the disciples to Israel.

13$^{1-35}$: Parables of the coexistence of good and bad in the present kingdom, and their gradual polarization.
18$^{1-14}$: Warnings to disciples against an attitude of superiority towards the erring, which condemns rather than reclaims.

23: Judgement on the old Israel in the persons of its religious leaders, in history.

B

7$^{13-27}$: Warnings against hearing the law without keeping it, i.e. not treating it as binding, and the consequences of this in the judgement.
10$^{24-42}$: The apostolic attitude characteristic of Christians, on which they will be judged.
13$^{36-52}$: Warnings of the final separation of good from bad in the judgement.

18$^{15-35}$: The basic purpose of the church discipline actually in force is not exclusion but forgiveness, and Christians will be judged on their practice of this.
24–5: The prospect of final judgement still to come.

There is tension here between the original mission of Jesus to Israel and the later (largely Gentile) Church which is the consequence of its rejection, and a gradual but perceptible shifting of weight from the first column to the second. But, further, it is difficult to restrict even the themes of the first column exclusively to the historical ministry of Jesus; the Christian mission to Judaism, for instance, was not completed during that period, and if the gospel sees the Jewish rejection of Jesus as itself a judgement on the nation, it nevertheless unmistakably regards the events of A.D. 70 as the execution of that judgement (see on 21^{43}, 22^{7}, 23^{37-9}, 27^{25}). If these themes are allowed to run consecutively, a limited 'sacred history' can be read off as follows: Jesus called disciples, and committed to them the definitive understanding of the law. He also sent them to proclaim the coming of the kingdom to his own people. The rejection of this mission by the religious leaders of Judaism has meant the progressive separation of the followers of Jesus from the old Israel; it is with them that the future of the kingdom lies (though some of them have needed to be warned against relapsing into the old exclusive Jewish attitudes). The old Israel which rejected has itself been rejected. This 'sacred history', superimposed by Mt upon the story of Jesus, represents his own view of the progress of the Christian gospel down to A.D. 70, the year of the Church's definitive separation from Judaism.

This anticipates certain conclusions about the original setting of the gospel which will be reached in due course.

THE BACKGROUND IN FIRST CENTURY JUDAISM

1. *A Jewish–Christian Gospel?*

Most of the features of Mt already noted, and especially his methods of scripture exegesis, stamp his writing as fundamentally Jewish in character. The list can be extended. Among *formal* characteristics we may mention:

(a) a fondness for number patterns (partly as a mnemonic device, and partly from a sense of the quasi-mystical significance of certain numbers which was widespread in the ancient world). Thus we find:

three divisions of the genealogy of Jesus (1^{1-17}), *three* temptations (4^{1-11}), *three* 'notable duties' (6^{1-18}), miracles narrated in *three* groups of *three* (Chaps. 8–9), *three* prophetic signs, *three* parables of judgement, and *three* controversial answers in Chap. 22;

five sayings discourses (see above), *five* antitheses (5^{21-48}), a *five*-fold arrangement of teaching in 19^{1-26};

seven parables of the kingdom (chap. 13), *seven* woes (23^{13-33}), *seven* parables of warning 24^{32}–25^{46}).

(b) a liking for *chiasmus* (i.e. a sandwich arrangement of his material, A B B A)[42] and *inclusio* (ending a passage by returning to the words with which it began), both of them characteristic of Jewish writing;

(c) in *terminology* Mt prefers 'kingdom of (the) heaven(s)', which he normally substitutes for 'kingdom of God' in his sources (see Note A, p. 232), and 'Father in heaven' (or 'heavenly Father'), a more distant and reverential and therefore more conventionally Jewish appellation for God than 'Father' (*Abba*), the intimate form of address used by Jesus himself (see commentary on 6^9).

At the same time, alongside these typically Jewish features stand others which imply that his gospel cannot be called Jewish without qualification. It is a Greek document, written for a Greek-speaking community whose Bible was the LXX, and its principal source is Mk, a gospel which as we have it was composed for a Hellenistic Christian community. It is fully committed to the Christian mission to the Gentiles, though it is careful not to imply that Jesus inaugurated this or anticipated it in his own ministry (interestingly, there is no reference to circumcision throughout the gospel). It is also marked by extreme hostility to the leaders of Judaism, particularly those whom it calls 'scribes and Pharisees', which suggests to a number of scholars not so much a 'gospel for Jews' as a 'gospel against the Jews'.

[42]See the note on this in Fenton, pp. 15f.

Mt thus reveals himself as both strongly Jewish and fiercely anti-Jewish. For the implications of this paradoxical character of his gospel to be understood, it needs to be studied against the background of Palestinian Judaism in the first century, and in particular of the changes that overtook it after the suppression of the rebellion of A.D. 66–70.

2. *Jewish pluralism in the first century*

One of the facts which the discovery of the Dead Sea Scrolls has forced upon the attention of students of the NT is the pluralist character of Palestinian Judaism in the time of Jesus.[43] Ever since the Maccabean revolt of c. 165 B.C. and the short period of independence which followed it, the nation had been stratifying into increasingly organized groups, with widely varying attitudes to the temple and its priesthood, to the interpretation of the law, and to the Roman occupation. Since the more prominent of these groups necessarily figure in a gospel commentary, it will be convenient to list them at this point.

(a) *The Sadducees* were the party of the aristocratic and priestly families (the most likely etymology of their name connects it with the priestly name *Zadok*), in control of the temple and its worship, and traditionally acting in concert with the *de facto* rulers of the country (who would in any case control appointment to the office of high priest). This in Jesus' time meant collaboration with the Romans, and it was in the fact of this collaboration, and not in their influence with the people, which was small, that their real power lay. They were naturally resistant to innovation, both political and religious, hostile to any movement that could jeopardize the understanding they had reached with the occupying power, and deeply suspicious of the suppleness of the Pharisees in the interpretation of the law (originally, as we shall see, the responsibility of the priest), as well as of the Pharisaic doctrinal

[43]See K. Schubert, 'Jewish Religious Parties and Sects', in A. Toynbee (ed.), *The Crucible of Christianity* (London, 1969), pp. 87ff.; M. Simon, *Jewish Sects in the Time of Jesus* (ET London, 1967).

innovations in the field of angelology and the resurrection of the dead.

(b) The *Pharisees*[44] (the name is probably derived from *parash*—'separate'— but whether this implies a breakaway from an earlier movement or simply denotes their exclusiveness remains unclear) were a lay movement concerned for strict observance of the law, which they were not prepared to leave, as it had traditionally been left, to the instructions of an often worldly and corrupt priesthood. Sociologically their strength lay in the urban middle class, though this did not exclude diversities of social background with which the running dispute between the followers of Shammai (conservative) and those of Hillel (liberal) may not have been unconnected. In any case they held the rural proletariat (the 'people of the land'), whose observance of the law was not meticulous, in great contempt. Though they did not reject the temple and its cultus, their influence was exerted mainly through the synagogues and the small confraternities (*haburoth*) in which the requirements of the law were studied. Their attitude towards the occupying power was broadly one of appeasement; they did not recognize its right to be there, but were generally unprepared to translate this into open opposition.

Their devotion to the letter of the law was balanced by flexibility in interpreting its requirements, and this and the fact that their interpretations continued to be transmitted orally until they were finally codified in the Mishnah (second century A.D.) and Talmud (fourth century) combined to create the fiction of an 'oral' law existing alongside the written one and, like it, believed to go back to Moses himself (cp. the saying in Mishnah *Aboth* 1[1] (Danby, p. 446): 'Moses received the Law from Sinai and committed it to Joshua, and Joshua to the elders, and the elders to the Prophets; and the Prophets committed it to the men of the Great Synagogue'.) This became an acute controversial issue between Pharisees and

[44]L. Finkelstein, *The Pharisees* (Philadelphia, 1940) contains valuable material, though not all agree with his historical and sociological evaluation of it.

other Jews, and not least with the emergent Christian Church. On doctrinal matters not covered by the Torah, such as resurrection and angels, they showed themselves, by contrast with the Sadducees, open and receptive.

On Jesus' own attitude to the Pharisees, see introduction to Chap. 23 (pp. 186 ff.).

Scribes[45] were never a party on their own. Responsibility for the sacred writings belonged originally to the priests, and those among them who were entrusted with transcription of the scriptures combined with this a limited function of interpretation (for which cp. Sir. $38^{24ff.}$). The latter came (largely through the rise of Pharisaism) to be taken over by professional lay scholars or *hakamim* ('wise men',), and the scribes (*soferim*) were more and more restricted to copying and correspondingly reduced in status. Eventually the scholars themselves came to be known as *soferim*. Mk's expression 'scribes of the Pharisees' (Mk 2^{16}) indicates that this transition had already taken place; it does not necessarily imply that other parties also had their scribes in this sense, but only that not all Pharisees were thus qualified. The significance of Mt's expression 'scribes and Pharisees', which seems to identify the two, is discussed below (see p. 30). Two references in Mt apparently to Christian scribes (13^{52}, 23^{34}) are probably using the word in its humbler sense.

(c) Of the *Essenes* little was previously known from the accounts of their contemporaries, beyond the fact that they lived an ascetic life in communes round the shores of the Dead Sea, and nothing whatever of their origins. But since the discovery of the writings of the Qumran community and its identification as an Essene group (this, though not unchallenged, is the view of the great majority of specialists),[46] it is possible to relate them more positively to the other tendencies in Judaism. It appears that like the Pharisees (the two movements may have common roots in the *hasidim* or

[45]See Bowker, op. cit., pp. 54f.
[46]Texts and select bibliography in Vermes (see p. x).

'pious ones' who made common cause with the Maccabees in their revolt) they emerged as a protest against laxity or compromise in the official priestly class, but whereas the Pharisees took the way of separation within the community, the Essenes took that of separation from the community, and in particular from what it regarded as a usurping priesthood and the temple now under its control. Possibly the breakaway was led by members of the priesthood; certainly the priestly emphasis survived in the organization of the Qumran covenanters and in their interpretation of the law (reserved to the priests of the community, and strongly conservative in character). But the community was shaped by its own subsequent history (the details of which can only be reconstructed conjecturally from its own writings) into a sect with a deep sense of its own identity, future destiny, and special role in God's final vindication of his people, and as such it is in some ways nearer to the Christians than any other Jewish grouping. Like them it largely stood aside from active opposition to the Romans, but it seems that it was Roman troops who finally destroyed the settlement at Qumran in A.D. 68, and it is possible that some survivors made common cause with the *sicarii* (see next section) in their final stand in the fortress of Masada (reduced in 73).

(d) It is easier to establish that a more or less organized attitude of all-out resistance to the occupying power existed, than that the term *Zealot* is correctly applied to it.[47] It was sufficiently widespread to be termed the 'fourth philosophy', over and above the three already named, by the historian Josephus; but he nowhere uses the Greek word of an organized party before the final stages of the Jewish war of 67–70, and then only in Jerusalem. The tradition of no compromise with alien rulers may go back in some sense to the Maccabees themselves;[48] it certainly received a new impetus from the

[47]The evidence is set out in K. Lake–F. J. Foakes-Jackson (ed.), *The Beginnings of Christianity* (London, 1920–23), i. 421–25.
[48]This is maintained by W. R. Farmer, *Maccabees, Zealots and Josephus* (New York, 1956).

revolt of Judas the Galilean against the Roman census of A.D. 6, and the momentum of this was maintained by members of Judas' family long after his execution. It is more than possible that some of Jesus' inner circle had been associated with this movement (see 10⁴), and some of his own more controversial acts (especially the cleansing of the temple) at least lent themselves to a construction of this kind. However the tendency of his sayings, and especially of his reply to the question about the tribute money (see commentary on 22¹⁵ᶠᶠ·), is in the opposite direction. It has not been possible to identify any special tenets of the extremists apart from this single principle; some scholars find it possible to regard them as no more than 'the action wing of the Pharisees', but although there may have been some overlapping, current expectations of imminent divine intervention on behalf of the oppressed people of God (apocalyptic; see introduction to Chaps. 24–5) which the Pharisees on the whole tended to play down, are a more likely ideological background for their policy. In the fifties of the first century the sub-group known to the Romans as *sicarii* ('dagger-men', from their habit of concealing long daggers under their clothes) stepped up the tactics of resistance to include the assassination of suspected collaborators, and it appears to have been this group which both precipitated the final revolt and held out in the last desperate resistance at Masada.

(e) A detached view of Palestinian Jewish *Christianity* would see it as originally no more than a further constituent in an already pluralistic Judaism, despite its missionary stance towards other Jews and the persecution which this from time to time attracted (such as that in which St. Paul was active before his conversion). It would seem that the sharper edges of Jesus' challenge to the Pharisees on the sufficiency of the law became blunted in the earliest period, until the emphasis of Paul (himself an ex-Pharisee) revived them; a proportion of Jewish Christians (though not necessarily their leadership) felt their position in Judaism compromised by the practice in the Hellenistic churches of admitting Gentiles to full membership without insisting on full observance of the law, and drew closer to their fellow-Jews in consequence. James, the 'Lord's brother', and leader of the Christian community in Jerusalem, was greatly respected by his contemporaries for his fidelity to the law; and though it is probable that the Christians always resisted Pharisaic teaching on the 'oral' law, a degree of peaceful coexistence between the two groups remained a practical possibility, if not always a fact, at least on their home territory. Like the Pharisees the Christians continued to use the temple, but found their real sources of cohesion and renewal elsewhere. Like the Essenes they saw themselves as an 'esschatological' community whose real significance would be shortly revealed in the 'age to come'. They shared with both groups a lack of interest in direct political action.

3. *Consequences for Judaism of the events of A.D.* 70[49]

The foregoing state of affairs changes drastically with the outcome of the Jewish war and the destruction of Jerusalem in A.D. 70. *Sadducees*, even if they had survived the conflict in any considerable numbers, would have had no significant role in a situation in which the temple had been destroyed, the functions of the priesthood were generally in abeyance, and such native Jewish institutions as persisted were not based on Jerusalem. No group calling itself *Zealot* or sharing the general aims of the extremists could have expected to survive the war or the reprisals which followed it. Any surviving settlements of *Essenes* would have been too cut off from the ordinary life of Judaism in Palestine to play much part in shaping its future. The *Pharisees*, on the other hand, were not only well adapted, by their lack of commitment to the rebellion against Rome, and their relative unattachment to the temple cultus, to

[49]On Judaism in the period immediately after A.D. 70 see E. Schürer, *The History of the Jewish People in the Age of Jesus Christ* (ET new ed., Edinburgh, 1973), i. 514ff; Schubert, loc. cit.; A. A. T. Ehrhardt, *The Framework of the NT Stories* (Manchester, 1964), pp. 103ff.; and from the Jewish angle J. Neusner, *A Life of Rabbi Johanan ben Zakkai* (Leiden, 1962), and L. Finkelstein, *Akiba* (Cleveland, 1962).

survive and take the lead in the reconstruction of Judaism; they had taken positive steps towards this end. Jewish tradition represents Rabbi Johanan ben Zakkai, the sole survivor of the Jerusalem Sanhedrin, as having made a spectacular escape from Jerusalem at the height of the siege (he is said to have had himself smuggled out in a coffin) and obtained permission from the Roman authorities to establish an academy of Jewish studies at Jamnia (Jabneh) near Joppa. It is not clear how literally this is to be taken. Jamnia certainly became in the years that followed, despite the existence of rival establishments in nearby coastal towns, both the real centre of the reconstruction of Jewish institutions in Palestine, and the authoritative source of official Jewish teaching. Its success in the first of these enterprises was short-lived; the second Jewish rebellion under Bar-Kokba in A.D. 132–4 and the severity with which it was suppressed finally reduced Judaism to the religion of a dispersed people. But its effectiveness as the source of Jewish teaching (to which we owe, among other things, the present canon of the OT, and ultimately the codifying of the oral tradition in the Mishnah) ensured that the Judaism which survived was Pharisaic Judaism. The dominant emphasis in this tradition was, as we have seen, on law, and it had become unreceptive to prophetic inspiration, which was held responsible for the apocalyptic extravagances which had fanned the spirit of rebellion among Jews in the years leading up to A.D. 70. In the synagogue, according to settled rabbinic opinion, there was 'neither room for the priesthood nor for prophecy'.[50]

The only serious contenders with the Pharisees' claim to represent true Judaism were the Christians. They too remained uncompromised by the rebellion (the Christian community of Jerusalem is credited with a withdrawal to Pella in the Decapolis during the siege),[51] and they were similarly free of dependence on the temple. There is a certain amount of

[50]Ehrhardt, p. 131.
[51]Eusebius, *H.E.*, III. v. 3. Some have questioned this, e.g. S. G. F. Brandon, *The Fall of Jerusalem and the Christian Church* (London, 1951), p. 168.

indirect evidence both inside and outside the NT that Christians at this time were making a definite bid for recognition by the outside world as the true successors of the old Israel (and thus as adherents, in Roman eyes, of a *religio licita*); and it would seem, from the references to them that survive in Jewish tradition, that the small number who actually returned to Palestine from Pella made a marked impression on the Pharisaic majority by their missionary zeal.[52] These two facts go a long way towards explaining the bitter hostility towards Christianity which from now on characterizes rabbinic writings, and which culminated, historically, in the addition, around A.D. 85, of the *birkath ha' minim*, the so-called 'Test Benediction', to the *Prayer of XVIII Benedictions* recited daily in the synagogue. This ran: 'let Christians and *minim* (heretics) perish in a moment, let them be blotted out of the book of the living and let them not be written with the righteous'.[53] No Christian could say Amen to this, or remain in the synagogue while it was recited; the inevitable, and intended, result was the exclusion of Christians from synagogues everywhere. In areas of mixed population this must have led to a large accession of Jewish Christians to the already separate churches of the Gentiles; in Palestine, wherever Jamnia was in effective control, it can only have meant the reduction of the Christians to a hated, if not actually persecuted, minority.

THE GOSPEL AND ITS AUTHOR IN THEIR HISTORICAL SETTING

It is widely agreed that it is to this stage in the emergence of Christianity from Judaism that Mt belongs. In the first place he is dependent on Mk, which is now usually dated little, if at all, before A.D. 70, and time would be needed for it to become current in the eastern Mediterranean. Secondly, Mt not only makes Jesus refer obliquely to the fall of Jerusalem

[52]See L. Goppelt, *Apostolic and Post-Apostolic Times* (ET London, 1970), p. 121.
[53]On this, and on the relation of Mt to rabbinic Judaism in general, see especially Davies, *SSM*, pp. 256ff. (for the text of the Benediction, p. 275).

and the destruction of the temple (22^7, 23^{38}, 24^3), but clearly understands these events as a judgement on Israel for its rejection of the Christ (cp. 21^{43}, $23^{34ff\cdot}$, 27^{25}). He sees the future as lying not with a revived Israel or a restored temple but in a new community founded on faith in Christ (16^{18}) and recruited from the Gentile world (28^{19}). And, thirdly, his repeated references to 'scribes and Pharisees', meaning the same people, must reflect a situation in which 'Pharisees' no longer distinguishes one Jewish standpoint from the rest, but, since theirs is now the only position that remains, the name has passed from the rank and file to their natural leaders, the professional teachers of the law, or, as we should now say, the rabbis.[54]

But within this area there is wide divergence between scholars, ranging from the view[55] that Mt represents a Christianity not yet fully separated from Judaism, to the conclusion[56] that the evangelist not only wrote for Gentiles but was one himself. Neither of these extreme positions is really tenable; Mt's repeated references to 'their (i.e. Jewish) synagogues' (4^{23}, 9^{35}, 10^{17}, 12^9, 13^{54}) must mean that the community for which he wrote thought of itself as already distinct from the synagogue (see also commentary on 18^{20}), while the evidence we have already found of a Jewish outlook and formation in the evangelist himself is too deep-rooted to be attributed simply to the written or oral sources at his disposal. The middle position,[57] which regards Mt as the work of a Jewish–Christian evangelist writing for a Greek-speaking community which lived, probably outside Palestine, in acute conflict with 'the

[54]Modern usage makes it difficult to avoid employing this word in its professional connotation, but in a NT context this is strictly an anachronism. It was used as an honorific form of address (see on 23^8) for any revered teacher (hence for Jesus in Mk and especially Jn, but this too may be anachronistic), and later restricted to Pharisaic scribes; but it does not become a synonym for the latter till well after NT times.

[55]Held by Bornkamm, Barth, and Hummel.

[56]Of, e.g., Strecker and, less explicitly, Trilling.

[57]Represented by Bacon, Kilpatrick, Davies, and Stendahl.

synagogue across the street',[58] more nearly accounts for the evidence than any other; it also allows for the possibility of some difference of attitude and even tension between the evangelist and some of the Christians for whom he was writing. It is fairly clear from the bitterness with which he attacks the Pharisees that he had undergone a conversion of some sort, and many scholars have been attracted by the suggestion first made by E. von Dobschütz, that 13[52] implies that he was a converted rabbi. This is at any rate a possibility. But it is by no means established that 13[52] uses the word 'scribe' in the later rabbinic sense, and some of the other evidence encourages an alternative explanation. D. R. A. Hare[59] has concluded from an examination of the passages in Mt relating to persecution of Christians by Jews (particularly 5[11f.], 10[17–23], 23[34–6]) that these refer to the persecution of Christian missionaries by official Judaism; that Mt had himself been involved in a Jewish–Christian mission to Jews which met with rejection and which he afterwards came to see as an error, since it failed to recognize in the events of A.D. 70 the execution of divine judgement on Israel for the rejection and crucifixion of Christ. There is much in the gospel to make this hypothesis very persuasive, and its implication is that the conversion which the evangelist underwent was not from rabbinic Judaism to Christianity but from Jewish particularism to universalism within Christianity itself. On this view he has not one controversial stance, but two. Externally he stands for Christianity against rabbinic Judaism, for the Christian Church as the true successor to the old Israel, and for the Gentile world as the area in which its future lies. Internally he seems to occupy a mediating position between those Christians who still wish to enforce observance of the whole Jewish law (see 5[17–20], and cp. introduction to Chap. 18) and possibly even look forward to a restored temple,[60] and

[58]Stendahl, *School²*, p. xi.

[59]*JPC*, especially pp. 8off. and the conclusion at pp. 146ff.

[60]Texts of Mt that can be construed as in some sense discouraging this include 12[7], 16[18], 18[20], 21[13], 23[39], 24[3,15], 26[61], 27[51], 28[16–20] (see commentary), but it is not clear whether the debate is going on within or outside the Church.

those who, whether explicitly antinomian or not, are tending to make light of ethical demands (see 7^{13-27}, and cp. 13^{41}, 24^{10-13}), and to take their final entrance into the Kingdom for granted (cp. 22^{11-14}, $25^{1-13,14-30,41-6}$).

This reconstruction of the evangelist's career implies that his personal roots, as well as those of the tradition he drew upon, particularly for the sayings of Jesus, lay in Palestine; on the other hand the geographical perspective of the gospel itself (see on 4^{24}), as well as its orientation towards the Gentiles, and the dominance of neo-Pharisaic Judaism within its own territory, suggests that the community for which he wrote lay outside Palestine, most probably in Syria. Precisely where is a matter of conjecture. Earlier scholars objected to Antioch on the grounds that this was the original centre of Hellenistic Christianity and therefore an unlikely place of origin for a predominantly Jewish gospel. This objection failed to take account of the change that came over Antiochene Christianity as a result of the fall of Jerusalem, from which it emerged as the successor to the church of Jerusalem, and the inheritor of much of its prestige.[61] It is likely that once Mt had reached Antioch that church was largely instrumental in circulating it to other Christian centres. But there is a little evidence that what was given this wider circulation was a slightly interpolated edition of Mt (cp. on 12^{40}, $13^{14f\cdot}$, 23^{34}, 28^{19}); and in any case Mt, though acutely alive to the dangers of wealth, does not quite suggest, culturally speaking, the cosmopolitan capital city that Antioch was. A situation nearer Palestine is really indicated.

Kilpatrick's general argument for a coastal area is not very cogent,[62] but his specific suggestion of the region of Phoenicia on the grounds of the alterations made by Mt to the story of the Canaanite (in Mk 'Syrophenician') woman (see on $15^{21ff\cdot}$) has more plausibility than any other so far advanced. It may be added in this connection that Mt's nearest relations (though it must be admitted, poor relations) are, within the NT, the

[61]See W. Telfer, *The Office of a Bishop* (London, 1962), pp. 70–72.
[62]*Origins*, pp. 131f.

Epistle of James, which has access to many of the sayings of Jesus found in Mt, and seems to be written for an affluent, Greek-speaking, but culturally not deeply Hellenized community on the Mediterranean seaboard;[63] and, outside it, the *Didache* (*Teaching of the Twelve Apostles*), a document for which, though the question remains disputed, a date not much later than A.D. 100 (but allowing for literary dependence on Mt at some points), and a situation in Syria, have commended themselves to many scholars.

Date and official authorship

The absolute *terminus a quo* for the date of this gospel is, for the reasons given above, A.D. 70, and it is unlikely that it antedates the 'Test Benediction' (see above, p. 29), usually dated about 85, though this can be only an approximation. The extreme *terminus ad quem* is the first external reference to it in the letters of St. Ignatius (c. A.D. 115; see above, p. 1); but if it was composed elsewhere than at Antioch time must be allowed for it to travel there and win acceptance. A date c. 90–100 seems indicated, but it is impossible to be more definite than this.

The ascription to 'Matthew' is puzzling. It is not of course part of the text, and there is some evidence that Mt was originally known (as it was, e.g., to Ignatius) simply as 'the gospel'. However the title is clearly known to Papias, since he offers an explanation for it. It may be connected with the substitution of 'Matthew' for Mk's 'Levi' in 9[9] and the corresponding designation of him as 'the tax collector' at 10[3]; but since these alterations can be plausibly explained on other grounds (see commentary ad loc.), it seems more likely that they were made the basis for an ascription of authorship after the gospel was first published, than that they formed part of

[63]James writes good Greek, denounces the rich (2[1ff.]), and speaks of the steering of big ships as of a familiar sight (3[4]). For points of contact between Mt and James see M. H. Shepherd, Jr, 'Matthew and James' in *The Authorship and Integrity of the NT*, SPCK Collections, no. 4 (London, 1965), pp. 98ff.

the author's design to publish his gospel pseudonymously (though this is a quite familiar phenomenon elsewhere in the NT, and one to which the ancient world raised no ethical objections). Suggestions such as that it was composed in an area which the apostle Matthew had a hand in evangelizing, or that its heading was transferred from an apocryphal gospel to our Mt as a more worthy candidate, can only remain conjectural.

MATTHEW'S PLACE IN EARLY CHRISTIANITY

Mt then derives from a stream which, apart from James, is otherwise virtually unrepresented in the NT. But the disengagement of the Church from Judaism, of which it represents a particular phase in a single geographical area, was a general problem for early Christianity; the different forms that it took account in great measure for the differences in theological outlook within the primitive Church, and it is by comparing Mt with these that its distinctive standpoint can be most clearly understood.

1. *Paul*

Paul and Mt are separated by thirty years or more; they worked in quite separate regions, and there is no indication that Mt was directly familiar with the writings of his predecessor. Yet, as C. H. Dodd[64] pointed out in an essay written before the Qumran material became available, there are striking parallels between them in their basic assumptions. This is not as surprising as it sounds, since Paul's Christianity certainly had deep Palestinian roots, and he himself, despite his close contacts with the speculative Hellenistic world, remained what many, as we have seen, have taken Mt for, a converted rabbi. Dodd noted parallels between them in three areas:

(a) The eschatological framework from which both were

[64]'Matthew and Paul' (1947), reprinted in *NT Studies* (Manchester, 1953), pp. 53ff.

working. Both Paul in 1 Cor. 15^{20-9} and Mt, especially in 13^{37-43} and $25^{31ff.}$, make a distinction between the kingdom (or reign) of Christ, which has been in operation from the resurrection, and the kingdom of God, to which it will give place at the final consummation after the judgement, which for Paul is to be executed by Christ as the agent of God (Rom. 2^{16}, 2 Cor. 5^{10}), in Mt by the Son of man (16^{27}, 25^{31}). It would seem that Mt does not add anything to the earlier conception of judgement except emphasis.

(b) The close correspondence of the provisions for church discipline in 1 Cor. $5^{1ff.}$ and Mt 18^{15-7}. Historically, as the discovery of a parallel procedure at Qumran confirms, this shows that the practice witnessed to by both derives from Jewish roots; theologically it reveals in both writers a deep sense of the continuing presence of Christ in and with his Church and especially in its solemn corporate acts (cp. 18^{20}), which Paul, but not Mt, interprets in terms of the activity of the Holy Spirit.

(c) Parallels are also noted between the diatribe against the Jews in Rom. 2 and the denunciation of the Pharisees in Mt 23 (both of which read like criticisms of Judaism from within). This is justly observed, but must not be allowed to obscure a significant contrast between Paul and Mt at this point. For whereas in Rom. 9–11, Paul, deeply torn between his sense of community with his unbelieving compatriots and his conviction that it is their rejection by God that has made room for the Gentiles, concludes that this rejection is not final and that God's will is to 'graft them in again', Mt sees no possibility of restoration for a people whose rejection of Christ, and of those sent by him, has been so decisive; they are not merely rejected but accursed.[65]

This reflects the far greater polarization between the two communities in Mt's day than in Paul's. It seems that the original Jewish–Christian community followed Jesus himself in confining its missionary effort to the Jewish people, in the

[65] See Hare, *JPC*, pp. 164–66.

belief that when these were converted the reception of the Gentiles, as foreshadowed in scripture, would necessarily follow.[66] Paul reacted to the Jews' initial rejection of the gospel by inverting the order, on the grounds of the shortness of the time left before the end; but in his time it was still possible to envisage as a consequence of this that once the Gentiles had responded to the message the Jews in their turn would do the same. The Jewish Christians for whom Mt in some sense speaks had evidently clung much longer to the original programme of evangelizing the Jews first, but they had finally been brought to the point of no return; not so much by the destruction of Jerusalem (though that would afterwards be appealed to as a sign of judgement exacted) as by the developments within Judaism which followed it, and in particular by the dominance there of an attitude which no longer recognized Jewish Christians as Jews. This was a far more traumatic blow than any that the Church of Paul's day had to face, and sufficiently explains the violence of their reaction.

There remains a more fundamental divergence between them, on the subject of the Christian understanding of the law.[67] For Mt, Jesus has come not to destroy the law, but to fulfil (i.e. 'realize') it (5^{17}), and though his emphasis is on the overarching requirement of love ($22^{24ff.}$) rather than on the observance of particular precepts as embodying this fulfilment, he is nevertheless content to rest the contrast between Christianity and Judaism at this point on the distinction between the written law of the Pentateuch, which remains fundamentally in force, and the 'oral' law of the Pharisees, which is rejected (cp. on $12^{1ff.}$, $15^{1ff.}$, $19^{1ff.}$). Righteousness for Mt remains fundamentally ethical righteousness, doing the will of God. The position of Paul is more revolutionary at this point, and cannot be fully reconciled with that of Mt. Paul also cites

[66]This is the view of J. Munck, *Paul and the Salvation of Mankind* (London, 1959).
[67]On this see G. Bornkamm, 'The Risen Lord and the Earthly Jesus', in J. M. Robinson (ed.), *The Future of our Religious Past* (London, 1971), pp. 228f.

the dominical ruling that love of neighbour itself constitutes 'fulfilment' of the law (Rom. 13$^{9f.}$); he calls the law 'holy and just and good' (Rom. 7^{12}), and he is not above quoting it as his authority in a controversial situation (1 Cor. 9$^{8-10}$). He is no antinomian in morals. But for him the function of the law as the means of a man's salvation is suspended; righteousness to him is no longer rightness of life before God, but right relationship with God, something given by God himself and received in faith, of which right conduct is the consequence. For Paul (as for Jesus) God is gracious before he is demanding; for Mt (as for the greatest of his Jewish opponents), God's graciousness is contained in his demand.

2. *Luke*[68]

Luke–Acts seems to be very close to Mt in date, and to be dealing with the same general problems from a rather different situation. Like Mt, its author has to make Christian sense of the fall of Jerusalem, the delay in the expected return of Christ, the shift in emphasis to the Gentile mission, and the need of the Church to secure recognition for itself as the authentic Israel. But its *milieu* is Hellenistic Christianity (with the Hellenistic Jewish synagogue of the dispersion in the background); hence a less comprehensive access (parables apart) to the sayings of the Lord, and a rather different, though overlapping, style of biblical exegesis. The major difference between Mt and Lk is in the perspective of their approach to history. The first generation of Christians had little sense of 'sacred history'; for them the 'Christ-event' and especially the resurrection were the first instalment of the end, and the rest was imminently expected to follow it. It was the failure of this to materialize at once that altered the perspective. Mt's reaction to the delay is, first, to admit a limited 'sacred

[68]For Lk's theological outlook see H. Conzelmann, *The Theology of St Luke* (ET London, 1960); J. L. Keck–L. E. Martyn (ed.), *Studies in Luke–Acts* (London, 1967); H. Flender, *Luke the Theologian of Redemptive History* (ET London, 1967); summaries in Rohde, op. cit., pp. 153ff.

history', in that the 'Christ-event' does not simply end with the passion and resurrection of Christ, but its repercussions run on until the judgement on Israel in A.D. 70 (see p. 20); and, secondly, to find meaning in the church life of the present, in which the risen and glorified Christ dwells until the end of time (28^{20}), and in which the actions of its individual members are to be of crucial importance for their judgement when it comes. Both themes are superimposed by Mt on the life of Jesus. The Church is already living under the signs of the approaching end ($24^{9ff.}$), and it is not implied that it will be delayed beyond the period necessary for taking the gospel to all the nations (cp. 24^{14}); but Mt's increased emphasis on the judgement of individuals looks like an accommodation to the probability that many will in fact die before the end comes.

Where Mt is writing instruction for a church, Lk is writing history for a literary public, and his response to the delay is to find theological significance in the historical interval between the Church's inauguration and the end. The progress of the Church (including its shift of centre from Jerusalem to Rome, the capital of the Gentile world) is for him itself a part of the divine plan, and is therefore not superimposed, as in Mt, on the life of Jesus but given a volume to itself, the Acts of the Apostles. It is not necessarily envisaged even here that the interval still remaining will be very long, but the open-ended conclusion of Acts undoubtedly does more than Mt, whether intentionally or not, to prepare the Christian imagination for the possibility that it may be. Lk's scheme also involves a different perspective on the person of Christ; the risen Jesus is thought of as enthroned on high until the time of his return, but not as constantly present with his Church in the interval (contrast Mt 28^{20}). The Spirit which he has sent to guide the Church through history until the end comes, and which in Acts regularly initiates new stages in its growth and progress, is once spoken of as the 'Spirit of Jesus' (Acts 16^{7}); but this identification is less emphasized in Luke–Acts than in any other major strand of the NT.

3. *John*

An earlier tradition of NT scholarship tended to make a hard-and-fast distinction between the three synoptists on the one hand and the fourth gospel on the other, the former being identified with historical fact about Christ and the latter with doctrinal interpretation of him. This had a certain plausibility so long as the synoptists were regarded merely as editors of written and oral source-material; but since they have begun to be seen also as authors each with his own theological viewpoint, as well as nearer in date, it is no longer self-evidently true. In the case of Mt it always raised special problems, since 11$^{25-7}$ has on the face of it a strongly Johannine flavour, and 28$^{18-20}$ expresses a Christology which in the submission of E. Lohmeyer is as exalted as any in the fourth gospel.

A number of general points of contact can in fact be observed between Mt and Jn. Each of the two books is the product of a tradition with some Palestinian roots (though Jn has moved further away from these into the world of Hellenistic culture and has a far less extensive acquaintance with the tradition of the sayings of Jesus). Both have a similar interest in the fulfilment of OT scripture expressed by a similar formula (for Mt see pp. 8f. above; cp. Jn 12^{38}, 13^{18}, 15^{25}, 18^{9}, 19^{24,36}); both see Christ as fulfilling the religious significance of the Jewish temple (cp. Mt 12^{6}, 16^{18}, 18^{20}; Jn 2^{22}, 7^{37} and the temple episodes in Jn 5–12 generally). Jn, like Mt, displays bitter hostility to the Judaism of the synagogue (cp. Jn 8 with Mt 23), and reveals traces of the working of the 'Test Benediction' (see Jn 9^{22}, 12^{42}, 16^{2}).

But it is in their Christology that the two gospels show the most striking and unexpected affinities.[69] It is well enough known that the Jesus of the fourth gospel is a divine person fully aware of his heavenly origin, omniscient, and the object of faith and worship even in his earthly life. Mt has not eliminated the human Jesus remembered by his followers from his source-material as systematically as this; the Christ of

[69]See E. P. Blair, *Jesus in the Gospel of Matthew* (New York, 1960), pp. 155f.

present experience is, as we have seen, superimposed on this, rather than fused with it as in Jn. But in those parts of it on which he has left his own stamp most clearly, such as the 'peak' sayings cited above (and $16^{18f.}$), and the healing narratives (see introduction to Chaps. 8–9), the same process is clearly at work. Jesus is addressed in the latter as *Kyrios* (Lord), with the liturgical overtones that this would have had in the worshipping community, and the attainment of faith in him (or, in the case of disciples, its confirmation and re-assurance—see on 'little faith' in 8^{26}, 14^{31}, 16^{8}) is treated as a matter of greater moment than the effecting of healing as such. The passion narratives of both gospels represent him as wholly in command of the situation, and his death as only possible by his free and full consent (for Mt see introduction to Chaps. 26–8; cp. Jn 10^{18}, 18^{4-8}, $19^{17,28-30}$). Both gospels show a pronounced liking for the expression 'my Father' on the lips of Jesus, i.e. the title 'Son of God' is being interpreted in terms not just of Messiahship as this had been understood in popular Judaism, but of transcendental divine Sonship; and both combine its use with that of the eschatological title 'Son of man' (see Note B, p. 237), though Mt's own use of this (as distinct from what came to him from his sources) seems to be governed by a 'future' understanding of it, whereas in Jn it denotes also, and indeed primarily, the pre-existent 'heavenly man' (cp. Jn 3^{13}). Indeed the principal difference between them, at this point and elsewhere, is that Jn thinks of Christ as a pre-existent divine being (see Jn 1^{1-18}, 6^{62}, 8^{58}, etc.) while Mt gives no clear indication of this.[70] The Johannine stand-point here has often been explained as the result of grappling with the speculations of Hellenistic philosophy; but though Jn is unquestionably nearer to the world of Greek thought than Mt, there was plenty in Hebraic sources (e.g. the speculations concerning the personified figure of Wisdom in the OT sapiential literature, and related ones about the Torah in the early rabbinic tradition) to prepare him for the

[70]The contrary argument of M. J. Suggs, *Wisdom, Christology and Law in Matthew's Gospel* (London, 1971) does not convince me.

position he arrived at. To label his Christology, and Mt's too at the points at which it approaches Jn's, as "Hellenistic"[71] in the sense of non-Judaistic begs too many questions to be illuminating.

Jn also distinguishes the person of the Paraclete (i.e. the Holy Spirit) from that of the exalted Christ. Mt, as we have seen, does not use this kind of language; he is less guarded about identifying the Christ of the Church's present experience with the glorified Lord of heaven and earth than any other NT writer, not excluding St. Paul. But the use of this concept by Jn conceals a further difference between them. For Jn part of the work of the Paraclete is to recall the teaching of Jesus and expound it afresh to the contemporary Church (cp. Jn 14^{26}, 16^{13-5}). For Mt the essential teaching is in the recorded words of the earthly Jesus (cp. 28^{19}) entrusted to the disciples, i.e. the Church;[72] reinterpretation will sometimes be necessary, and the disciples are invited to practise it (see 13^{36-52}), but the words themselves will not pass away even with the end of the world (24^{35}).

Mt and Jn are of course poles apart in their eschatology, since Mt still anticipates Christ's coming in judgement in the more or less imminent future, whereas Jn largely interprets both the return of Christ and the concept of judgement in terms of what is already true in the present (cp., e.g., Jn 3^{17-9}, 14^{18}, 16^{22}). But this reinterpretation seems to be personal to the fourth evangelist rather than characteristic of the Johannine stream in early Christianity as a whole, and the Apocalypse, which clearly draws on the same basic stock of imagery as the rest of the Johannine literature, has obvious points of contact with the type of eschatology found in Mt (see on 24^{31}).

[71]This is the view taken of Mt by Bornkamm, loc. cit., p. 213, and Stendahl, *School*[2], p. xiii. Contrast (for Jn) B. Lindars, *Behind the Fourth Gospel* (London, 1971), pp. 64ff., especially 72f.
[72]See Bornkamm, loc. cit., pp. 222ff.

RECEPTION OF THE GOSPEL BY THE CHURCH AT LARGE

How did a gospel deriving from a relative backwater come to win such immediate acceptance in the Great Church?

(a) Syria as a whole was far from being a *Christian* backwater; the originally Hellenistic church of Antioch not only enjoyed the prestige attaching to its situation in a great provincial administrative capital, but had inherited the spiritual leadership that had formerly belonged to the mother church of Jerusalem. Its influence on other churches, already not small, was later enhanced by the impression made by its great bishop Ignatius on his journey by way of Asia Minor to Rome and martyrdom. Once Mt had reached Antioch and had been accepted there, it was sure of a wide public. Streeter's conjecture[73] that it was Ignatius himself who brought the gospel of Mt to Rome has something to commend it.

(b) It was nevertheless as much by its own inherent qualities as by influential backing that Mt won recognition. It is the most comprehensive in its content, and the most lucid and systematic in its arrangement, of all the four gospels; and it had the advantage of entering the field at a time when it had only Mk to supplant.

(c) One consequence for Christianity of the Jewish revolt of A.D. 66–70 had been the dispersion of Jewish Christian refugees to many areas of the eastern Mediterranean and their influx into churches that had originally been predominantly Gentile, with resultant problems for the integration of local Christian communities (this has clearly left its mark on the Johannine writings, usually located in Asia Minor, and possibly also on the Epistle to the Ephesians). Mt, with its Jewish–Christian roots and its commitment to the inclusion of Gentiles in the Church, spoke effectively to this situation; as Stendahl has put it, 'Matthew is comprehensive by circumstance, and that makes it a rich and wise book'.[74]

[73]Op. cit., p. 525.
[74]*School*[2], p. xiv.

(d) As we have seen in connexion with Papias, a major concern of the second century Church was to combat Gnostic innovations with an appeal to the original gospel. The care with which Mt reproduces the sayings of Jesus *in extenso* catered for this need, and the gospel was held in correspondingly high esteen. Lk on the other hand was to some extent compromised by the use to which it was put by the heretic Marcion, and Jn was long suspected of a Gnosticizing tendency.

(e) Though the case has often been exaggerated,[75] the outlook of second century Christianity does on the whole represent on its ethical side something of a reversion to Judaistic moralism. A gospel which presented the Christian life as obedience to a renewed law was more readily understood and received than any writing expressing the Pauline viewpoint could have been.

(f) A special need of second century Christianity was the consolidation of local Christian communities thrown up by the great missionary expansion of the previous century. To the extent that Mt fulfilled this, it is proper to speak of it as the 'ecclesiastical gospel'. It certainly reflects the situation of such a community, having been written from first-hand familiarity with the problems of wavering faith, love grown cold, the prospect of judgement ignored, and, on the other hand, over-severity with the weak and erring. (It took the Church at large several centuries to catch up with the humanity of Mt's attitude to the forgiveness of the post-baptismal sins of Christians.)

(g) The expression 'liturgical gospel' needs to be used with caution. There is no necessary carry-over from a gospel shaped (if it was) by liturgical reading of its written sources to one which in its final form continued to lend itself to this function. It is nevertheless true that the compact sections of Mt's

[75]As by T. F. Torrance, *The Doctrine of Grace in the Apostolic Fathers* (Edinburgh, 1949); but cp. K. E. Kirk, *The Vision of God* (London, 1931), pp. 111–73.

narrative and the rhythmical quality of its prose helped to make it a favourite source for liturgical lections, and it retained this favoured position in the gospel lectionaries of most Christian communions down to the recent wave of reforms. Christian practice has universally preferred the fuller and more 'liturgical' form of the Lord's Prayer found in Mt to the informality of the shorter version preserved in Lk.

The consequences of this gospel's favoured position for the presuppositions of Christian faith and practice have been incalculable. If the actual teachings of Jesus have shaped the development of Christian ethical thinking, it is largely in their codified form in the Sermon on the Mount that they have done so. To Mt we owe, in addition to the familiar version of the Lord's Prayer, the Beatitudes (with their strong, if unobtrusive, influence on Christian spirituality), much of the traditional imagery of the last things, the fullest (if also the most problematical) of the accounts of the teaching of Jesus on marriage; and also, for better or worse, the principal texts used to support the papal primacy, those from which the doctrine of a double standard of Christian calling was developed, and, alas, those used to fasten guilt for the crucifixion of Jesus on the Jewish race. Some of these, and in particular the last, represent, as the commentary will attempt to explain, a misunderstanding of Mt's own position. All owe their influence in no small degree to the currency given to them by the Church's favourite gospel.

ADDITIONAL NOTE: PAPIAS ON MATTHEW

Papias' statement about Matthew is the last of a series of quotations from his writings preserved by Eusebius in the same context, and certain aspects of its vocabulary become clearer after examination of the other fragments. The following points are relevant:

(a) The lost work of Papias from which Eusebius was quoting was an 'Exposition of the Lord's *logia*' in five books (H.E. III. xxxix. 1).

(b) Papias shows a concern to go behind secondary authorities to the authentic voice of Christ himself:

'In fact, unlike most people, I did not care for men who gave the longest accounts, but for men whose teachings were true nor yet for men who reported the commandments of others, but for such as related those given by the Lord to be believed and stemming directly from the truth' (III. xxxix. 4).[1]

His motive for doing this, as has already been suggested (see p. 2), is the need to combat Gnostic innovations by an appeal to reliable tradition. How far he was successful in his object is another matter.

(c) Of Mark he says:

'Mark, who had been Peter's interpreter, set down accurately, but not word for word (*taxei*), all that he could remember of the Lord's sayings and doings. He had neither heard the Lord nor been his follower, but subsequently, as I said, he had been Peter's. Peter was in the habit of adapting his instruction to the needs of the occasion, without attempting to give a full account (*suntaxin*) of the Lord's *logia*; so that Mark was in no way to blame if his written account, based on his own recollections, was incomplete. His only concern was not to omit anything that he had heard, nor to falsify any item in it' (III. xxxix. 15).

(d) Finally of Matthew he says:

'Matthew . . . compiled (*sunetaxato*) the *logia* in the Hebrew language, and everyone translated them according to his ability' (III. xxxix. 16).

What is the meaning of *logia*? It is a more solemn word than that ordinarily used for 'sayings' (*logoi*), with the force of 'inspired utterances'; in a Judaeo–Christian context it normally means 'prophecies' or other texts of scripture that are taken as the voice of God himself, either individually, or

[1]Translation from J. A. Kleist, *Ancient Christian Writers*, vi (London, 1948), 115. The remaining versions are my own, though I have followed Kleist's interpretation of *taxei* in (c) (ib. 205, 207f.), a usage which has survived, as he says, in modern Greek.

collectively of the whole Biblical revelation.[2] The collective use could not be extended to the NT scriptures before the formation of the Church's canon of scripture (later second century), but already by Papias' time the scope of the *logia* of the Lord is beginning to be extended to include the recorded sayings of the Lord Jesus Christ.[3] Whether it could include his acts also[4] (God being understood to speak through both) is more questionable; it is true that, according to Papias, Mark remembered the 'sayings and doings' of the Lord, but these are not self-evidently the same as the *logia* which he did not reproduce in full, and restriction of the term to his sayings on the whole accords better with Papias' professed concern to get back to the authentic voice. It is still more doubtful whether the word can mean a 'gospel', in the sense of a particular kind of book. Papias does not appear to think of four gospels; the fragments preserved by Eusebius do not mention those of Lk and Jn, and Mk is compared unfavourably with Mt because he did not give a *suntaxis* of the Lord's *logia*. *Suntaxis* and the cognates also used by Papias are regularly associated with literary composition; their accent is not on logical or chronological sequence (the latter in particular would be inapplicable to sayings) but on completeness as opposed to summary or selection. Mk's account is pronounced reliable as far as it goes, and it is not denied apostolic authority, but it does not reproduce the sayings of the Lord in full as Mt does, and it is this that entitles Mt to be regarded as the gospel record *par excellence* (as it already was for Ignatius some thirty years before). The features of Mk picked out by Papias are recognizably those of the gospel we know, and the same is true of the *differentia* he notes between Mk and Mt; what he compared with Mk could hardly, at this date, be other than our Mt. The Lord's *logia* are this gospel, described in terms of its most

[2] See G. Kittel in *TDNT* iv. 139–41; Bauer, Arndt and Gingrich, *A Greek–English Lexicon of the NT*, s.v.; G. W. H. Lampe (ed.), *A Patristic Greek Lexicon*, s.v.
[3] As in 2 *Clement* xiii. 3–4; *Epistle of Polycarp* vii. 1.
[4] As Kittel suggests.

characteristic feature; Papias' 'Exposition' of them was, it would seem, the first gospel commentary.

It can therefore be inferred with some confidence that Papias had before him our Mt with its ascription to the apostle Matthew, a Palestinian and as such an unlikely author for a Greek gospel; it remains to be seen whether there is any historical substance in his convenient explanation of this difficulty. If the interpretation of *logia* which we have arrived at is correct, Papias cannot be saying, as some have suggested, that what Matthew did was to collect OT 'testimonies' (see, pp. 9f.) to the Messiahship of Jesus, which would in any case form an insufficient literary basis for a gospel. He could, so far as word usage goes, be saying that Matthew made a collection of the sayings of Jesus, such as that postulated as the source Q (see, pp. 5f.) but such a document (assuming it to have existed; the case must be argued on internal grounds) would need more than translation to produce our present Mt, and the arrangement of the sayings in the latter is patently the work of the evangelist himself. (Significantly, the only known literary parallel to the hypothetical Q is the so-called *Gospel of Thomas*,[5] a Gnostic conflation of canonical with manifestly spurious sayings and as such an example of the kind of work that Papias was probably attacking). There remains the hypothesis of an Aramaic proto-gospel behind canonical Mt. This is the most plausible account of what Papias thought to have been the case, and it has been the interpretation favoured by commentators for whom he represents authentic ecclesiastical tradition. But a narrative gospel which at the same time answered to the description of a compilation of the sayings of the Lord would be so close to our present Mt that it would be impossible to account for the latter's use of Greek written sources or to explain why it does not show more signs of having been translated. (Papias may, however, have had his own reasons for thinking that it had been. The apocryphal *Gospel of the Nazaraeans*,[6] a Syriac part translation, part paraphrase—

[5]See p. xi.
[6]*NTAp i*, pp. 139ff.

i.e. *targum*—of Mt, could have been already in circulation by this time; if Papias had been acquainted with it, at first or second hand, he could well have taken it for the original of Mt, though we know now that the dependence was the other way.)

.It thus seems impossible to reconcile what Papias says of Matthew with the findings of present-day scholarship. There is a similar problem in the case of Mark. While the presumed connection of Mk with Peter has been taken seriously by many scholars, it assorts uneasily with the general conclusion of form-criticism, that the bulk of the units which go to make up that gospel circulated independently before being incorporated in it. In both cases it is necessary to choose between 'tradition' and critical insights. While it is not impossible in principle that Papias had access to a line of tradition running back into the apostolic age, the tendency to supply gaps in what is known by conjectures which then take their place alongside the authentic material is too familiar to students of the development of oral traditions for us to place much confidence in his unsupported assertions. And the fact that his statements were repeated by later Christian writers of repute does not constitute support. A chain of tradition is only as strong as its weakest link.

THE GOSPEL ACCORDING TO

MATTHEW

PART I: JESUS THE CHRIST

I. THE ORIGINS OF THE CHRIST (CHAPTERS 1-2)

The infancy narrative with which Mt opens is no mere prologue to the gospel, but an integral part of it. If, as has been argued above, the purpose of the first ten chapters is to present to the reader the figure of Jesus the Messiah in its different aspects, the natural starting-point is an account of his origins, and this was the first point at which Mt found Mk incomplete.

It is probable that the earliest Christian apologetic attributed divine Sonship to Jesus only after, and by virtue of, his resurrection. But the tendency to anticipate this shows itself very early, and the gospel of Mk, Mt's only model, depicts him as Son of God from his first public appearance, at his baptism by John. Two logical developments, originally alternative, were possible from this point: either (as already in St. Paul, and fully worked out in the first chapter of Jn) a pre-existent divine being entered human life in the person of Jesus of Nazareth, or the inception of his life was itself an act in which God took the initiative. Mt takes the second alternative, as does Lk; neither of them betrays any interest in the question of Christ's pre-existence (see J. Knox, *The Humanity and Divinity of Christ* (London, 1967); R. H. Fuller, *Foundations of NT Christology* (London, 1965), especially p. 228; Lindars, *NTA*, pp. 189 ff.)

Mt obviously lacked material from his predecessor for Jesus' life prior to his baptism. Nor is what he has written paralleled in any other known source; Lk's account, though it has some formal correspondences with Mt's (see Kilpatrick, *Origins*, p. 54), is quite different in content. Either (i) Mt has drawn on eye-witness testimony or family traditions, or (ii) he is dependent on written sources unknown to us, or (iii) he found the material in the oral tradition of his own community, or (iv) he has improvised on the basis of OT texts, which for him were prophecies requiring fulfilment as the fore-ordained will of God. (i) is the kind of speculation which it is difficult to disprove, but the date at which Mt is writing, the lack of corroboration from other sources (even where it might be expected, as in the case of the massacre of the innocents), and the fact that the story is told from the point of view of Joseph, who was apparently no longer living at the time of Jesus' own ministry, all tell heavily against it. (ii) is not impossible in principle, but there are no agreed findings among scholars about the source-analysis of these chapters, which betray in addition certain characteristic marks of Mt's personal style. Between (iii) and (iv) there is considerable overlap, since Mt represents a tradition of the Christian interpretation of scripture of which the evangelist was not the first exponent, and, at the date at which he wrote, items of supposedly fulfilled prophecy may well have predominated over purely historical traditions in the material available to him. In any case, these chapters show clear signs of having been written round selected OT texts; those explicitly cited are the clue to the evangelist's own purpose in writing, but further layers of OT allusion can be detected underneath them, and these are not all necessarily due to Mt himself.

The texts, whether cited or not, are treated in accordance with the exegetical principles current in contemporary Judaism, and the stories which are hung on them are rightly classified as examples of Christian *haggadah* (see Introduction, p. 11). We should not therefore look for literal history in these chapters, but read them as their author presumably intended them to be read, for imaginative insight into the person and mission of Jesus, in the light of hints and suggestions offered by the OT scriptures. This has to be done from the following angles:

(a) *Typological*: Jesus Christ is the fulfilment of the old Israel; therefore its history, and that of its representative figures Abraham, Jacob, Moses, David, etc., is recapitulated in his personal history.

(b) *Prefigurative*: since the events of the ending of Jesus' earthly life, his passion and resurrection, and the universal mission of the Church which was their consequence, were divinely fore-ordained, the evangelist sees these as fore-shadowed in the events of his infancy; this is particularly true of Chap. 2 which is heavy with forebodings of persecution and suffering to come.

(c) *Controversial*: Christians had to meet the objection of contemporary Judaism that the Christian Messiah was a Galilean, and possibly also Jewish allegations that he was illegitimate and had learned black magic in Egypt. (It is true that the rabbinic sources in which these latter slanders are found are later than Mt, and could even be dependent on his gospel. But certain features of the narrative are more easily understood if the dependence is the other way.)

(d) *Apologetic*: the aim of these chapters is not limited to answering misrepresentations against the person of Jesus. They also argue positively that, irregular as his background appears, it nevertheless fulfils the accepted scriptural require-ments for Messiahship. Chap. 1 does this in terms of the persons from whom Jesus is descended, Chap. 2 in terms of the places from which he comes. See the illuminating analysis of K. Stendahl, 'Quis et Unde', in W. Eltester (ed.), *Judentum, Urchristentum, Kirche* (Festschrift für J. Jeremias, Berlin, 1960), pp. 94ff. (in English).

1: 1–25 *Son of David and Son of God*

The solemn opening introduces not only the genealogy but the whole infancy narrative, and, in a broader sense, the whole gospel. The Gk word *genesis* can mean not only 'gene-alogy' (as at v. 1 RSV; cp. Gen. 5¹), but also 'birth' (as it probably does at v. 18) and 'creation' (cp. Gen. 2⁴ and the traditional title for the first book of the OT—though it is not certain that this figured in the LXX text in Mt's day). It is likely that the word picks up a reference to Gen. 1¹ in Mk's word *archē* ('beginning') at Mk 1¹ (cp. Jn 1¹); in any case Mk's opening is the starting-point for Mt's. It sets the scene for an account of the personal origins of Jesus, in two parts: his continuity with the Israel of the OT, and his supernatural relationship to God.

1: 1–17 (a) Jesus in the Davidic line

For the character of the genealogy see M. Johnson, *The Purpose of the Biblical Genealogies* (Cambridge, 1969), pp. 139ff. It is an artificial construction in three sections of fourteen generations each (though the third actually has only thirteen). The first two sections are based on similar genealogies in the OT (1 Chr. 2¹⁻¹⁵; Ruth 4¹⁸⁻²²; 1 Chr. 3¹⁰⁻¹⁷); for the names after Zerubbabel no continuous source is known. The dividing points between the sections are the reign of David and the exile, the peak and the trough respectively of the fortunes on the kingdom of Israel; this points to the coming of Christ as the restoration of the kingdom and the fulfilment of the Messianic hope.

1. *Son of David:* a Messianic title, found by Mt at Mk 10⁴⁷ and constantly used by him. Jewish expectation awaited the fulfilment of God's promises to David (see 2 Sam. 7) in a Messiah (Christ) descended from him. The primary purpose of the genealogy is to establish Jesus' claim to the title; cp. on v. 17.
   son of Abraham: Abraham, the father of Israel, is shown to be the father of the representative figure of the new Israel, and through him of all its members, whether or not literally descended from him. For Mt as for Paul (Rom. 4; Gal. 3) these will include Gentiles; cp. 3⁹. The covenants with Abraham and David both involved the birth of a son, and in Abraham's case the greatest birth miracle of the OT.

2. *and his brothers:* not strictly necessary to the argument from descent, but included either to express the solidarity of Israel or as an instance of the overruling of the ordinary law of primogeniture.

3. *Tamar* was Judah's daughter-in-law, and her conception by him the result of prostitution; see Gen. 38.

5. *Rahab:* the prostitute of Jericho (Jos. 2). Dt. 23¹⁷ forbade (cult) prostitution in Israel. *Ruth:* morally blameless, but a Moabitess, and

therefore subject to the ban on Gentile wives (see Dt. 7³, etc.). The book of Ruth appears to be an early protest against this kind of exclusiveness.

6. *the wife of Uriah:* Bathsheba, whom David seduced and then married after contriving her husband's death in battle (2 Sam. 11). She is, significantly, referred to by the name of her Gentile husband.

These four women (not usually mentioned in Hebrew genealogies) are introduced for a reason. What have they in common? Three were unchaste, and three (possibly all four) were Gentiles. (The mother of the original son of David was both). Either condition was an irregularity disqualifying them for inclusion in a table of legitimate descent (since it called for obligatory divorce). Yet in each case the divine purpose overruled it. The parallel with the irregular introduction of Jesus into the Davidic line (see vv. 18ff.) is obvious, and deliberate.

7–15. The names of Ahaz, Joash and Amaziah are missing from this section, presumably to keep the number of the generations down to fourteen (see on v. 17).

7. *Asa:* the Gk has *Asaph*, but these are only variant forms of the same name. Another Asaph figures in the OT as a contributor to the Psalter (which was reckoned prophetic).

10. *Amos:* the Heb. of 1 Chr. 3¹⁴ has (correctly) *Amon*, but the MSS of LXX vary between 'Amon' and 'Amos'. and the same is true of other passages where this king is mentioned. It is still possible that Mt by his choice of forms in these two places sought to include at least an oblique reference to the OT prophets in the genealogy of the Lord who fulfilled them; but not very much can be built on this.

11. *Jechoniah and his brothers:* this is at variance with the OT data, since Jechoniah (Jehoiachin) was Josiah's grandson and had no recorded brothers, though his father Jehoiakim had several. Suggested solutions to this problem include confusion of similar names, complications arising out of Mt's scheme of generations, and rabbinic preoccupation with the figure of Jechoniah; see Johnson, pp. 182–4.

16. The text is disputed. The RSV reading is that of the bulk of MSS. Some MSS of the 'Caesarean' family and some versions have some form of the expression '. . . Joseph to whom being betrothed Mary a virgin gave birth to (*egennēse*) Jesus'. One version (Syriac) has '. . . Joseph, and Joseph to whom Mary a virgin was betrothed was the father of (*egennēse*) Jesus'. The first of these alternatives is clearly a compromise. The second is either a statement of Joseph's paternity, or an assimilation of this item in the genealogy to the rest. On the latter view it is by definition a correction of Mt and not the original reading; on the former it can only be claimed as original if Mt took the genealogy from a source, since he would hardly himself have written such an apparent contradiction of the virginal conception to which he elsewhere holds unambiguously. The source theory is not

very probable. See further C. S. C. Williams, *Alterations to the Text of the Synoptic Gospels and Acts* (Oxford, 1951), pp. 25ff.

17. The most plausible explanation of the repeated emphasis on the number *fourteen* is that it represents, by the method known as *gematria*, the numerical value of the name *David* in Hebrew (D W D=4+6+4 =14). So, cautiously, Davies, *SSM*, pp. 74ff. For alternative explanations see Johnson, pp. 189ff. What is here expressed numerically is the finality of Jesus the Messiah, as the fulfilment to which the whole history of Israel has been leading. There is no fully satisfactory explanation of the fact that the last section actually contains only thirteen generations. Possibly Mt thought of a further generation elapsing between the birth of Jesus and his effective assumption of Messiahship (see on 26[64], 28[18]). Cp. the frequent deprecating references to 'this generation' (11[16], 12[39ff.], 23[36], etc.).

1: 18–25 (b) The virgin birth of Jesus

Having established the Davidic descent of Jesus Christ, Mt goes on in the second half of the chapter to relate this to what is known of his personal origins. Stendahl sees this as a continuation of the theme of the genealogy, an account of the 'grafting' of Jesus the Son of Mary into the Davidic line; this rather underplays the paradox of the Son of David who is at the same time supernaturally born (cp. 22[42ff.]). It is therefore an exaggeration to say with him that the virgin birth in Mt is 'theologically mute' (is there no connexion between the child's conception 'by Holy Spirit' in vv. 18, 20, and the meaning of 'Emmanuel' in v. 23?); but it is true that it remains theologically subordinate, and the probable implication of this is that the doctrine itself is no part of Mt's own haggadic improvisation, but was received by him as a *datum*. The apologetic motive which many see in the narrative would point in the same direction. Later rabbinic writers referred to our Lord as Yeshua ben Pantera (Pantera may either be a proper name, with the imputation of illegitimacy, or a corruption of the Gk *parthenos*—virgin—which would presuppose the virgin birth tradition). This particular form of the slander is not attested earlier than A.D. 130 and may not have been current in Mt's day (it may even be dependent on his gospel); but allegations of illegitimacy against Jesus must have been already in circulation when Jn 8[41] was written. The virgin birth story probably lies behind these, and if Mt's account is intended to counter them, the tradition must have been current before he wrote. How long before, it is impossible to say (the argument of J. Daniélou, *The Infancy Narratives* [ET London, 1966], goes considerably beyond the evidence); but the silence of Paul and Mk (representing early Gentile Christian communities) and the continuing rejection of it by the Ebionite sect (deriving, it would seem, from the position of early Palestinian

Christianity) together point to some area of Greek-speaking Jewish Christianity as the setting in which it emerged (see Fuller, op. cit., p. 195). The evidence of Mt is fully consistent with this. Jewish thinking was not altogether inhospitable to the idea of a virgin birth in connexion with an outstanding figure; for Isaac (son of Abraham, cp. v. 1) see Fuller, p. 202; for Moses, Daube, *NTRJ*, pp. 5ff.

18. *birth*: Gk *genesis*, as in v. 1. Stendahl argues that there is no change of meaning, Mt's purpose being simply to explain how one born as Jesus was known to have been born fitted into the Davidic line. Hence the story is told from the point of view of Joseph through whom the descent was traced. More probably there is a play on the two meanings of the word, emphasizing both the continuity with Israel and the divine intervention. One family of MSS. has *gennēsis*, a word with the unambiguous connotation of parenthood, which links this section directly with v. 16. *betrothed*: a more solemn step in Jewish practice than engagement is with us, normally followed by co-habitation (though apparently not in Galilee). *Holy Spirit*: i.e. by the supernatural intervention of God. References to the Holy Spirit are as rare elsewhere in Mt as they are in the synoptic tradition generally.

19. *a just man*: i.e. a faithful observer of the law, which (as interpreted in the first century) required a man to put away his betrothed if he had evidence of her unchastity (Dt 24¹). *and unwilling . . . shame*: cp. *NEB* 'and at the same time wanting to save her from exposure'. Joseph wants to do the right thing both by the law and by Mary, of whose guilt he is not convinced. *divorce*: RSVCE 'send her away', to avoid any judgement on the validity of the marriage; but the distinction is an unreal one in a Jewish context.

20. *in a dream*: a recurrent motif of these chapters; possibly the name Joseph recalls the OT Joseph, 'this dreamer' (Gen. 37¹⁹). Dreams were regarded in antiquity, as they have been in many cultures, as communications from the unseen world; in these chapters they express God's overruling of human intentions. The oracle which follows is composed in the rhythms characteristic of Hebrew poetry, a feature which recurs at solemn moments in the gospel, e.g. 5³⁻¹⁰, 11²⁵⁻³⁰, 16¹⁷⁻⁹, 28¹⁸⁻²⁰).

21. *Jesus*: the Gk form of the Hebrew *Yeshua* (Joshua), a name in very common use in first-century Palestine (cp. on 27¹⁵), meaning 'Yahweh is salvation'. *he will save . . . sins*: evidently offered as an interpretation of the name *Jesus*, but, linguistically speaking, a very free one. The wording is reminiscent of Ps. 130⁸, but it seems not to be a direct quotation.

23. Is. 7¹⁴, quoted, with one alteration (see below), directly from LXX, unlike Mt's other special quotations. *a virgin*: the Heb. '*almah*' used in Is. 7¹⁴ means simply 'a young woman'. The LXX in using the Gk

parthenos to translate it may have been perpetuating a Jewish tradition that Isaiah had prophesied the birth of the Messiah from a virgin (this is the assertion of Justin Martyr [*Dial.* 71]); nevertheless the Gk is the only form of the OT text itself that can be used to support this idea. In any case Mt is more interested in the Messianic aspects of the text; he is not trying to establish by it that Jesus was born of a virgin, but that one so born can yet be the Messiah. *his name shall be called:* lit. 'they shall call his name'. LXX has 'you shall call', which is altered because Joseph has already been instructed to call the child by another name. *God with us:* added to the quotation by Mt from Is. 8¹⁰. In the OT this is a semi-technical expression of God's helping presence with individuals (see W. C. van Unnik, 'Dominus vobiscum' in A. J. B. Higgins (ed.) *NT Essays: Studies in Memory of T. W. Manson* (Manchester, 1959), pp. 270ff.). For Mt's further use of it, cp. 18²⁰ and especially 28²⁰.

25. *knew her not:* there is nothing here about the perpetual virginity of Mary, either for or against. Mt is only concerned to establish her virginity at the time of the birth; he is not answering any questions about what happened afterwards (though he does not see his later allusions to brothers of Jesus at 12⁴⁶ᶠᶠ·, 13⁵⁵ as a matter calling for explanation).

2: 1–23 *From Bethlehem to Nazareth*

'Mt 2 is dominated by geographical names' (Stendahl, op. cit., p. 97). The problem that underlies this chapter (cp. Jn 7⁴¹ᶠ·) is: how, if the Messiah was born at Bethlehem (as, according to the prophecy, he must be), did he come to be associated with Galilee (as the tradition unanimously asserts that he was)? The question of how this happened is answered by Mt with an outline itinerary taking Jesus from Bethlehem to Egypt and back to Nazareth, which serves as the framework for the contents of the chapter (note that the four OT texts actually cited all contain place names); the question of why it happened receives the answer: because of persecution by his own people. It is given in such a way as to prefigure the future history both of Jesus (crucified in Judaea; seen risen by his disciples in Galilee, 28¹⁶⁻²⁰) and of his Church (the new Israel, rejected by traditional Judaism, but received by the Gentiles). 'From this point of view the whole series of incidents in Mt 2 are portents presaging the great acts at the close of the gospel. Jesus is treated as a king, yet rejected by Herod; he is thrust out to Egypt, the house of bondage and the symbol of death; but Herod's evil intentions are defeated, so that Jesus is able to return to live in Galilee.' (Lindars, *NTA*, p. 218). At the same time, since the child Jesus represents the new Israel, his story is told in a way which recapitulates that of the old Israel and of representative figures in it.

1. *born in Bethlehem:* this is assumed (in view of the prophecy at v. 6), not described. It is a secret to be revealed to Israel, and it is Gentiles who learn of it first. *Herod the king:* Herod the Great, an Edomite and a friend of Julius Caesar, became governor of Galilee in 47 B.C., and was given the title of king of Judaea by Antony and Octavius in 40 B.C., a position which he held till his death in 4 B.C. (see A. H. M. Jones, *The Herods of Judaea* [Oxford, 1939]). Both Mt and Lk—our only authorities—place the birth of Christ in his reign; this may be no more than an inference from the known approximate date of the crucifixion, but it does not follow that they were the first to make it. (The traditional division of B.C. and A.D. rests upon a miscalculation by an unknown chronicler.) Herod's reputation for cruelty and duplicity long survived him (see the account in Jos., *Ant.* xvi. 392ff., xvii. 32ff.) and Mt may be presumed to have been familiar with it. But his Herod is clearly a representative figure; in him the *de facto* ruler of Judaea (and an Edomite and Roman nominee at that) is confronted by the claims of the true Davidic king of Israel. *wise men* (Gk *magoi*) *from the East:* the term 'magi' originally denoted the priestly class in ancient Persia, which had an extensive reputation as astrologers and diviners. Some time before Mt wrote, it had acquired the more general and pejorative connotation of magicians or sorcerers. Although king and 'magus' are not mutually exclusive terms, Mt's preference for the latter in a passage clearly influenced by Is. 60[3] and Ps. 72[10] calls for some explanation:

(a) Central to the whole episode is the opposition of king Herod to the newly born 'king of the Jews'; this would stand out in less clear relief if the Gentile visitors who worshipped while Herod set out to destroy were themselves represented as kings.

(b) The part played by the star called for observers skilled in astrology.

(c) Later rabbinic tradition alleged that Jesus had learned sorcery in Egypt. Mt could be answering a slander of this kind if it was already current: so far from instructing him in Egypt, the 'magi' offered him worship (and perhaps surrendered their trade and its ill-gotten gains —see on v. 11) before his journey there, from which in any case he returned while still a child.

2. *his star*: the OT text 'just under the surface' (Stendahl) is Nu. 24[17]: 'a star shall arise out of Jacob'—a passage already studied at Qumran, and later to be exploited by the last Jewish claimant to Messiahship, Simon Bar-Kokba ('son of the star'), whose rebellion was put down in A.D. 135. There is a significant parallel to Mt's story in a legend of the birth of Abraham preserved in a late Jewish *midrash* (see Vermes, *Scripture and Tradition in Judaism*, pp. 68ff.). In this too the birth is revealed by the appearance of a star, and the predictions of greatness which follow lead to an attempt on the part of 'magi' to kill the child, which his father Terah frustrates by hiding him in a cave for three years.

Pagan parallels are of a more general kind and a guide to the contemporary imagination. Since the principal military threat to the Roman empire at this time was the Parthian kingdom to the east of it, it was to the east that subject peoples, especially near that frontier, projected their dreams and hopes of future liberation, and this was a fertile source of predictions and rumours throughout the first century. Astronomical portents at the birth of kings and other great men are a commonplace of classical literature, e.g. Augustus (Suetonius, *Aug.*, p. 94) and Alexander the Great, whose star was declared by Asian 'magi' to forebode evil for their country (Cicero, *On Divinity*, p. 247). Tiridates, king of Armenia and himself a 'magus', travelled with other 'magi' to Rome to do homage to Nero, because he had observed the star of the expected king of the world in the west (Pliny, *Natural History*, XXX. ii. 17).

In view of the legendary background of the story it is not really profitable to attempt to identify the astronomical phenomena associated with it. (For suggestions that have been made, see H. Montefiore, *Josephus and the NT* [London, 1962], pp. 8ff.) *in the East*: it is doubtful if the Gk (*anatolē*, singular) can mean this; a more probable rendering is 'at its rising' (cp. NEB 'we have seen the rising of his star')—a technical term for time at which it first became observable. But the word is also used in LXX as a designation of the Messiah (Zech. 3[8], 6[12]), and there may be a hint of that here.

6. Mic. 5[2] is quoted in a composite form widely divergent from the Heb. and even more from LXX with which it has only six Gk words in common. The key word is the name *Bethlehem*, and the quotation lacks the usual introductory formula 'that it might be fulfilled . . .', because it is part of the answer of the Jewish authorities, and the birth of the Messiah at Bethlehem was part of current Jewish expectation and needed no specifically Christian justification. *by no means least*: The Heb. implies the insignificance of Bethlehem. Mt's text has completely altered the meaning by the insertion of a negative. *who will govern . . . Israel*: these words, though they have their counterpart in the Micah text, are actually quoted from the LXX of 2 Sam, 5[2].

7. *ascertained*: a technical term in astrological observations.

9. *went before them:* this has not been implied for the earlier part of their journey, but the idea would raise no difficulty for ancient minds: cp. Virgil, *Aeneid*, ii. 694ff. (of the star which led Aeneas to the place where Rome was to be founded). Bethlehem is in fact only three hours' journey from Jerusalem. There may be a deliberate contrast between the brilliance of the star and the obscurity of the birthplace, symbolizing that between the destiny of the royal child and the insignificance of his earthly background. *came to rest over:* see Jos., *BJ* v. 289 for the star said to have stood over Jerusalem shortly before the city's destruction.

11. *worshiped:* this primarily means the prostrations customary before a king (cp. Ps. 72^{11}), as is also implied by the gifts (see next note), but this, as elsewhere in Mt, shades off into the adoration due to a divine figure. *gold and frankincense and myrrh:* cp. Ps. 72^{15} (gold), Is. 60^6 (gold and incense), Ps. 45^8 (myrrh), Song of Songs 3^6 (incense and myrrh). All these are found in a royal context; they are also characteristic of the east, especially Arabia. It is also possible that the gifts represent the stock-in-trade of 'magi'—incense and myrrh being used to accompany their incantations, and gold standing for the money they make by them—all of which are now surrendered and laid at the feet of the child-king.

12. *warned:* i.e. by God (the Gk word is often used of oracles). The 'magi' on account of their profession, like Joseph because of the associations of his name, are held to be specially open to the language of dreams.

13–23. The scene now changes. Bethlehem has played its predestined part in the coming of the Christ, but persecution by the ruler of the earthly Israel makes it impossible for him to remain there.

Two OT types may have played their part in the formation of this section. Jesus' escape to Egypt and return from it seems to be compared and contrasted with Moses's escape from Egypt and return to it (Ex. 2–4), with Herod in the role of Pharaoh; and Daube (*NTRJ*, pp. 189ff.) draws attention to the striking parallel between Herod's persecution of Jesus and Laban's persecution of Jacob as recounted in the contemporary Jewish Passover *haggadah*. The significance common to the two is their association with the Exodus; the true Christian fulfilment of this is in the death and resurrection of Christ, but Mt sees these as prefigured in the events of the infancy.

15. *Out of Egypt . . . son:* Hos. 11^1, quoted in a form very close to Heb. but different from LXX. There is more to its use here than the fact that it contains a reference to Egypt; in its original context it speaks of God's deliverance of his people from bondage, and Jesus is seen as representative of that people.

16. Nothing is known of this massacre from any contemporary source—although Josephus lost no opportunity of recording the crimes of the Herods.

18. Jer. 31^{15}, cited in a version agreeing neither with LXX nor Heb., but closer to the latter than any other Gk version. Three matters call for further comment:

· (i) The *Ramah* of the original prophecy is about five miles north of Jerusalem, on the route which the Hebrew captives had to take to exile in Babylon. It is thus nowhere near Bethlehem. The link between the text and its application is probably the traditional tomb of Rachel at Ramoth-rachel between Bethlehem and Jerusalem (see Gen. 35^{19}, 48^7).

(ii) Mt, not for the last time, goes out of his way to name Jeremiah as the source of the prophecy, and this is a clue to his purpose in using it. Jeremiah is the prophet associated with the destruction of Jerusalem in 586 B.C., and Mt is deeply preoccupied with the repetition of that destruction in A.D. 70, which he sees as a judgement on Israel for its rejection of Christ (see on 23$^{37ff.}$, 27$^{3ff.}$). The price of Jewish obduracy, as in the former instance, was a visitation in which the innocent were caught up (cp. 27^{25}); this is foreshadowed in the manner in which the Bethlehem innocents pay for Herod's hardness of heart.

(iii) The verse which follows the prophecy in Jeremiah is nevertheless a message of comfort and hope, and Mt means this to be taken up. There is indeed a future for the remnant of the old Israel, but it lies in Galilee (v. 22), i.e. among the Gentiles (see on 4$^{15f.}$), where the people of God are now to be found.

19. *Herod* died in 4 B.C., and his kingdom was divided among his sons, Archelaus the eldest receiving Judaea, Samaria and Idumaea (Edom). Augustus refused to confirm him in his kingdom until he had proved himself by good behaviour, and in A.D. 6, partly at the request of the Jews themselves, removed him and replaced him by a prefect (not styled 'procurator' until the reign of Claudius, A.D. 41–54) acting under the legate of Syria—the office afterwards held by Pontius Pilate. The tradition of Mt's day seems to have remembered that Archelaus was a more dangerous man than his brothers.

20. A reminiscence of Ex. 4^{19}—the return of Moses not from, but to Egypt.

23. *that what was spoken by the prophets might be fulfilled:* no prophets are named, and the quotation which follows is found nowhere in the OT. See Gundry, *Use,* pp. 97ff., for a full list of the explanations that have been offered; among the more plausible are the following:

(i) The quotation is a gloss, and the formula really points forward to 4$^{15f.}$. But elsewhere the formula always introduces a text, and in this chapter one closely connected with a place-name. And the absence of any text here would leave Mt's conclusion to this chapter in mid-air.

(ii) *Nazarene* is connected with Heb. *nazir* (a Nazirite). and the reference is to Jud. 13^7. This is unlikely both etymologically and because 'Nazirite', though apt for John the Baptist, is hardly applicable to Jesus (cp. 11$^{18f.}$).

(iii) There is a play on the Heb. *neser* (branch), and the reference is to Is. 11¹, cp. 4², Jer. 23⁵, 33¹⁵, Zech. 3⁸, 6¹². In favour of this is the fact that Mt refers to *prophets* in the plural, and this is the only interpretation to which there is multiple prophetic witness (several of the texts have influenced the gospel elsewhere). The words will then be a summary in indirect speech (as in AV) rather than a quotation. Gundry makes the important observation (*Use*, p. 104) that both rabbinic and Qumran literature interpret the 'branch' passages of the lowliness and obscurity of the Messiah; this accords well with Mt's own conception of the role of Christ, and suggests an acceptable scriptural justification of a Galilean Messiah.

Nazarene: RSV conceals the fact that Mt (like Lk and Jn) prefers the form *Nazorean*. His derivation of it from Nazareth is etymologically possible for either form (cp. G. F. Moore in *The Beginnings of Christianity* (ed. Lake and Foakes–Jackson), i. 426ff.); on the other hand there are scattered indications of a 'baptist' movement in the Jordan valley which used the title 'Nazorean'. There is evidence in the NT (e.g. at Acts 18²⁴ᶠ·, 19¹ᶠᶠ·) that the early Christians sometimes had difficulty in dissociating themselves from the followers of John, to whom they were linked by their origins and the rite of baptism. If a title with 'baptist' associations had come to be applied contemptuously first to Christians and then to their Master (cp. the references in the Talmud to Christians as *nosrim* and to Jesus as *nosri*) it would have been natural for Christians to try to draw its sting by reinterpreting it as of our Lord's place of origin.

2. THE INTRODUCTION OF THE CHRIST TO ISRAEL (CHAPTERS 3:1–4:16)

3: 1–12 *John the Baptist*; cp. Mk 1²⁻⁸

Mk, on whom Mt is able to draw from this point, makes the preaching of John the starting-point of the gospel of Jesus. For Mt, who has begun his version of the gospel further back, the ministry of John is the means by which the true, and so far hidden, identity of Jesus is first revealed to his people.

The NT writings invariably present John in relation to Jesus. His significance as a person in his own right, and the impression he made on his contemporaries, can be judged by comparing the account of Mt's Jewish contemporary Josephus (*Ant.* xviii. 116 ff.); if we had only this to go by, it would be necessary to regard him as historically a more significant person than Jesus himself, who is not mentioned in the authentic part of Josephus' history. Josephus too calls him the Baptist, meaning not only that baptism was reckoned his characteristic activity but that he administered it himself (in contrast to the self-baptism of Jewish proselytes or the Essenes of Qumran), and seems to have grasped, in a confused way, its primarily moral rather than ceremonial significance, as well as that Jews themselves underwent it; though he misses the connexion of both these facts with the coming judgement which John preached. (The character of John's baptism is discussed by, e.g., W. F. Flemington, *The NT Doctrine of Baptism* (London, 1948), pp. 13ff.; G. R. Beasley-Murray, *Baptism in the NT* (London, 1962), pp. 31ff.).

Mt's account of John is on the other hand a Christian account compiled from Christian sources, with little or no purely biographical interest. Besides Mk, he is able to draw on a fuller form of John's sayings than Mk actually reproduces; though it seems that he also attributes to the forerunner a few sayings which belonged in the tradition to Jesus himself. There are reasons for this. Mt develops Mk's identification of John with the Elijah whose return was to herald the coming of the Messiah (Mal. 4^{5f}; cp. Mk 9^{11-3}; see 11^{14}); this enables him at once to safeguard the uniqueness of Jesus (see on vv. 13–15 below), and to represent not only John but the prophetic tradition which he sums up as in line with the teaching of Jesus. See on 11^{2ff}, and cp. W. Wink, *John the Baptist in the Gospel Tradition* (Cambridge, 1968), pp. 27ff.

1. *in those days:* used at Mk 1^9 of Jesus' first appearance on the scene; here transferred to John's. In either case it is not an indication of date, but signifies in OT language that the 'last time' is near.
2. The content of the Baptist's preaching has been assimilated with that of Jesus at 4^{17} (cp. Mk 1^{15}). Until Jesus' first public appearance John is the representative of the kingdom. *Repent:* i.e. a complete change of heart and mind. Mt does not say, as Mk does (and as John's prophetic sign clearly implied) that the baptism was for remission of sins; this may be due to reflection on the fact that Jesus underwent it, but more probably to a desire to attribute the remission of sins to the death of Christ alone (see Mt's addition to the saying over the cup at 26^{28}).

On either interpretation the baptism administered by John is distinguished from that received by Christians (cp. on 20²²).

3. *the voice . . . straight:* Is. 40³ (quoted, as in Mk, from LXX).

4. John reproduces the exterior appearance of Elijah; see 2 Kings 1⁸. Locusts, surprisingly, were not regarded as unclean beasts; Lev. 11²² allows them to be eaten, and they appear as an article of diet in the writings of the Qumran community.

7. *Pharisees and Sadducees:* an unlikely combination in John's day. Except at 22²³ᶠᶠ· (taken from Mk, and involving a point of specifically Sadducean doctrine), Mt mentions Sadducees only in association with Pharisees (here and at 16¹ᶠᶠ·). Together they stand for the Jewish leadership in the time of Jesus, whereas Pharisees by themselves or in association with scribes often carry overtones of the Christian dispute with the synagogue of Mt's own day. (But cp. Note C, p. 247). *brood of vipers:* sometimes understood as a reference to young snakes escaping from a bush fire, as an image of flight from the fire of judgement. But as the phrase is elsewhere (12³⁴, 23³⁷) used vituperatively of the Pharisees, it is probable that Mt has projected his own hostility to these upon John as he later does upon Jesus. There may be a reminiscence of the serpent of Gen. 3¹; cp. Jn 8⁴⁴.

9. A hint of what is eventually to come about. For non-Jewish Christians as the sons of Abraham, see the argument of Rom. 4, and for Abraham as a point of controversy between Jews and Christians, cp. Jn. 8³³ᶠᶠ·.

10. *every tree . . . fire:* found as part of a larger context at 7¹⁹. Mt therefore probably received it as part of the tradition of the sayings of Jesus himself; though it may be proverbial in origin, and this would make its transference to John easier to explain.

11. *he who is coming after me:* i.e. one who is my disciple. *whose sandals I am not worthy to carry:* Mk has 'untie'. In either case the action is that of a slave. It was generally acknowledged that a rabbi's disciple owed a slave's duty to his master. But R. Joshua ben Levi held that a disciple should do anything a slave would do for his master except remove his shoes. Mt's alteration may therefore be in accordance with rabbinic sentiment. John is thus represented as saying that he has a disciple whose disciple he is himself unworthy to be. This prepares the reader for the encounter at vv. 13–15. *with the Holy Spirit and with fire:* Mk has only 'with the Holy Spirit'. Either (i) Mt has conflated Mk with another tradition which lacked Mk's christianizing interpretation of 'fire' as 'Holy Spirit', or (ii) he has followed an alternative source which originally spoke of 'wind and fire', i.e. the fiery stream of the divine judgement (Dan. 7¹⁰). The association of wind and fire is found also in the Pentecost narrative of Acts 2. But (i) is probably to be preferred.

12. *winnowing fork:* a wooden shovel used for throwing corn into the air to separate the grain from the chaff.

3: 13-17 *The baptism of Jesus*; cp. Mk 1[9-11]

The primitive Christian community remembered that the ministry of Jesus had been preceded, and very possibly inaugurated, by his baptism by John, and the narrative of this episode must have been overlaid with hints of its theological significance for his person and mission even before it reached Mk. In Mk it reveals to the reader in advance the true identity of Jesus to which the eyes of the disciples are only opened very gradually (see Nineham, *Mark*, pp. 55f.). It could no longer perform this function in a gospel which begins its account of his Messiahship with his birth; and its presence posed a problem for later Christians in that it represented the Messiah as having been baptized by the forerunner. Mt therefore makes one addition and one significant alteration to the account he found in Mk:

(a) He inserts the story of the Baptist's hesitation. This has often been taken as a disclaimer that Jesus, the sinless one, required baptism for remission of sins. This thought is undoubtedly present in a fragment of the apocryphal *Gospel of the Nazaraeans* (probably written in Syriac, but dependent on our Mt; see *NTAp i*, p. 139): 'Behold, the mother of the Lord and his brethren said to him: John the Baptist baptizes unto the remission of sins, let us go and be baptized by him. But he said to them: Wherein have I sinned that I should go and be baptized by him? Unless what I have said is a sin of ignorance' (ib. i. 146f.). But it is very unlikely in Mt, who has already suppressed Mk's note that John's baptism was for remission of sins (see on 3[2]). More probably he is answering a question which exercises all the later evangelists: why did Jesus, the mightier one foretold by John, submit to baptism by him? Lk forestalls it by making the unborn John salute from his mother's womb the unborn Jesus (Lk 1[41]); Jn meets it by not only stressing the priority of Jesus (Jn 1[15,31]) but suppressing the account of the baptism altogether; Mt on the other hand finds a theological reason of his own for its appropriateness.

(b) The words of the heavenly voice after the baptism, which in Mk are addressed to Jesus himself, are in Mt put in the third person and addressed to the witnesses. Mt's more advanced Christology has no room for a revelation to Jesus of his own relationship to the Father as late as this point; for him the recipient of the revelation is not Jesus but Israel.

13. *to be baptized by him:* the emphasis is on the deliberate intention of Jesus, who, here as in the passion narrative, is in full control of the situation.

15. *it is fitting for us:* i.e. for John and Jesus acting together. *to fulfil all righteousness:* these words must be interpreted in the light of their use elsewhere in Mt, especially in 5^{17-20} where they are again found together. For Mt's conception of righteousness as 'rightness of life before God' see p. oo. *all righteousness* is to be taken as 'the opposite not of sin but of partial righteousness' (Schlatter). Jewish piety was content with a 'predominant' righteousness; the demand of God on Christ, as of Christ on the disciple, is for all or nothing.

Mt uses the word *fulfil* in two connexions: Jesus fulfils the prophecies of the OT by himself, as the true representative of Israel, embodying or bringing about what they foretold, and he fulfils the law by giving it a new and more radical sense ($5^{17, 21ff.}$). In either case the sense of the word (which is a Semitism, and the image it contains not really adequate to its metaphorical use) is best conveyed by a different word, e.g. 'realize'. In the Sermon on the Mount Jesus 'realizes' the righteousness contained in the law by his teaching; here he 'realizes' the righteousness proclaimed by John, the last of the prophets, by his example. The representative of Israel submits to the prophetic sign laid upon the whole people. His example is, in particular, one of humility or meekness. This is inculcated in the Beatitudes (5^5), and presented as part of the Messianic example from which disciples are to learn at 11^{29}; and it is itself seen as the fulfilment of Messianic prophecy, indirectly at 2^{23} and $12^{18ff.}$, and directly at 21^5. Mt has thus linked the answer to the Baptist's question to his whole theology of Messiahship.

16. *the heavens were opened:* see Ezek. 1^1, the model used by various apocalyptic writings to describe a revelation of the last things; cp., in the NT, Jn 1^{51}, Acts 7^{56}, Rev. 4^1, etc. Mt's alteration of Mk ('he saw the heavens opened') brings the words closer to Ezekiel. *descending like a dove:* basically a reference to Gen. 1^2, but possibly transferred to the thought of the Exodus seen as a new act of creation by the intervention of God (cf. Is. 43^{16-21}). See below.

17. *a voice from heaven:* rabbinic tradition was familiar with heavenly utterances (usually in the form of scriptural quotations) to which it gave the name of *Bath qol* ('daughter of the voice'). *This is my beloved Son:* RSV mg ('my Son, my Beloved') is to be preferred. Three OT

passages in particular lie behind the heavenly voice: Ps. 2^7; Is. $42^{1ff.}$ (quoted in full at 12^{18-21}); Gen. 22^2.

The heavenly voice, the figure of the dove, the descent of the Holy Spirit and, in effect, the opening of the heavens are all found together in one of the earliest rabbinic commentaries on Exodus (the *Mekilta*). This makes it probable that Mt sees the baptism and the events connected with it as a new Exodus repeating the pattern of the old. On this see Davies, *SSM*, pp. 36ff.

4: 1–16 *The Temptation of the Son of God*; cp. Mk 1^{12-3}, Lk 4^{1-13}

This section is continuous with the baptism story both in theme and in source. Mk follows his account of the baptism with a brief allusion to forty days of temptation in the wilderness, but says nothing of the nature of the temptations. Lk's version is, with some variations in the order, substantially the same as Mt's. What is the ultimate source of the narrative? It is unlikely that Mk and Mt–Lk are wholly independent of each other, because the story could hardly have circulated independently of its context; either (i) there is a single version behind Mt and Lk, which Mk has abbreviated, or (ii) the version of Mt–Lk has expanded Mk and therefore presupposes familiarity with Mk's gospel. In this case its author is doing precisely what Mt himself set out to do, and if it is allowed that Lk could have known Mt (see Introduction, p. 6), the most economical solution makes Mt the author. Of these alternatives, only (i) is compatible with the Q-hypothesis; its attraction has lain in the possibility of assigning the story to an early date and, consequently, of finding a place for it in the recollected experience of the Lord himself. It has even been argued that the third of the temptations is political in character and would have had no significance for the situation of the later Church; but in that case the Church was no more likely to have preserved the story than to have created it. Among the considerations which tell against an early date are: (1) The narrative is formal and stylized and quite different from the 'pronouncement-stories' in which the tradition of Jesus as a controversialist has mostly been handed down (e.g. $9^{10ff.}$, $22^{15ff.}$). (2) The three episodes in the story all grow out of the answers to Jesus, each of which is a quotation from Deuteronomy. All are cited from LXX, which implies that the story as we have it was composed for a Greek-speaking church; (3) The narrative speaks of *the devil*, not *Satan*, whereas the earlier strands in the tradition of the words of Jesus leave the Hebrew form untranslated, as does Mk. (4) The point of the story is lost without the expression 'Son of God', uncharacteristic of the early tradition but very prominent in Mt.

It seems then that Mt has taken Mk's brief and enigmatic sketch and expanded it into a meditation or *midrash* which weaves together a series of OT texts and themes. For this view of it see Gerhardsson, *Testing* (though Gerhardsson's attachment to the Q-hypothesis forces him to postulate a floating *midrash* of Jewish–Christian origin; in view of the admitted midrashic character of Chaps. 1–2 this is to multiply sources unnecessarily). The central theme carries over from the baptism; Jesus submits to baptism as the representative of Israel, and in doing so is revealed to be the Son of God (for this as a designation of Israel itself cp. Ex. 4$^{19ff.}$, Dt. 8$^{2ff.}$, Jer. 31^9, Hos. 11$^{1ff.}$, etc., and see Gerhardsson, *Testing*, pp. 19ff.). The Exodus-theme of Israel in the waters leads on to that of Israel in the wilderness; but whereas the first Israel repeatedly put God to the test there, Israel's antitype is himself tested, and found obedient.

1. *led up by the Spirit*: Mt's emendation of Mk's *the Spirit drove him*. Mk's Christ is driven into the wilderness like Adam driven from paradise; Mt's is led as Israel was led through the wilderness by the presence of God in the cloudy pillar. A text in the background is Is. 63, especially v. 14. *wilderness*: Mt takes over this word from Mk where it sets the scene for the whole temptation episode, and is probably to be understood as the home of demons and the natural place for spiritual conflict with them. In Mt it is the scene of the first temptation only, and, besides recalling the wanderings of Israel after the Exodus, it is specifically 'the place for a humiliating and testing hunger' (Gerhardsson, *Testing*, p. 40). *to be tempted by the devil*: the earlier strands in the OT commonly speak of God himself tempting man; later Jewish thinking was markedly more reserved about the divine activity in general, and on the source of evil or temptation its expression became progressively more dualistic, though without ever depriving

God of ultimate responsibility. Mt maintains this tension; if the devil is the author of the temptations, it is by the guidance of the Spirit, and therefore by divine permission, that Jesus goes out to meet them. *devil*: the Gk *diabolos* is an attempt to render literally the meaning of the Heb. *satan*, which means 'accuser', but had long been treated as a proper name.

2. *fasted forty days and forty nights*: cp. Dt 9⁹⁻¹⁸ (Moses on Horeb), 1 Ki. 19⁸ (Elijah on his way to Horeb). As Moses' fast preceded the delivery of the law, and Jesus' Sermon on the Mount is not far ahead, there may well be a thought of Moses at this point. But the main reference is certainly to Israel's forty years in the wilderness (Dt. 8²ff·).

3. The temptation presupposes that Jesus' fast is a command of God, and that to abandon it under pressure of bodily hunger would mean disobedience and failure to trust in the divine guidance, even before the outset of his ministry. For craving for food as an expression of rebelliousness, see Nu. 11⁴ff·, Ps. 78¹⁸ff·, 106¹⁴; all are in connexion with the manna.

4. quoted from Dt. 8³, which refers in its turn to Ex. 16 (the hunger of Israel and the feeding with manna).

5. There is a striking shift of scene from the wilderness to the temple, the spiritual heart of the nation and the place of divine protection (see Gerhardsson, *Testing*, pp. 56ff.). The first temptation tested the personal fitness of the Son of God for his mission, his singleness of heart; the second looks forward to the conflict between that mission and the expectations of the official Israel. It foreshadows the actual temptation on Golgotha (27⁴⁰·⁴²), when Jesus is invited to save his own life, and in doing so to be the kind of Messiah that the Jewish people can accept. *holy city*: Jerusalem, cp. 27⁵³, and Is. 48², 52¹, etc. *pinnacle*: the Gk *pterugion* (lit. 'wing', diminutive), may have been used (though we lack other evidence) to denote some position high up on or above the roof of the temple, e.g. a balcony or parapet (for a summary of suggestions offered, see Gerhardsson, *Testing*, p. 59). But 'wings' is used frequently in the Psalter as a symbol of the divine protection, and particularly in Ps. 91 which is central to this passage (probably suggested by Mk 1¹³), and this word-association is possibly more significant for Mt's meaning than the precise identification of the place.

6. The quotation is from Ps. 91¹¹f·. Jesus' temptation here is not to impress witnesses by a spectacular display of power; none are mentioned. It is indeed to demand a sign from God, as Israel did at Massah, but a sign to himself; and that not as support for wavering faith but as confirmation of God's faithfulness. 'Satan exhorts Jesus to endanger himself by his own act so as to challenge God to save his life in accordance with the covenant promises' (Gerhardsson, *Testing*, p. 60).

7. Dt. 6¹⁶, referring back to Ex. 17 (Israel's demand for water, and the

striking of it from the rock); note especially Ex. 17[7]: '. . . because they put the Lord to the proof by saying "Is the Lord among us or not?"'

8. The scene shifts again for the climax of the narrative, the temptation on the mountain. Jewish law was familiar with the ancient custom by which the owner of a property would take a prospective buyer to some vantage-point from which he might 'receive it with his eyes' (Satan, says Daube, 'was a good lawyer'; see Gerhardsson, *Testing*, p. 63); and a high mountain as a vantage-point from which to survey the world is a commonplace of apocalyptic writing (e.g., *II Baruch* lxxvi. 3; *I Enoch* xxiv–xxv.). But the mountain most likely to have been present to Mt's mind is Pisgah, from which Moses had his preview of the promised land (Dt. 3[27], 34[1ff.]). For Mt the promised land of the new Israel is clearly the territory of the Gentiles (cp. 4[15f.], 28[18ff.]). Jesus in the days of his flesh will not see this, but his disciples will take possession of it in his name, and his temptation now is the anticipation of theirs.

9. 'If you are the Son of God' is missing from this temptation. The first two assume that Jesus has power; the third offers it to him. The risen and exalted Christ is to receive 'all authority in heaven and earth' (28[18]); till then the Gentile world remains *de facto* in the power of the devil (cp. 1 Jn 5[19], Jn 12[31], 14[30], 16[11]; 2 Cor. 4[4] actually calls him 'the god of this world').

10. *Begone, Satan:* the Gk wording is the same as in Jesus' rebuke to Peter at Mk 8[33] (par. Mt 16[23]). *it is written:* at Dt. 6[13]. No specific episode in Exodus is cited, but the worship of the golden calf in Ex. 32 is an example of what it forbids. The gospel as a whole hardly represents idolatry as a live option for Jesus; and though Christians on trial before the Roman authorities were often under pressure to save their lives by a token offering of incense to the emperor's image, the evidence of Mt does not suggest that his church has yet undergone that kind of persecution (cp. Hare, *JPC*, pp. 96ff.). What sort of temptation is then envisaged?

(i) The mission of Jesus the Messiah is to be achieved in obscurity and weakness (see on 2[23], and cp. 11[29], 12[18ff.], 21[5]); he is the first of the meek who will inherit the earth (5[5]). This is not compatible with reliance on the world's power-structures, which belong, as yet, to the devil.

(ii) Idolatry and covetousness are closely linked in the OT and in later Jewish writings (cp. Dt. 6[10ff.], 8[11ff.]; also Col. 3[5], and see Gerhardsson, *Testing*, pp. 64f.). 6[24] represents 'mammon' as a rival to the sovereignty of God, and Mt elsewhere (cp. 19[21ff.]) warns against the dangers of wealth (itself of course a form of the power that tends to corrupt). He could be saying here that Christian penetration of the Gentile world must not be at the cost of compromise with its characteristic vices.

Gerhardsson (*Testing*, pp. 71ff.) suggests that the three temptations correspond to the three ways of loving God enjoined in the *Shema* (Dt. 6⁵; see on 22³⁷), as expounded in the Mishnah (*Berakoth* 9⁵; Danby, p. 10): 'You shall love the Lord your God with all your *heart* (i.e. with undivided heart; see on 5⁸), and with all your *soul* (i.e. above one's own life, if demanded), and with all your *strength* (understood as wealth)'. The influence of this text is reflected also in the Beatitudes (5³⁻¹⁰).

11. The note of conflict with the devil is subdued throughout this gospel as compared with Mk and Jn; Mt's Jesus does not fight Satan, but masters him with his word. *angels . . . ministered to him:* Mt takes over this reminiscence of Ps. 91¹¹ from Mk 1¹³. There the angels' ministry is continuous throughout the period in the wilderness; here it is a recognition of Jesus' mastery of the devil as a fulfilment of his Messianic role. Cp. also 1 Ki. 19⁵⁻⁷ (angels' ministry after fasting); Ps. 78²⁵ ('angels' food').

12–16. These concluding verses are formally parallel to 2²²⁻³. Both narrate a withdrawal to Galilee under pressure of external circumstances, which is nevertheless in accordance with the will of God, since it has been foreshadowed in scripture.

13. Mt accepted the tradition which explained Jesus' title of 'Nazarene' as connecting him with Nazareth (see note on 2²³). But, with some support from his sources, he clearly regards Capernaum as the principal centre of Jesus' Galilean ministry (cp. 9¹⁰). By transferring him there at this point he is able to make a geographical connection with Is. 9¹ᶠ·; his real interest in this text lies in the justification that it affords of a Messianic mission in Galilee. *Capernaum:* generally identified with Tell Hum near the north end of the Sea of Galilee. The site has been excavated, and a synagogue, later in date than the NT, discovered.

15–16. This version of Is. 9¹ᶠ· has points of contact with both Heb. and LXX, but does not consistently follow either. *Galilee of the Gentiles:* so LXX. Galilee was an area of mixed population. Mt finds great significance in the fact that the gospel was originally preached in a partly Gentile region, which for him prefigures the eventual mission to Gentiles (see especially the setting and content of 28¹⁸ᶠᶠ·); the LXX wording offered support for this. *sat:* Heb. has 'walked'. Mt may be influenced by Ps. 107¹⁰. *light has dawned:* cp. Nu. 24¹⁷ (see on 2¹ᶠᶠ·), Mal. 4².

3. THE TEACHING OF THE CHRIST (CHAPTERS 4:17–7:27)

The title 'Sermon on the Mount' is first and foremost an indication of context in this gospel; the context created by Mt for the first of his five arrangements of collected sayings of Jesus. Because it is also the most comprehensive and the most familiar of the five, it is common to find it regarded as the heart of the moral teaching of our Lord. That a large part of its contents ultimately derives from him is not in question, but the composition as we have it is the work of Mt himself, and his selection and arrangement are as important for our understanding of it as the materials with which he is working.

As part of his presentation of Jesus as the Messiah, Mt here introduces him as the teacher of Israel. Jewish sources differ sharply over the extent to which the Messiah was expected to maintain, supplement, or supersede the role of Moses in relation to the Torah (law). Some would deny him a teaching function altogether, some (possibly under indirect Christian influence) actually hint at the possibility of a new Torah. But the mainstream view was that the Messiah would not promulgate a new law, but rather offer a new interpretation of the old; in short, that he would be the archetypal rabbi (see the cautious discussion in Davies, *SSM*, pp. 156ff.; more positively, Barth, *TIM*, pp. 153ff.). For this understanding of the figure of Jesus elsewhere in the gospel, cp. 23[8], 28[20].

In thus presenting Jesus as the Messianic interpreter of the Torah, Mt is faced with a double task. He has to state a Christian attitude to the OT law itself, and he has to relate to it the positive teaching of Jesus, which some lines of Christian teaching, notably that of St. Paul, were already tending to think of as 'the law of Christ' (Gal. 6[2]; cp. 1 Cor. 9[21], and see Davies, *SSM*, pp. 189f.). Clearly not all sayings of Jesus were relevant to the Christian understanding of the law; Mt selects those which he regards as appropriate, and reserves the rest for his four remaining discourses. The material he uses in the Sermon falls under four headings:

(a) a series of 'antitheses' (originally three) contrasting commandments of the law as commonly interpreted and as interpreted by Jesus;

(b) a similar series of contrasts between the three principal aspects of conventional Jewish piety and the corresponding requirements from disciples;

·(c) a collection of Jesus' sayings on ethical matters available to both Mt and Lk, the full extent of which is difficult to determine (since it presupposes an answer to the question of whether Lk could have drawn on Mt), but which probably included at least a form of the Beatitudes and the injunctions to non-resistance and to love of neighbour and against judgement of others;

(d) miscellaneous sayings preserved in the tradition.

(a) and (b) may well have comprised a single source, especially if both were based on a threefold division.

How has Mt handled these materials?

(a) He has expanded the antitheses by packing in other sayings of Jesus originally independent of these contexts (5^{21-37}); and he has constructed two further antitheses out of the material common to him and Lk (5^{38-48}).

(b) The contrast between Jewish and Christian prayer has been enlarged by the insertion of a digression centred on the Lord's Prayer (6^{7-13}).

(c) Further sayings are gathered under the heading of 'acts of mercy' ($6^{19}-7^{12}$); for the connexion of this with what precedes it see commentary ad loc.

(d) These three sections, which together form the core of the Sermon ($5^{21}-7^{12}$), are introduced by a further group of sayings which are intended to elucidate the attitude of Jesus (and thus the true Christian attitude) to the OT law (5^{17-20}).

(e) The Beatitudes stand at the head of the Sermon both in Mt and Lk; but Mt's enlarged version outlines the spiritual qualities which disciples are to bring to their observance of the law (5^{3-16}; see commentary).

(f) A final series of sayings is worked up into a solemn warning against 'hearing and not doing' (7^{13-27}).

The whole tendency of the Sermon as Mt has built it up is thus to bring as much as possible of the teaching of Jesus into contact with the Torah or with traditional Jewish piety; i.e. he treats it here as *halakah* or commentary on the commandments of the law, to be understood not as a completely fresh departure but in relation to the older teaching which it reinterprets. He does not see it as an 'impossible ideal' designed to bring a man to despair, and thus to reliance on 'the righteousness which is by faith'. Mt's standpoint and language are not those of St. Paul; for him 'righteousness' 'denotes the conduct of a man which is in agreement with God's will, which is pleasing in his sight, rightness of life before God' (Barth, *TIM*, p. 139). In this he is at one with the best traditions of rabbinic Judaism. But the Sermon is not therefore to be regarded as an alternative version of the more liberal rabbinic approach to the law, as suggested by H. Windisch (*The Sermon on the Mount*, [ET Philadelphia, 1951]); despite some close parallels of detail, the range of Jewish and Christian influence is too wide, and the foundation in the teaching of Jesus too revolutionary, to justify so narrow a definition (see Davies, *SSM*, especially pp. 425ff.). For Mt, Jesus is not a rabbi in the company of other rabbis, he is *the* rabbi to supersede the whole rabbinic tradition; and the righteousness which he demands of the Christian disciple is a more radical righteousness than theirs. It is an 'easy yoke and light burden' (11³⁰)—implying that the gospel does not add commandments to the law, but rather simplifies the interpretation of its requirements—and yet at the same time it is to 'exceed that of the scribes and Pharisees' (5²⁰); it is no cheap let-out but a commitment with unlimited liability, not less but more demanding. What does this involve? First, that the right understanding of the law is summed up in the double commandment of love (Dt. 6⁵ with Lev. 19¹⁸). At 22⁴⁰ Mt makes this the fundamental principle for the interpretation of the whole law (see Barth, *TIM*, pp. 76ff.), and this is partly anticipated at 7¹²; if this point is grasped the rest will follow. Secondly, the spirit in which the disciple is to approach its demands is set out in the Beatitudes with which the Sermon opens, the message of which may be epitomized as single-minded dedication, generosity, and dependence on God. This is the counterpart in Mt's understanding of the Christian life to the Pauline teaching on faith; without it the new interpretation of the law of God would remain a religion of the letter.

4: 17–5: 2 The setting

The sermon presupposes that the gospel has already been preached and that men have responded to its demands by becoming disciples. This is outlined in the introductory verses.

17 *From that time:* an emphatic indication (obscured by the paragraphing of RSV) that a new stage in the gospel story has been reached. The content of Jesus' preaching (identical with that of John at 3²) reinforces this. John's arrest (v. 12) has put the proclamation of the kingdom unambiguously in the hands of Jesus. *is at hand:* lit. 'has drawn near'. The Gk probably distinguishes imminence from actual arrival.

18–22. As in Mk (1¹⁶⁻²⁰) the preaching of the gospel of the kingdom is followed by these illustrations of the absoluteness and urgency of the demands it makes upon men. But Mt's purpose is also, as is made explicit at the opening of the Sermon (5¹), to depict Jesus as a rabbi with disciples.

19. *fishers of men:* cp. Jer. 16¹⁶, Am. 4², Ezek. 29⁴ᶠ·. But in OT use of the image men are always caught for judgement, not salvation.

23. This first verse of the summary of healings is repeated word for word at 9³⁵; in both cases it introduces a section of the gospel devoted to the teaching of Jesus. *their synagogues:* cp. 9³⁵, 10¹⁷, 12⁹, 13⁵⁴. Mt's care to dissociate himself from those who worship in synagogues implies that he is writing at a period when the breach between church and synagogue is complete.

24. *Syria:* the list in the following verse takes Syria as including the various districts of Palestine. This suggests an author who regarded himself inclusively as a Syrian rather than as a Palestinian. Note that he suppresses Mk's reference to Tyre and Sidon—possibly his own district (see Introduction, p. 32).

25. *Decapolis:* the name given to a confederation of Greek cities, originally ten, liberated from Jewish control by Pompey in 60 B.C.; they included Pella, Gadara, and Gerasa (Jerash), with Damascus at a distance from the rest.

5: 1. *mountain:* unnamed, and obviously symbolic. Mountains as settings for divine revelation are common in the OT, but in view of the Exodus-typology of the previous two chapters, as well as of the character of the teaching delivered here, Mt must be thinking particularly of Sinai. *sat down:* the customary teaching posture of a rabbi (cp. 23²), as is implied also by the reference to *disciples. came to him:* for instruction by him as their rabbi. Mt frequently uses the word in this sense; e.g. 13¹⁰,³⁶, 15¹², 18¹, 24³.

5: 3–16 *Introduction: on Discipleship: the Beatitudes*

The Beatitudes stand at the head of the Sermon as the Ten Commandments stand at the head of the Torah (Ex. 20¹⁻¹⁷). But whereas the law of Moses is introduced by a series of prohibitions, the disciples of Jesus are first given a summary of the essence of true discipleship, and only then faced with the positive demands of the law of God.

Sayings expressing (generally in proverbial form) the happiness of particular categories of people are common in the OT; cp. Sir. 25⁷⁻¹⁰, Ps. 1¹, 32¹⁻², 112, 119¹⁻², 128¹⁻⁴. It would therefore have been a natural form for our Lord to use. Comparison with Lk 6²⁰ᶠᶠ· suggests that the beatitudes which actually go back to him are four in number:

> Blessed are the (*or* 'you') poor
> Blessed are the sorrowful
> Blessed are the hungry
> Blessed are you when men hate you, etc.

The fourth of these stands rather apart from the rest, and may belong to another occasion, especially if it is addressed to disciples, as the other three seemingly are not (cp. J. Dupont, *Les Béatitudes,* ii. (Paris, 1969), 281ff.). These, particularly the first two, are reminiscent of Is. 61¹ᶠᶠ·; they form a kind of opening text for the preaching of the kingdom of God, which is to come as inheritance of riches for the poor, comfort for the sorrowful, and food for the hungry.

Lk has preserved the original content of the Beatitudes as he received them, but has interpreted them in his own way by introducing a contrast between present and future and by supplying a corresponding series of 'woes'. He thus turns them into a *peripeteia* or 'turning of the tables', a form of composition familiar in Hellenistic literature (see C. H. Dodd, *More NT Studies* (Manchester, 1968), pp. 1ff.). Mt on the other hand expands the list by the addition of four further beatitudes, of which one is a direct quotation from the Psalter and at least two others reminiscent of it. His beatitudes are neither an anticipation of the overwhelming joy of the kingdom (as in the original), nor a promise of relief to the unprivileged and oppressed (as in Lk), but a statement of the moral and spiritual qualities which are characteristic of discipleship, and of the rewards that go with them. These are arranged in pairs, not in simple juxtaposition but dovetailed: the poor and the meek, the mourners and the hungry, the merciful and the peace-makers, the single-hearted and the sufferers for righteousness. The result is a rhythmical hymn in eight lines, A B A B C D C D, tied together by the use of *righteousness* in the last line of each quatrain, and by the repetition *for theirs is the kingdom of heaven* from the first line to the last (an instance of *inclusio*, see Introduction, p. 21).

3. *poor in spirit:* it is probable that what Jesus himself said was simply 'poor', but that he used it in its religious sense of the downtrodden remnant of the people of God, as in Is. 61¹ (cp. Is. 11⁴, 29¹⁹, and the Psalter *passim*), perhaps with special reference to tax-collectors and other Jewish outcasts. Lk, who has a rigorist attitude towards material wealth, take the word literally and contrasts the blessedness of the poor with the doom of the rich. Mt's gloss 'in spirit' excludes this, but nevertheless qualifies the literal meaning of the word, and the exegesis of the whole expression should not stray too far from that. It does not in any case have to cover the whole range of meaning implicit in the 'religious' sense of 'poor', since Mt has separated out from that the connotations of humility and persecution, which are expressed in separate beatitudes (vv. 5, 10). Moreover the gloss is his own, and is therefore likely to reflect the situation for which he is writing, rather than that of the ministry of Jesus (this rules out, as far as the gloss is concerned, a reference to the despised Galilean 'people of the land'; see Introduction, p. 23). Mt elsewhere sees affluence as a grave threat to committed Christian living (cp. 6¹⁹ff. and especially 19²¹ff.)—he seems to have been writing for a rich community—and this suggests that the poverty he has in mind is in respect of perfectly real wealth, but that the attitude enjoined is one of spiritual detachment from it, as opposed to material deprivation of it.

It is interesting that the Heb. equivalent of Mt's 'poor in spirit' is found in the Qumran War Rule (1 QM 14⁷; V, p. 142), though the text is too fragmentary for any certain conclusion about the meaning.

One suggestion (K. Schubert in *SNT*, p. 122) is that it means 'poor in will', i.e. voluntarily poor.

The paraphrase 'those who know their need of God' offered by NEB involves taking 'in spirit' as qualifying an already non-literal sense of 'poor'. The beatitude certainly expresses dependence on God (as does that on hunger and thirst for righteousness, v. 6), but in a more concrete and restricted sense than the translators supposed. *for theirs is the kingdom of heaven*: a present claim to future inheritance (see Note A, p. 232). The other verbs expressing reward are all future.

4. *those who mourn*: cp. Is. 61²ᶠ·, Ps. 126⁵. There is little to indicate what Mt understood by mourning as a spiritual disposition. If the formal correspondence with v. 6 is pressed the counterpart of hunger for righteousness is to lament one's lack of it; and the fact that Mt introduces the word into his version of the saying about fasting at 9¹⁵ shows that its meaning is in any case penitential. *they shall be comforted*: the passive (as also in vv. 6, 7, 9) is a reverential circumlocution for the action of God.

5. *meek*: i.e. humble, those who claim nothing for themselves. This beatitude has been constructed from the LXX of Ps. 37¹¹. The same Heb. word (*anaw*) lies behind *meek* here and *poor* in 5³; the distinction is therefore possible only in Gk. That the beatitude is nevertheless Mt's own and not, as some have suggested, a later interpolation, seems certain from the importance he attaches to humility elsewhere in the gospel; cp. 18¹⁻⁴, 23⁸⁻¹², and for Jesus as himself exemplifying it, 3¹⁵, 11²⁹, 12¹⁸⁻²¹, 21⁵.

Some MSS. put this beatitude second, probably through observing its close correspondence with the first. But the total pattern is more intelligible if it is left where it is.

6. Mt makes two additions; thirst is added to hunger, and both are spiritualized by the addition of *for righteousness*. For thirst as an image of spiritual longing cp. Is. 55¹, Ps. 42¹ᶠ·, but especially Sir. 24²¹, 51²⁴ (hunger and thirst for wisdom; see on 11²⁹ᶠ·). *righteousness* is the spiritual quality which corresponds to the kingdom and admits to it; cp. 5²⁰, 6³³. *they shall be satisfied*: i.e. God will satisfy them. Righteousness is a gift which he will not withhold from those who truly seek it.

7. Possibly Mt's version of Lk 6³⁶; cp. Jas. 2¹³. The quality of mercy is a theme running right through the gospel; cp. 6¹²,¹⁴ᶠ·,¹⁹⁻7¹², 18²³ᶠᶠ· (especially 18³³), 23²³, and the two citations of Hos. 6⁶ at 9¹³ and 12⁷.

8. *pure in heart*: the key beatitude, and crucial to Mt's understanding of the Christian ethic. The emphasis is not primarily on sexual purity, though it is applied to that at 5²⁸; the central thought is a double one:

   (a) singleness of heart, integrity; cp. Dt. 6⁴ (the *Shema*, recited daily by devout Jews), 'You shall love the Lord your God with all your heart', and the thought of seeking the Lord with 'the whole heart' at Ps. 119²,¹⁰. 'The ideal is the integrated and uncomplicated personality wholly consecrated to the service of God' (Gerhardsson, *Testing*, p. 48). For this thought elsewhere in Mt cp. $5^{28ff.,48}$, $6^{19ff.}$, 18^{35}, 19^{21}, 22^{37}.

The opposite of a 'pure' heart is a divided heart (cp. Jas. 4^8), and for Jewish thought what divides the heart is the evil *yetzer* (inclination), the source in particular of the sexual and acquisitive instincts in man. This is implanted by God and so far good, but divisive in its effects on the personality when not controlled and directed by the higher self (called, in some sources, the good *yetzer*). Cp. a rabbinic comment on Ps. 119^{80}: 'David said, Master of the world, when I am occupied in thy law, allow not the evil *yetzer* to divide me . . . but make my heart one, so that I be occupied in the Torah with soundness (or perfection)' (quoted by S. Schechter, *Some Aspects of Rabbinic Theology* (London, 1909), p. 278). See further W. D. Davies, *Paul and Rabbinic Judaism* (London, 1948), pp. 20ff.; Gerhardsson, *Testing*, pp. 49f.; and for Jewish texts, C. Montefiore–H. Loewe, *A Rabbinic Anthology* (London, 1938), pp. 295ff. The parallel with the *libido* in the thinking of Freud is striking.

(b) (arising out of [a]) the inward and spiritual as well as the outward and cultic: see Ps. 24^{3-4}: 'Who shall ascend into the hill of the Lord . . . he that has clean hands and a pure heart'; cp. Ps. 15^2, 51^{10}, 73^{13}, Jas. 4^8; elsewhere in Mt, $6^{1-6,16-8}$, 12^{34}, 15^{1-20}, $23^{3,5ff.,25ff.}$. *see God*: see Ps. 24^3, quoted above, and cp. Ex. 24^{9-11}. What the ascent to the temple (or the mountain, in the latter case) was for the Jew, the vision of God in his kingdom is to be for the disciple. But cp. Ps.–Jonathan on Lev. 9^6 (quoted by Schechter, p. 292): 'Remove the evil *yetzer* from your hearts, and the divine presence will at once be revealed to you'. Cp. also Heb. 12^{14}.

9. *peacemakers*: the Gk word (found only here in the NT) denotes the active pursuit of peace. The basic OT text is Ps. 34^{14}; cp. the comment of R. Hillel: 'Be of the disciples of Aaron, loving peace and pursuing peace, loving mankind and bringing them near to the law' (Mishnah *Aboth* 1^{14}; Danby, p. 447); and *Sifra* on Nu. 6^{26}: 'He who practises peace is a child of the world to come'. *sons of God*: cp. Dt. 14^1, and R. Akiba's comment on it: 'Beloved are Israel, for they were called children of God; still greater was the love in that it was made known to them that they were called children of God'.

The combination of the two thoughts appears to be unique.

10. The persecuted (Mt characteristically adds *for righteousness' sake*) are one class of the spiritually poor, and they have the same reward.

Mt's final beatitude is a generalized form of the original, which could not be fitted as it stands into his rhythmical composition, but is nevertheless appended in the two following verses.

11–12. Cp. Lk 6^{22-3} which appears to derive from independent tradition and to be nearer to the original. Mt seems to have adapted it to the experience of a community some of whose members have undergone actual persecution; cp. on 10[16-23] and see Hare, *JPC*, pp. 118ff., 130ff.). *persecute*: this word is introduced by Mt. *falsely*: omitted in some MSS. *prophets*: those addressed are in the true line of succession to the prophets, and not only by virtue of sharing their persecution; see on 23[29ff.].

5: 13–16 Salt and light

The qualities required of disciples include an outward-looking attitude; Mt illustrates this with a cluster of short parables. The framework in which he sets them, with its parallelism of salt and light (the parallel, though known to classical literature, is not really close) is probably his own. The thought behind his use of both metaphors is similar to that expressed in the *Epistle to Diognetus* (second century A.D.) which speaks of Christians as 'the soul of the world'.

13. *You are the salt of the earth*: *You* is emphatic. The disciples, in contrast to the exclusiveness of neo-Pharisaic Judaism, are to allow their influence to be felt in the world at large; they are not to become another sect. *has lost its taste*: this represents the meaning of Jesus' original saying (cp. Mk 9[50]) rather than that of Mt's Gk, which means literally 'becomes foolish' and seems to rest either on a mistranslation of the Aramaic (also at Lk 14[34]) or, less probably, on a secondary interpretation of it (salt is used to stand for wisdom in the rabbinic literature). Salt cannot, strictly speaking, lose its salinity; but Palestinian Jews normally gathered it in an impure form, combined with other matter which would remain after the salt proper had been dissolved by water, and be useless without it. The original form of the saying was probably a warning not to disciples but to a hostile audience. (See Jeremias, *PJ*, pp. 168f.).

14. *light of the world*: for Israel as the light of the world cp. Is. 49[6] (at Jn 8[12] it is Jesus himself). The expression could also be used for a distinguished rabbi. The two short comparisons which follow were originally independent of one another. *A city set on a hill*: perhaps originally proverbial, but especially appropriate to Jerusalem on account both of its situation and of its symbolic importance for Judaism. Jerusalem and its temple are both called 'the light of the world' in later Jewish writing.

15. cp. Mk 4[21], Lk 11[33]. Jeremias (*PJ*, pp. 120f.) has a purely domestic explanation of the parable; Derrett (*LNT*, pp. 189ff.), more plausibly, a religious one. The *lamp* is that lit in the house for a festival, in particular for that of Dedication (cp. 1 Mc. 4[49f.]), and the *bushel* (i.e. the bushel measure) would be turned over the lamp, not to extinguish it, but to hide it (Derrett mentions possible motives for doing this). But its proper place is the lampstand (a link with the temple and thus with v. 14). *Let your light so shine*: this verse takes up

the words *shine*, *light* and *men* in the three preceding ones, and is therefore probably Mt's comment on them as a whole. *good works:* a common Jewish expression not elsewhere favoured by Mt. For the Jew a certain category of works was 'good'; for Mt the disciple's whole behaviour is 'good'. *give glory to:* i.e. as the author of the 'goodness' of the disciple. *Father who is in heaven:* see on 6⁹.

5: 17–7:12 *The New Righteousness*

5: 17–20 *Preface: Jesus and the Law*

On the question of the true Christian attitude to the Mosaic law, Mt himself steers a middle course between conservatives who continue to regard every letter of it as sacrosanct and radicals for whom it is altogether superseded. But he had received from the tradition (and therefore probably accepted as uttered by Jesus) a number of sayings expressing the former viewpoint (cp. 10^{5,23}, 23$^{2f.}$); and it is possible that, like St. Paul at Corinth, he was faced with an antinomian current in the church for which he was writing (see on 7$^{13ff.}$). Against this the sayings enjoining the observance of particular commandments could be a useful argument, while their scope remains carefully defined by the context in which he places them, as well as by actual verbal modifications. The section falls into three parts:

17. (a) This saying represents Mt's own position, possibly expressed in his own words. For the meaning of *fulfil* see on 3^{15}. The fact that the true meaning of the Torah as revealed by Jesus transcends the older understanding does not imply that the Torah is itself abolished; cp. Rom. 3^{31}.
law and the prophets: the prophets are not strictly required in the immediate context, and if Mt is using a source may not have formed part of the original saying. But Jesus' Messianic authority covers both parts of the OT revelation, and it is important that no wedge shall be driven between them. Note that the adversaries of 7^{15} are called 'false prophets', i.e., probably, prophets who reject the law, who are no more tolerable than scribes impervious to prophecy (cp. 9^{13}, 12^7). See further on 22^{40}.
18–19. (b) Two sayings with a Jewish–Christian bias which in their original form insisted that the individual precepts of the whole Mosaic law remained binding on the Christian. *Until all is accom-*

plished apparently duplicates *till heaven and earth pass away*, and in its original sense probably meant the same; but comparison with 24³⁵ (par. Mk 13³¹) suggests that the opening phrase was formulated by Mt. Its introduction enables him to reinterpret the concluding one, taking it in the same sense as his own *fulfil* (v. 17). Until the end of the world (which only the words of Jesus will outlast, 24³⁵) every scripture has its place in that fulness of meaning which the Messianic interpreter brings to the whole; cp. NEBmg 'before all that it stands for is achieved'. In the final analysis the law is to be fulfilled in much the same sense as the prophets. *iota:* the Gk equivalent of *yod*, the smallest letter of the Heb. alphabet. *dot:* the precise reference of the Gk word (lit. 'horn') is uncertain, but it evidently denotes a part (perhaps a stroke) of a Heb. letter. *these commandments:* the original force of this saying must have had in view the OT law as it stands; but the following verse, and the section it introduces, suggest rather that Mt takes it to mean the law as reinterpreted by Jesus. At 28²⁰ it is his own commandments which Jesus requires his disciples to teach their converts to observe. *least in the kingdom of heaven:* Mt's retention of this expression here and at 11¹¹ shows that despite the parable at 19³⁰ᶠᶠ· he did not completely reject the idea of gradations in the kingdom. But for indications that the saying had been used in a sense of which he disapproved, see introduction to Chap. 18.

20. (c) The corollary of the two statements already made—(i) Christ came to fulfil the law (v. 17); (ii) this fulfilment embraces individual precepts (vv. 18–9)—is that the fulfilment must be worked out in terms of specific commandments. This saying is therefore the prelude to the antitheses of 5²¹⁻⁴⁸, *scribes and Pharisees:* Jeremias (*Sermon on the Mount* (London, 1961) pp. 22f.) suggests that the antitheses are aimed at the scribes (i.e. rabbis, learned interpreters of the law), and the three injunctions against hypocrisy (6¹⁻⁶,¹⁶⁻⁸) against the Pharisees. But Mt's regular identification of the two makes it unlikely that he intended a distinction here, and both style and content of the verse are typically Matthaean.

5: 21–48 *The Old and the New Righteousness contrasted: five antitheses*
We do not know at what point the teaching of Jesus on specific precepts of the law was first given this antithetical formulation (E. Käsemann attributes it to Jesus himself). Of the five, three (vv. 22, 28, 34) intensify the existing law (and it is to these, significantly, that rabbinic parallels are found); the last two come nearer to contradicting it. These latter are the two that Mt has constructed from material found also in Lk; the remainder he received from a separate, and perhaps

early, source. (The number five is arrived at by treating the antithesis on divorce—also introduced by Mt—as subordinate to that on adultery. Most commentators reckon it separately.) *the men of old* (vv. 21, 33): the quotations are all from the Torah, but what is really being attacked is the oral tradition of casuistry; for this see Introduction, p. 23.

5: 21–26 On murder and anger

The Mosaic commandment (Ex. 20¹³, Dt. 5¹⁷) confined itself to the external action of killing, and the judgement attached to it would be external also, that of legal proceedings (cp. Ex. 21¹²). The new interpretation extends it to cover attitudes and passions which if indulged can lead to murder; the only judgement on these can be the hidden judgement of God.

22. This contrast is somewhat blurred by the present confused state of the saying in v. 22. The penalties named seem to be arranged in ascending order of severity: (i) judgement by a local court; (ii) judgement by the Sanhedrin (the Jewish supreme court); (iii) hell-fire. But it is not at all clear that the offences listed are arranged in a similar ascending scale, and the distinctions between them have a legalistic ring about them. *Mōre* (fool) seems to be roughly the Gk equivalent of *Raca* (see RSVmg) and both are no more than expressions of the anger already condemned in v. 22a. It is possible that *Mōre*, like *Raca*, really transliterates a Hebrew term of abuse, and sanctions against both words have been introduced from a rabbinic Jewish source (which would take care to reproduce the exact words forbidden); and that the original antithesis ran something like this: 'You have heard that it was said . . . "You shall not kill", and that whoever kills shall be liable to the judgement; but I say to you that every one who is angry with his brother shall be liable to the hell of fire'. See Davies, *SSM*, pp. 235ff.; for alternative explanations, C. F. D. Moule in *Expository Times*, lxxxi (1969/70), 10ff.

The connexion between murder and anger was not unfamiliar to the rabbis; behind them lies Lev. 19¹⁷ᶠ·; cp. also Sir. 10⁶, 28⁷. *brother*: probably used by Jesus himself in the regular Jewish sense as the equivalent of 'neighbour'; cp. Lev. 19¹⁷, Dt. 15². Mt turns the Jewish 'brother' into the Christian 'brother', i.e. fellow-disciple; see especially 18¹⁵·²¹. *hell* (Gk *geenna*) *of fire*: The valley of Hinnom (Heb. *ge-Hinnom*), to the west of Jerusalem, was used as the rubbish dump of the city, and the smouldering of fires there was seen as a symbol of eternal punishment, a doctrine drawn from the OT (e.g. Is. 66²⁴) by contemporary Jewish teachers, and assumed in this and other instances (e.g. Lk 16²³) by Jesus.

Mt adds two short illustrations of the need for reconciliation:

23–24. *Reconciliation before worship:* for a Jewish precedent cp. the saying in Mishnah *Yoma* viii. 9 (Danby, p. 172): 'For transgressions that are between a man and his fellow the Day of Atonement effects atonement only if he has appeased his fellow'. The original saying of Jesus still had the temple in mind; by Mt's time it would probably have been applied to Christian worship. Cp. the injunction in *Did.* xvi. 1 to confess sins before the Sunday eucharist 'that your sacrifice may be pure'.

25–26. *Agreement with one's accuser:* cp. Lk 12⁵⁷⁻⁹. Jeremias assumes that the situation envisaged is that of a man arrested for debt, a practice which, like imprisonment in general, was unknown to Jewish law. 'Jesus is deliberately referring to non-Jewish legal practice which his audience considered inhuman' (*PJ*, p. 181; cp. 18²⁵,³⁴). The original message of this parable was probably the imminence of the final crisis and the urgency of the hearer's situation. By using it simply as an illustration of the need to be reconciled with one's enemy, Mt offers a domesticated version with the eschatological dimension removed. *guard* (Gk *hupēretēs*): according to Jeremias (*PJ*, p. 27n) a synagogue official; if so the word alters the original setting of the parable (see above). *penny:* the *quadrans* or ¼ *as* (¹⁄₆₄ of a *denarius*), aptly rendered 'farthing' in AV, was the smallest coin in the Roman currency.

5: 27–32 On adultery, lust and divorce

Again the Mosaic commandment (Ex. 20¹⁴; Dt. 5¹⁸) is intensified, but this time without reference to any penalty associated with it (though Mt half supplies this by his insertion from Mk 9⁴³ of the command to pluck out the offending eye rather than let it be the cause of one's ruin). Rabbinic opinion in general was also severe on the lustful look; e.g. R. Simeon ben Lakish: 'the eye: lest you should think only he who sins with his body is an adulterer; he who sins with his eye is also an adulterer' (with a reference to Job 24¹⁵; *A Rabbinic Anthology*, no. 1441).

28. *committed adultery . . . heart:* Jewish moral teaching in the time of Jesus already extended the scope of the seventh commandment (apart from strictly legal contexts) to cover any sexual activity outside the married state (cp. Derrett, *LNT*, pp. 370f.). Jesus' comment simply carries this further. It does not mean that there is no distinction between the act and the thought, but only that there is no hard and fast boundary. A man's life must be all of a piece; where the physical act is wrong, the lustful design is wrong too, though not necessarily in the same degree. There is here a particular application of the beatitude on the pure in heart (5⁸).

31–32. Since the objection here to *divorce* is that it incurs, for somebody, the guilt of adultery, Mt's insertion of this saying is properly taken not as a completely fresh antithesis but as subordinate to that on adultery. It is here reproduced in the most ancient form in which it has come down to us; it is thoroughly Jewish in its assumption that divorce is the prerogative of the husband and adultery the 'matrimonial offence' of the wife. On this, and on the problems of the saying generally, see Note D, p. 248.

31. The quotation is from Dt. 24¹. *certificate of divorce:* to protect her against a charge of adultery in the event of her remarriage.

32. *except on the ground of unchastity* (Gk *porneia*): the word is not the ordinary one for adultery (*moicheia*), though it is occasionally used in this sense in the Gk Bible (e.g. Sir. 23²³). It is also used to mean 'false marriage', i.e. within the prohibited degrees, or premarital unchastity, whether before or during betrothal. It is not clear that any one of these meanings is to be preferred to the rest. All fall within the scope of the strict interpretation of 'some indecency' in Dt. 24¹, and the quasi-legal phrasing of the exceptive clause strongly suggests that it has this text in mind. The question whether Jesus was himself the author of it is discussed in Note D. *makes her an adulteress:* a woman sent away by her husband would normally (unless it was still possible for her to return to her father's house) be forced to cohabit with another man, or else starve. Jesus puts the responsibility for this situation squarely on the husband.

5: 33–37 On swearing

The Mosaic law expressly commanded swearing by the name of God (Dt. 6¹³, 10²⁰); but later Jewish opinion was very much alive to the possibility of abusing this and sought to restrict it. For the rabbis see C. G. Montefiore, *Rabbinic Literature and Gospel Teachings* (London, 1930), pp. 48ff.; for the Essenes, CD 15¹ᶠ·, 16²ᶠᶠ· (V, pp. 108f.), and the comments of Davies, *SSM*, pp. 240ff. One or two of the rabbinic parallels are very close in form to the saying here; e.g. R. Huna: 'the yes of the righteous is a yes; their no is a no'; R. Elazar: 'yes is an oath; no is an oath'; but the latter saying at least is taking a strict view of what constitutes the binding validity of an oath rather than forbidding swearing as such. The conclusion of Montefiore seems justified: 'I do not think that the . . . "unqualified truthfulness in speech" which Jesus demanded was not also demanded and was not also regarded as part of the moral ideal by the Rabbis . . . On the other hand, so far as Jesus means: Never swear; do not say more than Yes and No; merely "affirm", he goes beyond the rabbis' (op. cit., p. 50).

The text used is composite and probably derived from Jewish catechetical material (cp. *Did.* ii. 3 for the first half); unlike 5²¹·²⁷

it is cited not from the Decalogue but from Lev. 19[12] and Nu. 30[2] (cp. Dt. 23[21]). The former text may conceal a reference to the third commandment (Ex. 20[7]); it is an injunction not to profane God's name by misusing it. The latter is concerned with the performance of vows. vv. 34b–36 have a surface resemblance to 23[16–22], which is directed against the Jewish casuistry which allowed some vows to be circumvented on a technicality. But the passage as a whole is not about vows but about speaking the truth at all times.

34–36. cp. Is. 66[1], Ps. 48[2]. For current circumlocutions for the name of God in oaths, see on 23[16–22], and for a parallel to swearing by one's head, Montefiore, op. cit., p. 49.

37. For a slightly different version of this command see Jas. 5[12]. There can be little doubt that behind both lies an authentic saying of Jesus which had a pervasive influence on the NT and beyond it (see especially 2 Cor. 1[17ff.], and cp. in this gospel 26[63–4,72,74]). The command not to swear was taken with extreme literalness in the pre-Nicene Church; see, e.g., the stringent conditions exacted from serving soldiers and civil officials who offered themselves for the catechumenate (Hippolytus, *Apostolic Tradition*, xvi. 17–18; G. Dix (ed.), p. 26).

5: 38–48 The two remaining antitheses differ from the foregoing ones in the following ways: (i) they are found in non-antithetical form in Lk; (ii) they show no signs of containing interpolated material; (iii) the single text cited in each is not a prohibition of the kind found in the Decalogue which needs to be taken deeper, but a positive enactment which limits the goodness required of those who observe the law (contrast 5[48]). Hence the conclusion that Mt has formulated them himself, and that they represent, more unambiguously than the rest, his own understanding of what is meant by 'fulfilling' the law.

5: 38–42 On the duty of non-retaliation and non-resistance: cp. Lk 6[29–30]

The *lex talionis* (the name is derived from the Roman *Law of XII Tables*, but the principle is widespread and at least as old as the Code of Hammurabi at Babylon [eighteenth century B.C.]) originally enacted not the duty of revenge but a restriction on the right to it, as against the unlimited pursuit of a vendetta. The biblical sanction here cited for it is found at Ex. 21[24], Lev. 24[20], Dt. 19[21]; but in Jesus' time only the Sadducees observed it literally, the Pharisees normally substituting fines. This makes it an unlikely starting-point (in the original context) for the piece of dominical teaching which follows, but a convenient one for a statement of Mt's position in relation to that of the rabbis, since it is a point of law which the latter themselves did not press.

The instruction on non-resistance which follows is a particular application of the command to love one's neighbour (in the inclusive sense; see on vv. 43ff.) to the situation of the individual who finds himself imposed upon or exploited. It is significant that the examples include being pressed into service by the forces of the occupying power (see on v. 41), the most resented form of exploitation in Roman-occupied Judaea (though not, in Jesus' time, in Galilee); here Jesus explicitly dissociates himself from the extremist policy of all-out resistance to the Romans. The grounds for his attitude were, probably, his transcendental, as opposed to national, conception of the kingdom of God, and his belief that its coming was so imminent as to make any thought of national liberation irrelevant. That all participation in resistance movements or wars of liberation or self-defence is therefore, in any conceivable circumstances, to be condemned is more than can be established from this text; it concerns the attitude of the individual to his oppressors, and it depicts this, in vividly concrete terms, as unlimited love and generosity.

39. *one who is evil*: not the 'evil one' (as generally in Mt), but the human aggressor.

40. Mt's version envisages a legal action, Lk's a commandeering which is more likely to be original (see next verse). *coat* (Gk *chitōn*): the sleeved under-tunic or shirt. *cloak*: (Gk *himation*): the garment worn over it, and also used to sleep in at night. Note that that the OT law forbids a plaintiff to claim this (Ex. 22²⁶ᶠ·, Dt. 24¹²ᶠ·).

41. *forces* (Gk *angareusei*): the *angaros* was the courier of the Persian royal mail service (cp. Herodotus viii. 98; Esther 3¹³), who had authority to commandeer the services of men and animals. The verb came to be used of any form of compulsory requisition or conscription, such as was common under the conditions of the Roman occupation. *mile*: a Roman measurement of distance, again suggesting the demands of the occupying forces. 'The first mile renders to Caesar the things that are Caesar's; the second mile, by meeting oppression with kindness, renders to God the things that are God's' (Manson, *SJ*, p. 160).

5: 43–48 On love of one's neighbour: cp. Lk 6²⁷ᶠ·,³²⁻⁶

The command to love one's neighbour as one's self at Lev. 19¹⁸ is in its original context restricted to the Jewish neighbour; and the typically Semitic opposition of *love . . . hate* (meaning, in effect, to love A more than B; cp. 6²⁴) accurately conveys its original scope, though the OT (despite Ps. 26⁵, 139²¹) contains no explicit parallel to the language. A direction to 'love all the sons of light and hate all the sons of darkness' is found in the DSS (1 QS 1⁹ [V, p. 72]; cp. 9²¹ᶠ· [V, p. 88]); but Mt's gloss more probably reflects the sense in which Lev. 19¹⁸ was regularly taken by his Jewish contemporaries (i.e. the 'tradition').

The contrast highlights both the originality of the teaching of Jesus, in that he transformed the scope of the precept by universalizing the meaning of 'neighbour' (see especially the parable of the Good Samaritan, Lk 10²⁵ᶠᶠ·, and on it Bornkamm, *Jesus of Nazareth* [ET London, 1960], pp. 111ff.), and the sense in which, for Mt, it has 'radicalized' the requirements of the OT law.

45. *sons of your Father who is in heaven*: the expression is unique in the NT, but used at Sir. 4¹⁰ of those who, like God (Ps. 146⁹), care for the orphan and widow. Mt has a particular fondness for ben-Sirach, and may have been influenced by him in his formulation of this saying.

46–47. *tax collectors . . . Gentiles*: Lk uses the one word 'sinners'. Mt's two words reappear together at 18¹⁷ (clearly a community saying) as does the contemptuous tone which is uncharacteristic both of Jesus and Mt (cp. 8¹¹, 9⁹ᶠᶠ·); probably it represents a Judaizing strain in the tradition Mt was drawing upon. Some MSS. read 'tax collectors' for *Gentiles*.

48. *perfect, as your heavenly Father is perfect*: the basic OT text for the imitation of God is Lev. 11⁴⁴ᶠ·: 'be holy, for I am holy' (quoted at 1 Pet. 1¹⁶, and probably made the basis for a good deal of early catechetical teaching; see P. Carrington, *The Early Christian Catechism* [Cambridge, 1935]). Mt's *perfect* and Lk's 'merciful' seem to be alternative developments of the OT conception of holiness, though, as Dalman pointed out (*Words of Jesus* [ET Edinburgh, 1902], p. 204), 'merciful' in the OT is always used of God, never of men, and is therefore more appropriate to a passage enjoining the imitation of God than 'perfect', which is always used of men, never of God. *perfect* (Gk *teleios*) is the word used in LXX at Dt. 18¹³ (RSV 'blameless'; NEB 'wholehearted'). It is clearly to this Jewish usage and not to the Hellenistic connotation of 'mature' found in the Pauline literature (which would be inapplicable to God) that we must look for the elucidation of Mt's meaning, which is closely related to that of 'pure in heart' at 5⁸. *teleios* expresses both consistency (being 'all of a piece'), and total commitment and generosity (cp. NEB 'there must be no limit to your goodness'). Cp. 19²¹ (on this, Davies, *SSM*, pp. 209ff.); also Jas. 1⁴, 3².

v. 48 sums up not only this section but the whole account of the Christian attitude to the law in 5²¹⁻⁴⁷.

6: 1–18 *True and False Piety*

The Sermon now passes from the requirement of 'wholeness' in the observance of the law to that of 'inwardness' in the practice of external acts of piety. It does this in terms of almsgiving, prayer, and fasting, the 'three notable duties'

which the Christian ascetical tradition took over—with the
help of this passage—from Judaism; see Tobit 12⁸. But the only
one of these that Mt lingers over is prayer.

1. *piety:* lit. *righteousness,* which links this section with the foregoing one.
Some important MSS. have 'almsgiving', with which in later Jewish
practice 'righteousness' came almost to be identified. But Mt reserves
this emphasis for vv. 19ff.

6: 2–4 Almsgiving

2. *sound no trumpet:* trumpets were sounded during the public fasts in
time of drought, which were accompanied by public prayer in the
streets and very possibly by collections of alms. This custom is
probably the background of the whole section. *hypocrites:* the Gk word
came to be used regularly of an actor, but without moral significance.
In Jewish circles however, and particularly in the gospels, it represents the Aramaic *hanipha,* which originally meant a 'profane person',
but by Jesus' time had evidently acquired the connotation of 'in
sincere' or 'flattering'. In *Did.* viii. 1 it appears to be a regular (?Jewish)
Christian term of abuse for observant Jews, as here. *they have their
reward:* the Gk word *apechein* is a commercial one, found also in
papyrus receipts. *left hand . . . right hand:* the Jews, like many non-
European peoples, distinguished carefully between their two hands;
the right was for giving, receiving, and blessing, the left for cursing
and for activities considered shameful. See Derrett, *LNT,* p. xlv.

6: 5–6 Prayer

5. *stand:* the normal attitude for prayer among Jews (cp. Lk 18⁹ᶠᶠ·),
as also among early Christians, for whom kneeling expressed extreme
penitence.

6. *room:* Gk *tameion,* i.e. the storeroom, the only room in the house which
it would be possible to lock, and without a window to light it. It is
used as a symbol of secrecy at Is. 26²⁰, to which this passage is
obviously indebted, and at Lk 12³ (where Mt suppresses it in his
parallel, 10²⁷).

6: 7–15 *Digression: Prayer and the Lord's Prayer*

Mt here inserts into a passage, which by itself merely shows
the disciple how not to pray, a positive instruction on prayer.
This allows him to place the Lord's Prayer at the very centre
of the Sermon. But he introduces it with a further negative
warning: the Lord's Prayer is to be seen as the pattern of all

prayer; it is not to be treated as an empty, stereotyped and repeated formula, such as pagans use.

7. *heap up empty phrases:* Gk *battalogein*, a word otherwise unknown before A.D. 530; its meaning must be more or less equivalent to *many words* in v. 7b, but its etymology can only be conjectured. It is likely to be either connected with *battalos* ('gabbler'), the nickname bestowed on the Attic orator Demosthenes for his astonishing fluency, or onomato-poeic like the word 'babble' coined by Tyndale to translate it (so NEB). *Gentiles:* Christian prayer is distinguished from pagan practice as well as from Jewish. Pagan popular piety was certainly dominated by the use of incantations and magical formulae, some of them known to us from papyri, which were supposed to depend for their efficacy on the actual recitation, irrespective of the intention behind it.

6: 9–13 The Lord's Prayer

This has come down to us in two recensions, the shorter form at Lk 11$^{2-4}$ and the longer and more familar text here. Both have doubtless been shaped to some extent by the worshipping tradition of the local Christian communities through which they were transmitted; but it is a reasonable inference that Lk's shorter recension stands nearer to the original. Mt's fuller and more rounded version not only has a rhythmical structure of its own (distinct from Lk's), but a degree of formal correspondence with the *Shemoneh Esreh* or *Prayer of XVIII Benedictions* recited daily in the synagogue. Davies (*SSM*, pp. 309ff.) suggests that the Lord's Prayer was deliberately reshaped as a Christian counterpart to the *Shemoneh Esreh* either in its full or abbreviated form. The *Didache*, which reproduces Mt's version of the Prayer with slight variations, significantly directs its recitation three times a day (viii. 3). The language of the additions in Mt is close enough to Mt's own to suggest that he stood very near to the source of the reshaping. (The first century form of the *Shemoneh Esreh* is given by C. W. Dugmore, *Influence of the Synagogue on the Divine Office* [^{2}London, 1964], pp. 114ff.; the abbreviated form of the modern version by R. M. Grant, *Historical Introduction to the NT* [London, 1963], p. 283. On the interpretation of the Prayer in general see C. F. Evans, *The Lord's Prayer* [London, 1963]; Jeremias, *PrJ*, pp. 82ff.; E. Loh-meyer, *The Lord's Prayer* [ET London, 1965].)

9. *Our Father who art in heaven:* Lk's 'Father', representing the Aramaic *Abba* (according to Jeremias a very familiar diminutive used by children, as in Palestine to this day), is clearly original; as a form of address to God it is unparalleled in Jewish religious literature, and is probably to be attributed to our Lord's own deep personal awareness of his filial relation to God, in which the disciples are invited to share.

(See *PrJ*, pp. 11ff., especially 57ff.). Mt has substituted a more reverential form common in Jewish worship and teaching. But he too restricts the application of God's Fatherhood to disciples; it is not a universal Fatherhood of all men. Cp. (outside the Sermon) 13⁴³, 23⁶; and see H. F. D. Sparks, in D. E. Nineham (ed.), *Studies in the Gospels* (Oxford, 1955), pp. 241ff. *Hallowed be thy name:* either (i) the first of the petitions of the Prayer (in the first three the Gk verb is in the emphatic position at the beginning of the sentence), and in that case almost equivalent to the petition which follows; cp. Ezek. 36²³, Sir. 36⁴, and the Jewish Prayer called *Kaddish:* '. . . Let thy great name be magnified and hallowed"; or (ii) a *berākāh* or expression of praise to God for his mighty acts already performed (see on 11²⁵, and cp., e.g., Lk 1⁴⁷⁻⁹). This normally preceded petition in Jewish prayers, including the *XVIII Benedictions*, and it would be natural to expect it here. Possibly those who re-shaped the Prayer took in this sense a petition which originally expressed sense (i).

10. *Thy kingdom come:* the heart of the Prayer. For what it would have meant to Mt see Note A., p. 232. *Thy will be done . . . heaven:* Mt only. The whole phrase is a unity, and explanatory of the preceding petition, possibly of the preceding two. God's will is perfectly done in heaven, and man's praise is the participation in that. God's will is not yet perfectly done on earth, and the coming of the kingdom will be the realization of that. In any case the petition, though it may owe something indirectly to Jesus' reported prayer in Gethsemane (contrast Mk 14³⁶ with Mt 26⁴²), is not an expression of resignation to God's will but a prayer that men may everywhere fulfil it.

11. *Give us this day our daily bread:* the Gk word, *epiousios*, here translated *daily*, is, as Origen noted, unique in Greek literature, though it has since turned up in a papyrus fragment of an account-book (published in 1889 and later lost) which reads '½ obol for *epiousi* . . .' The only clues to the meaning are (i) the possible (but not demonstrable) equivalence of the Latin *diaria* (daily rations) found in a similar account scratched on a wall at Pompeii; (ii) etymology, which on the whole supports the meaning 'for the coming day'. See Evans, pp. 46ff.

Black (*AA*, pp. 203ff.), suggests that behind the Gk word lies an Aramaic phrase meaning literally 'today and tomorrow' (i.e. 'day by day'); cp. Lk 13³². He suggests that Mt's version has translated the two halves of the expression separately ('give us our bread today for tomorrow'), whereas Lk's 'each day' translates the whole expression correctly, but has had the word *epiousios* introduced into it at some subsequent stage from the other version.

If Black is right, the petition is simply for daily material needs, of which bread, as the most obvious, is made the symbol. If, with Evans, we regard *epiousios* as representing a word in the original meaning 'for the coming day'; there are two possibilities. Either (a) the petition is closely connected with the command not to be anxious for to-morrow (see on 6²⁵ᶠᶠ·), and prayer for tomorrow's bread is the obverse of trusting God to provide it; or (b), as Evans himself holds, the bread of the petition is not common bread, but the symbol of the kingdom which is to come as bread to the hungry (cp. 5⁶). This is wholly in keeping with the eschatological meaning of the Prayer as originally delivered.

12. *our debts:* the Aramaic *hobha* (debt) is regularly used to mean 'sin' in rabbinic writings. *have forgiven:* the perfect is peculiar to Mt, whose version assumes that those who ask God's forgiveness have already tendered their own. Cp. Sir. 28², and see on vv. 14f., below.

13. *lead us not into temptation* (NEB 'do not bring us to the test'): God does not tempt in the sense that Satan does in 4¹ᶠᶠ·, by actual enticement to evil; but he does permit his elect to undergo trials which are a severe test of their faithfulness, and the apocalyptic tradition from Daniel onwards anticipated a trial 'of cosmic proportions' (Evans, p. 67). Jesus started from this inherited outlook, and it is probable that in this petition he was teaching his disciples to pray that they might not be overwhelmed by the 'Messianic woes'. Cp. 26⁴¹. *but deliver us from evil:* Mt only. RSVmg 'from the evil one' is almost certainly right. The petition is a kind of positive counterpart of the previous one, and may have been inserted because of misunderstanding of it. Jas. 1¹³ has already to insist that God 'tempts no one'; for glosses to the same effect in Tertullian, Cyprian and Augustine see Evans, pp. 64f.

The doxology printed in the mg 'For thine is the kingdom and the power and the glory, forever. Amen'. is not found in the majority of the earlier MSS., and probably owes its present form to liturgical usage. But the habit of concluding the prayer with a doxology of some sort is attested as early as the *Didache* (viii. 2) and is fully in line with Jewish practice at least on more formal occasions.

14–15. *if you forgive . . . .:* a reinforcement of the petition in 6¹², to which Mt attaches great importance; see especially the parable of the unmerciful servant (18²³ᶠᶠ·), which is the climax of a whole section on forgiveness; also 5²³ᶠ·. Cp. Mk 11²⁵.

6: 16–18 Fasting

This is the final item in Mt's comparison of true and false piety, to which he now returns. 9¹⁴ᶠᶠ· (par. Mk 2¹⁸ᶠᶠ·) suggests that the disciples of Jesus, by comparison with those of John, were not conspicuous for asceticism. It does not necessarily follow that this saying was not spoken by Jesus, but it at least makes it likely that it was not originally addressed to the circle of his close followers. It takes for granted the forms of piety observed by devout Jews, and shows the spirit in which they are to be practised. 9¹⁴ᶠᶠ· also implies that the early post-resurrection Church did practise fasting, and the *Didache*, which may be very near to Mt in date and *milieu*, enjoins it on similar lines to the Jewish practice, only on different days of the week; see *Did*. viii.

17. *anoint:* the outward sign of rejoicing.

6: 19–7:12 *Acts of Mercy*

R. Samuel the Just (first century A.D.) is reported to have said: 'By three things is the world sustained: by the Law, by the (Temple) service, and by deeds of loving kindness'. Davies (*SSM*, pp. 305ff.) suggests a corresponding division of the main body of the Sermon, with Christian devotion substituted for the worship of the temple; in that view this final section represents the 'deeds of loving kindness'. It has been questioned whether R. Samuel understood this expression in its conventional sense; but, be that as it may, it admirably expresses the connecting theme of the contents of this section. For Mt's understanding of 'mercy' or 'loving kindness' cp. 5^7 and his use of Hos. 6^6 at 9^{13}, 12^3. The section falls into two parts:

6: 19–34 (1) *Generosity with money:* four sayings.

In all these, to be merciful (5^7) is found to involve poverty of spirit (5^3) and singleness of heart (5^8).

19–21 True riches and the single heart

Jeremias insists that 'it is not a question of contrasting earthly with heavenly treasure, but of where the treasure is stored' (*PJ*, p. 202n). In that case the saying must refer to the giving away of wealth, and this is what is enjoined at 19^{21}. Money given away is equivalent to property wisely stored, in conditions in which it will not depreciate.

Cp. Jas. 5^{1-3} for a fierce denunciation of the rich in a Christian congregation based on this saying. *moth:* the enemy of fabrics. *rust:* more probably consumption by some kind of vermin—worm (so RSVmg and *Thomas*, 76) or mice—the enemy of foodstuffs. The saying presupposes Palestinian conditions, with the storing of goods in kind in barns (cp. v. 26, and Lk $12^{13ff.}$), not money in coin. *heart:* see on 5^8.

22–23 The single eye

See Jeremias, *PJ*, p. 163, for the original meaning of this little parable, which treats the eye, in accordance with ancient physiology, as the source of light for the whole body; if it is not to get it from there, where is it to get it? The point is thus similar to that of the salt that has lost its taste (5^{13}). Mt's use of it as an invitation to generosity depends on the literal meaning of the two adjectives which RSV has obscured by paraphrasing. *sound*: lit. 'single', the single eye corresponding to the single (undivided) heart (v. 21). *not sound*: lit. 'evil'. The 'evil eye' was a familiar Semitic expression for jealousy or meanness (cp. 20^{15} and mg; Dt. 15^9). As the eye is, so is the whole man.

24. Singleness of service

This saying, perhaps originally proverbial, would have been understood as a call to absolute commitment; cp. 10^{37-9}. The application to worldly wealth (v. 24b) is probably secondary and may be due to Mt himself. *hate . . . love*: a characteristic Semitic antithesis, meaning that he will love one more than the other. *mammon*: an Aramaic expression for 'property', found in the Heb. version of Sir. 31^8; cp. Lk 16^{11}, 1 QS 6^2 (V, p. 80). Any personification is entirely due to the context.

25-34 Trust in God's goodness: the priority of the kingdom

This is the most extended and the most beautiful of the poems of our Lord that has been preserved for us. The version at Lk 12^{22-31} seems to have been independently transmitted and is probably closer to the original (cp. v. 26, and see Manson, *SJ*, pp. 111ff.). Mt offers it as a general counsel to all disciples; but it is likely that its original reference was more restricted. The charge given to the disciples sent out on mission requires them to take no provisions with them, but to live on what those who receive them set before them (see $10^{9f.}$ and cp. especially Lk $10^{7f.}$); and this principle was so taken for granted in the apostolic church that St Paul has to make a formal *apologia* for diverging from it (see 1 Cor. 9^{1-18}). This is the situation which the saying fits and in which it was doubtless preserved. Those upon whom God lays a special task are to undertake it with confidence; God knows their needs and will see that they are provided for. The context suggests that Mt is using it as an encouragement to those deterred from generosity by the thought of finding themselves without provision.

25. *be anxious*: the Gk *merimnān* can mean either this or 'make an effort'. The use of *zētein* ('seek', 'strive') as an equivalent (vv. 32f.) strongly favours the latter, as does the comparison with birds and flowers, which are depicted as not working, not as not worrying (see Jeremias, *PJ*, pp. 214f.).

26. *birds of the air*: Lk's 'ravens' is probably original, as it is particular and parallel in this with *lilies* (really 'wild anemones'). Ravens (which are masculine in Aramaic) are here associated with men's tasks, and lilies (which are feminine) with women's. A reference to Ps. 147^9 (which speaks of 'young ravens') is therefore unlikely. But the thought of the raven being an unclean bird (Lev. 11^{15}, Dt. 14^{14}) may sharpen the point.

27. *span of life:* the word can equally well mean 'stature' (so RSVmg);
but a cubit (18 inches or approx. 47 centimetres) is rather a large
addition to a man's height, and the context seems to require a very
small one.

30. *men of little faith:* the expression (also found in Lk) seems to have caught
Mt's eye, since he uses it several times subsequently (8^{26}, 14^{31}, 16^{8},
cp. 17^{20}) to express the doubt of a believing disciple.

33. *and his righteousness:* a characteristic addition by Mt, for whom
kingdom and *righteousness* are correlatives: *righteousness* the present and
qualifying attitude, *kingdom* the future and contingent fulfilment; cp.
$5^{3,6,10}$. Note that in the Lord's Prayer the petition for the coming of
the kingdom precedes that for daily bread.

34. Mt's concluding comment on the poem, and possibly an indication
of how he understood the word translated 'daily' in the Lord's Prayer.
Let the day's own trouble . . . day: probably a traditional proverb; cp.
Prov. 27^{1}, Jas. $4^{13f.}$.

7: 1–11 (2) *Mercy received as well as given:* four sayings.

The connecting theme between the remaining sayings of this
section appears to be that the disciple must act as one who hopes to
receive mercy himself (cp. $18^{23,35}$, 1 Cor. $4^{4f.}$).

1–2. On judging others

A shortened version of the saying at Lk $6^{37f.}$, where it goes closely
with that on love of enemies. It has sometimes been taken as a
prohibition of all litigation, and 1 Cor. 6^{1-8} suggests that this may
have begun early.

3–5. Judgement begins at home; cp. Lk 6^{41-2}.

Mt uses this as a concrete application of the meaning of vv. 1f.,
but, though found in the same context in Lk, it was originally
independent of it. A parallel saying ascribed to R. Tarphon (late
first century A.D.) has survived in the Talmud. If both rest on a
Palestinian proverb, this saying, like 19^{24}, shows our Lord drawing
on proverbial wisdom for the grotesque exaggerations which are a
mark of his own personal style. But it is conceivable that an original
saying of his passed (anonymously) into wider Jewish currency.
speck: i.e. of straw or sawdust.

6. Christian discrimination

An epigram with a strong anti-Gentile bias (*dogs . . . swine;* cp.
$15^{26f.}$), probably framed by earlier Jewish Christians as a comment
on the mission to Gentiles, is turned by Mt into a general injunction
to 'reserve in the communication of religious knowledge'. Disciples
will be answerable for their care of what is committed to them. *what
is holy:* A. Meyer suggested that this is a mistranslation of an Aramaic

word meaning a 'ring', i.e. of gold; this would give admirable parallelism with *pearls*. In any case Mt is reinterpreting the metaphor, a process carried further in *Did.* ix. 5, where it is referred to food blessed at the agape-meal (or, less probably, the eucharist) of which the unbaptized are forbidden to partake. The invitation to communion 'Holy things for holy people' is found in Greek–Syrian liturgies from an early date. *they trample* (i.e. the *swine*) . . . *and turn to attack you* (i.e. the *dogs*): a perfect example of *chiasmus*.

7–11. Trust in God's goodness: the prayer of petition

This little poem stands in a corresponding position to 6²⁵⁻³³, and, like it, is an encouragement to believe the best of God, as vv. 1–5 are an invitation to think the best of men. Those who show mercy themselves stand in need of receiving it.

12. Conclusion: the Golden Rule

The 'Golden Rule' was well known to contemporary Judaism; cp. Tob. 4¹⁵, *Did.* i. 2 (deriving from a Jewish source), and especially the saying of R. Hillel: 'What is hateful to you you shall not do to your neighbour; this word is the whole law, and all else is commentary' (Talmud, *b. Shabb.* 31a). But all the Jewish authorities put it in this negative form; to state it positively was, it seems, the great innovation of our Lord himself. For Mt it sums up not only the section on works of mercy, and in it especially the injunction not to judge others, but the righteousness which exceeds that of the scribes and Pharisees (who know only the negative form) (5²⁰), and the Christian understanding of law and prophets (5¹⁷; cp. 22³⁷⁻⁴⁰). Hence its position at the conclusion of the central section of the Sermon.

7: 13–27 *Final Warnings against Unfaithfulness*

See Introduction, p. 19, for the tacit change of audience in the final section of each of the 'five discourses'. Like 13³⁶ᶠᶠ· and 24–5, the present section with its warning against 'hearing and not doing' (vv. 24–7) is addressed to the evangelist's contemporary Christians in the light of their impending judgement; and like them it mentions 'lawlessness' (Gk *anomia*—concealed by the RSV rendering 'evildoers' at 7²³, 13⁴¹; cp. 24¹²) and the influence of *false prophets* (7¹⁵, 24¹¹; the 'causes of sin' at 13⁴¹ may have a similar reference). Barth (*TIM*, pp. 73f.) maintains that Mt is challenging an explicitly antinomian group in his own church. Antinomianism was a predictable reaction to Christian revaluation of the law in any of its forms (cp. 1 Cor. 5–9, and, nearer to Mt in time and place, Jas. $1^{22ff\cdot}$, $2^{14ff\cdot}$), and though the laxity attacked here could proceed from indifference (cp. 'love . . . will grow cold' at 24^{12}) as much as from deliberate rejection of a morality based on law, *false prophets* suggests propaganda rather than drifting.

13–14. The two ways

Mt seems to have conflated the saying about a gate found also at Lk $13^{23f\cdot}$ with another about two ways, one leading to life and the other to death. The latter idea, deriving ultimately from Dt. $30^{15,19}$ (for the wording cp. also Jer. 21^8), became a commonplace of Jewish catechetical teaching which left its mark on the early Church; cp. *Did.* i, *Ep. Barn.* xviii–xx (both probably dependent on a single Jewish source). In v. 13a RSVmg 'for the way is wide and easy' is possibly right.

15–23. The two trees and their fruit

15. *false prophets:* who are these? The revival of prophetic activity was a striking feature of early Christianity (see 1 Cor. $12^{10,28}$, 14 *passim,* Eph. 4^{11}, Acts 11^{28}, $21^{10f\cdot}$), and Mt not only regards the disciples (i.e. the Church) as being in the prophetic succession (5^{12}) but gives 'prophets' pride of place in his list of Christian emissaries to the Jewish people (23^{34}). But by the end of the first century bogus prophets were becoming a problem in a number of churches; cp. 1 Jn 4^{1-3}, Rev. 2^{20}, *Did.* xi–xiii. Mk 13^{22} makes the appearance of 'false prophets' a distinguishing mark of the end-time, and Mt's parallel at 24^{11} backdates this to the period of preliminary tribulation in which the Church is already living. It is not altogether clear whether these latter are prophets in the technical sense or are so called because of their influence over others. Here however v. 22 suggests that at least some of those involved exercised a prophetic gift; i.e. they were prophets first, and only afterwards, through misuse of their gift, *false prophets.*

15. *sheep's clothing:* i.e. they are within the Christian fold, as is confirmed by their activities in v. 22. *wolves:* cp. Ezek. 22^{27}, Zeph. 3^3.

16. *You will know them by their fruits:* note the repetition at v. 20, enclosing sayings which illustrate it (*inclusio*). For these cp. 3^{10}, 12^{33}.

21. The 'fruits' in which the 'false prophets' are wanting. *Lord, Lord:* 1 Cor. 16^{22} shows that the use of 'Lord' in a quasi-liturgical formula addressed to Christ goes back to Aramaic-speaking Christianity. The frequent use of the Gk *Kyrie* in petitions for healing in the miracle stories of this gospel (see Held, *TIM,* p. 265) probably also reflects liturgical practice. The reduplicated form recurs at 25^{11} expressing despair in a similar eschatological situation. *he who does the will . . .*

heaven: this could serve as a definition of the word 'righteous' as Mt understands it.

22–23. cp. Lk 13²⁶ᶠ·. *in your name:* use of the name of Jesus in healing, exorcism, etc. (cp. Acts 3⁶, 19¹³) implied unity with its owner and possession by him. This is now shown to be no automatic guarantee of admission to the kingdom. *depart . . . evildoers* (lit. 'doers of lawless-ness') : Ps. 6⁹.

7: 24–27 The two houses: cp. Lk 6⁴⁷⁻⁹

The concluding parable uses the floods which, in Palestinian conditions, follow the autumn rains, and which only a well-founded building will survive, as an image of the divine judgement (see Jeremias, *PJ,* p. 194). Is. 28¹⁶, Ps. 46⁴ apply it to the holy city Jerusalem, the rabbinic tradition to the man who knows and obeys the Torah. Mt is here closer to the latter; but at 16¹⁸ he uses the image of the Church, the re-founded Israel.

24. *wise man:* used commonly in Hebrew proverbial literature to denote the man who understands the realities of his situation. For Jesus (and Mt) these are eschatological realities (see Jeremias, *PJ,* p. 46n)—how he will stand in the judgement of God. Cp. the use of the word in 25¹⁻¹³.

27. *great was the fall of it:* a proverbial expression for complete collapse.

4. THE MIGHTY ACTS OF THE CHRIST (CHAPTERS 7:28–9:34)

Mt's summary of authoritative teaching from the mouth of Jesus is followed by a series of acts of power performed by him. The parallel is intentional; 'he intends . . . to portray Jesus as the Messiah in Word and the Messiah in Deed' (Jeremias, *Sermon on the Mount,* p. 17). It is possible to reckon the number of miracles as ten, and some commentators have argued that this number was suggested by the plagues of Egypt (i.e. Jesus is acting, as he has already taught, as the new Moses). But the Moses-typology, though it may be present, is not sufficiently prominent for this to be pressed (for Davies [*SSM,* pp.88 ff.] the thought is of 'the creative activity of God'); and the miracles fall more naturally into three groups of three. They are all, with one exception, drawn from Mk, but their order is completely rearranged, and the details abbreviated; not however for abbreviation's sake, but with a definite method and theological purpose which are analysed by Held (*TIM,* pp. 165ff.). His findings can be summarized as follows:

(a) Mk's diffuse style and abundance of detail is reduced to a stereotyped formal pattern; non-essential people and actions are omitted, and the essential actions—the request for healing, the healing saying and the actual healing—are held together by catchwords.

(b) All the attention is concentrated on the dialogue at the centre of the story; little is paid to the actual healing.

(c) The miracle is closely connected with the faith of the person healed, and the purpose of the dialogue is to elicit an expression of this.

(d) The way the figure of Jesus is presented and addressed implies both a high Christology and the consequence that what happened in the gospel ministry can still happen in the Church to which Christ has promised his presence (18^{20}, 28^{20}).

28–29. The first of Mt's recurrent formulas which follow the five great discourses; cp. 11^1, 13^{53}, 19^1, 26^1. In each case the formula marks the transition to a new section, rather than the conclusion of the discourse itself. *crowds*: mentioned at 5^1; they have been listening in on a discourse addressed primarily to disciples, those who have already accepted the call to follow Jesus (see $4^{18ff.}$). As always in Mt (cp. 12^{23}, 13^2, 23^1) the word denotes the uncommitted masses, the raw material from which the future Church will be recruited.

29. *as one who had authority*: originally Mk's comment on the discourse of Jesus in the synagogue at Capernaum, which he does not report in detail. Mt has not only, as it were, supplied the content, but he uses the comment to convey his own conception of Christ as the authoritative interpreter of Torah. This is confirmed by the 'signs' of the present section. *their scribes*: this dissociates Jesus (and his disciples) from the official teachers of Judaism; cp. 4^{23} etc.

8: 1–17 *Three Healings of Excluded Persons*

The feature common to the subjects of these three healings is that they are all persons excluded from full participation in Israel's worship; a state of affairs which it is implied will be reversed in the kingdom of heaven (see Davies, *SSM*, p. 90).

8: 1–4 (i) A leper: cp. Mk 1^{40-5} (Held, pp. 213ff.)

3. *was cleansed*: in Mk, the leper; in Mt, awkwardly, the leprosy; the consequence of trying to abbreviate and still keep the catchword.

4. *say nothing to any man:* a detail taken over from Mk; see on 12[16ff.].
   show yourself to the priest: as prescribed at Lev. 14[2ff.]. *for a proof to the people* (lit. 'for a testimony to them'; cp. RSVmg): Mk's explanation of Jesus' injunction to obey the provisions of the ceremonial law (itself fully consonant with what can be recovered of his attitude) to readers who presumably no longer observed it. For Mt it depicts Jesus as the 'fulfiller' of the law (cp. 5[17]); this is a testimony to Jews, as the proclamation of the gospel (24[14]) is to Gentiles. V. 12 hints at its rejection.

8: 5–13 (ii) A Gentile: cp. Lk 7[1–10], Jn 4[46–54]

This is Mt's only non-Marcan miracle story, and, like the rest, reduced by him to the essential dialogue. The fact that Lk reproduces this dialogue almost *verbatim*, but seems to be otherwise independent, strongly suggests that he took it from Mt, and constructed his own narrative to introduce it. The points of contact with the story of the official's son in Jn are sufficient to justify the conclusion that the two traditions go back to the same episode, and where they diverge it is often Jn who seems to have the earlier version (see C. H. Dodd, *Historical Tradition in the Fourth Gospel* (Cambridge, 1963), pp. 188ff.). Thus both locate the episode at Capernaum in Galilee. Galilee, having its own tetrarch until the death of Herod Agrippa I in A.D. 44, was not under Roman military occupation in Jesus' time (though it had become so by Mt's), and therefore a centurion was unlikely to have been found there; Jn calls him a *basilikos* (an official of the royal administration, whether civil or military), and this is true to the situation in the time of Jesus. The significance of the story for Mt lies in its prefiguration of the admission of Gentiles to the Kingdom (see vv. 10–12).

6. *servant:* the Gk *pais* ('boy') can mean (like its English equivalent in some former outposts of empire) both 'son' and 'servant'. It is found in the former sense at Jn 4[51], and there is no obstacle in Mt's account to taking the sick boy as the centurion's son. It is Lk (7[2]) who has confused the sick boy of v. 6 with the obedient slave of v. 9.

7. The words are probably better understood as a question, expressing surprise or even indignation: 'Shall I (a Jew) come and heal him?' There is thus a close parallel (of which Mt is aware) between this story and that at 15[21ff.].

8. For healing by the word of God, cp. Ps. 107[20], 33[9].

9. *under authority:* i.e. with authority upon him. But there may be an element of mistranslation from the Aramaic; see Black, *AA*, p. 159. The centurion sees an analogy between his own relation to the imperial power and that of Jesus to God, and Mt sees this as an illustration of 7[29].

10. *not even in Israel:* the variant reading 'with no one in Israel' (see mg)

better expresses Mt's understanding of this episode. Cp. 15²⁸ for another commendation of faith in a Gentile.

11–12. The theme of Gentiles admitted to the kingdom and Jews excluded becomes increasingly prominent in the later chapters of Mt; the language of v. 12 is characteristically Matthaean (cp. 13⁴²,⁵⁰, 22¹³, 24⁵¹, 25³⁰). *east and west:* cp. Ps. 107³. *sit at table:* i.e. at the Messianic banquet, a common image of fulfilment in the kingdom (anticipated in the table-fellowship of Christians). *with Abraham, Isaac and Jacob:* as the true heirs of the promises made to those patriarchs. *sons of the kingdom:* a Semitic expression for those who should inherit it, i.e. the Jewish nation. *outer darkness:* i.e. Gehenna (see note on 5²³).

8: 14–15 (iii) A woman: cp. Mk 1²⁸⁻³¹ (Held, pp. 169f.)

The healing of Peter's mother-in-law is the only pericope in Mt which shows Jesus taking the initiative in healing; this is explained by the prophecy quoted in 8¹⁷ which Jesus the Messiah fulfils.

15. *she arose and served him:* Mk has 'them'. Held points out that whereas in Mk Jesus is accompanied into the house by the four disciples already called, Mt leaves the impression that he went in alone. Mt thus focuses all the attention on the figure of Jesus himself. But there may also be a hint that whereas in the temple cultus a woman had to remain at a distance, in the new order of things she may offer direct personal service to the Lord himself. For the presence of Christ in the Christian (domestic) praying community, cp. 18²⁰.

8: 16–17 Summary of healings: cp. Mk 1³²⁻⁴

A general statement of the healing activity of which three particular examples have already been given. *with a word:* cp. 8⁸.

17. The formula quotation of Is. 53⁴ is quite different from LXX but close to the Heb., and may, as Stendahl suggests (*School*, p. 107), be Mt's own rendering of it. The Heb. however uses *took* in the sense of 'took upon himself'; here it is clearly understood as 'took away'. For this meaning of the Gk *lambanō*, cp. 5⁴⁰, 15²⁶, and for the general sense Jn 1²⁹. There is nothing here about vicarious suffering.

8: 18–9:17 *Three Signs of Power*

8: 18–27 (i) The stilling of the storm: cp. Mk 4³⁵⁻⁴¹

18–22. The episode is prefaced by two warnings to would-be disciples. Bornkamm (*TIM*, pp. 54ff.) shows that these belong closely with what follows, and declare it to be, for Mt, itself a story about discipleship.

19. *a scribe:* for Mt, probably an unconverted Jew. *Another of the disciples* (v. 21) would suggest that he was a disciple already (cp. 13⁵²); but

the address *Teacher* (v. 19) is elsewhere in Mt found only in the mouths of non-disciples (see 12³⁸, 19¹⁶, 22¹⁶·³⁶, 26²⁵·⁴⁹), and implies at the very least that the speaker has not understood the distinction between following (i.e. being a disciple of) any other rabbi and following Jesus. He is prepared to follow Jesus in the Jewish sense.

20. *Foxes . . . head:* Jesus' reply has a proverbial ring, though no parallel to it has been discovered. Possibly a saying first spoken of hunted humankind in general was obliquely and ironically applied by Jesus to himself. But it may equally well have been original to him. *Son of man:* see Note B, p. 237.

21. *bury my father:* an application of the fifth commandment of the Decalogue which had such priority for observant Jews that it dispensed from the duty of reciting the *Shema* (see on 22³⁷).

22. *leave the dead:* either 'dead' =non-disciples, or there is some element of mistranslation from the Aramaic. Manson (*SJ*, p. 73) suggests either (a) 'leave the dead to the buriers of their dead' (not very likely as the normal 'buriers of the dead' were their own sons), or (b) 'leave the burying of the dead completely alone'. Black (*AA*, pp. 207f.) thinks that the original read 'let the waverers bury their dead'. In any case the original point of the saying is the absolute priority of the demands of the kingdom.

23–27 On the storm see Bornkamm, loc. cit.; Held, pp. 200ff.

23. *followed:* in Mk the disciples take Jesus with them. Mt's alteration deliberately connects their 'following' of Jesus into the ship with the 'following' of Jesus which is required for discipleship. Mt is thus the earliest exegete to interpret the ship as the Church, 'the ark of salvation'.

24. *storm* (Gk *seismos*): lit. 'earthquake'; not in Mk, and an unusual word for a storm at sea, but used elsewhere in Mt of the terrors of the end-time (24⁷; cp. 27⁵⁴, 28²), of which the storm is here taken as the symbol. The Church, frail craft as it is, will have to weather the final storm, but despite the fears of its members it can come to no harm, for Jesus is with them (cp. 28²⁰).

26. *O men of little faith:* a favourite expression of Mt's, addressed always to disciples, but as representing the contemporary Church, of which 'little faith' (i.e. failure of confidence in those living by Christian profession) was clearly a regular feature. Cp. 14³¹, 16⁸, 17²⁰, and see Held, pp. 291ff.

27. *the men:* i.e. not the disciples but others aboard the ship. Bornkamm suggests that they represent those who encounter the story through preaching.

8: 28–34 (ii) The exorcism of the Gadarene demoniacs: cp. Mk 5¹⁻²⁰ (Held, pp. 172ff.)

The sequence of storm-stilling-exorcism is taken over from Mk, for whom it is probably a fulfilment of Ps. 65⁵. Mt, though as usual he abbreviates, keeps the main outline of Mk's narrative; but unlike Mk he shows no interest at all in the men cured. He relates the story simply as a revelation of divine power in the destruction of demons. This is in line with his general tendency to play down the incidence of exorcism in Jesus' ministry which is so prominent in Mk.

28. *Gadarenes:* the most likely reading in Mt, as against 'Gergasenes' or 'Gerasenes' (mg); in Mk the reading is a very vexed question, but Mt seems to have altered whatever it was in the interests of probability. Gadara was a Greek town a few miles S.E. of the lake. *two demoniacs:* Mk mentions only one, and it is not clear why Mt duplicates; possibly because he has omitted the story of the exorcism in the synagogue (Mk 1²¹ᶠᶠ·), possibly to bring the total number healed in this section (if Matthew the tax collector is counted in) up to twelve.

The question of demoniac possession, and Jesus' own attitude towards it, is discussed in connection with 12²²⁻³².

29. *Son of God:* Mk here represents the demons as countering Jesus' formula of exorcism with magical counter-formulas of their own (these can be checked from contemporary magical papyri). Mt omits Jesus' own formula, and thus turns the saying of the demons into a Christological confession. *torment us before the time:* a clue to Mt's own eschatology. Mt distinguishes much more sharply than Mk between Christ's first coming and his second (cp. introduction to Chaps. 24–5). Jesus has overcome Satan in his own person (cp. 4¹⁻¹¹), but the devil will not be finally put down till the coming of the kingdom in the end-time (cp. 13³⁹, 25⁴¹). The present assault on the demons is therefore an anticipation of the end; cp. 12²⁸.

30. *many swine:* it is impossible now to trace the pre-history of this macabre tradition which Mk reproduces, and therefore questions about the morality of the action attributed to Jesus (which would in any case be a small price to pay for the restoration of a human being to sanity) are really beside the point. The part played by the swine in Mk's version (apart from the affinity of unclean beasts with unclean spirits) is to indicate the number of demons ejected from the possessed man (his name is given as 'Legion', and the number of the pigs as about 2000). Mt omits these details, but retains the episode as confirmation that the demons were actually destroyed (which exorcism by itself would not imply).

32. *perished:* better 'they perished'. The Gk makes clear that the subject of the verb is not the herd but the demons.

9: 1–8 (iii) Pardon and healing of the paralytic: cf. Mk 2¹⁻¹²
(Held, pp. 175ff.)

Mk's account contains two episodes, imperfectly integrated and probably originally separate: the command to the paralytic to pick up his bed and walk, and the dispute over the Son of man's authority to forgive sins. All Mt's emphasis falls on the second.

It appears that Jesus' undertaking to forgive sins was a major bone of contention between him and the Jewish religious authorities. The current teaching about forgiveness was that (a) it belonged to God alone, and (b) it would take place with the establishment of his kingdom in the end-time. Jesus' action is probably to be interpreted less as a direct claim to the divine prerogative than as a sign that the kingdom of God was dynamically present already in his mission (cp. 12^{28}). But to the strict Jew the claim was either blasphemy or the exercise of divine power. Mt's basic assumptions are sufficiently Jewish for him to accept this dilemma, while his Christology is sufficiently developed for him to have no hesitation in taking the second alternative. He therefore makes the episode the climax of his three signs of power.

2. *your sins are forgiven:* the passive implies that the forgiving is the act of God himself, the regular Jewish circumlocution.

6. *Son of man:* see Note B, p. 237. Mk probably, and Mt certainly, here uses the title as a designation of Jesus himself, though perhaps in an inclusive rather than an exclusive sense (see next note).

8. *who had given such authority to men:* Mt's addition, anticipating his special interest in the forgiveness of sins in and through the Church acting in Christ's name; cp. 16^{19}, 18^{18}.

9: 9–17 The call of Matthew and other sayings: cp. Mk 2$^{13-22}$

The material which follows is already attached to the healing of the paralytic in Mk. Mt retains it in this position, probably because the thought of the Son of man's authority to forgive sins leads on naturally to that of Jesus' mission to sinners, of whom the tax collectors, as collaborators with the occupying power and frequently given to extortion to fulfil–or exceed–their quota, are throughout the synoptic tradition the representative figures.

9. *Matthew:* the alteration from Mk's 'Levi' makes the recipient of this striking call one of the twelve representative disciples (cp. 10^3). Possibly Mt is insisting that the company of disciples included reclaimed 'sinners' from the beginning, as it was afterwards to include 'sinners of the Gentiles' (Gal. 2^{15}); cp. the emphasis of Chap. 18. On the possible connexion with the official authorship of the gospel see Introduction, pp. 33f.

10–13. A 'pronouncement-story' attached to the call of Matthew by the common theme of Jesus' concern for tax collectors.

10. *in the house:* in Mk this is Levi's house; Mt implies that it is Jesus' (cp. 13^{1,36}), and probably sees it as prefiguring the Church, in which there is room for sinners excluded by the old Israel.

11. Tax collectors were not, with minor exceptions, ceremonially unclean,

as is often asserted (see Jeremias, *NT Theology* i, p. 111), but their moral reputation was such that those who ate with them would be gravely compromised in the eyes of law-abiding Jews.

12. This, the punch-line of Mk's story, may well have been, like 8²⁰, a proverbial saying used by Jesus (or possibly, but less likely, put into his mouth). A similar saying is attributed to the Greek Cynic philosopher Diogenes (fourth century B.C.): 'neither does a physician who is capable of giving health practise among those who are well'. In Mk the saying is followed immediately by that in v. 13b, a secondary elucidation of it by the evangelist or by some hand in the tradition behind him. Mt. separates them by his insertion of the quotation from Hos. 6⁶ (repeated at 12⁷). *mercy and not sacrifice* (for the common Semitic antithesis cp. on 5⁴³, 6²⁴) means that 'God is gracious before he is demanding' (Barth, *TIM*, p. 83); to demand reform before extending forgiveness, as the Pharisees do, is to invert the true priorities.

14–15. Fasting, as the question implies, was a normal practice of the Pharisees, and a natural accompaniment of the Baptist's call to repentance. Jesus' divergence from both was a consequence of his teaching about the kingdom, which he saw as already operative in a proleptic sense in his own ministry (cp. 11¹⁶⁻⁹, 12²⁸).

The saying in its Marcan form, however, is likely to have derived from the post-resurrection Church, and to have been the result of a tension between Jesus' own remembered attitude and the continued or revived practice of fasting among his followers.

15. *wedding guests:* lit. 'sons of the bridechamber', a characteristic Semitic expression. *mourn:* altered by Mt from Mk's 'fast', though, as the context shows, without any real change of meaning. Possibly there is a reference back to the beatitude at 5⁴. *bridegroom:* see Hos. 2¹⁶⁻²⁰, Is. 54⁵ᶠ·, 62⁴ᶠ·, Ezek. 16⁸ᶠᶠ·, for passages which speak of God as the bridegroom of his people; Christian usage eventually applied the image to Christ (2 Cor. 11², Eph. 5²²ᶠᶠ·, and cp. Mt 25¹ᶠᶠ·). But it is not used of the Messiah in the OT or later Jewish literature (see Jeremias, *PJ*, p. 52), and therefore can hardly have been used by Jesus in this sense. Here it probably refers to a wedding as a time of joy; in v. 15b it is referred allegorically to Jesus himself—clearly the thought of the post-resurrection Church.

16–17. A pair of parables originally independent of the question of fasting. The point of both is the newness of the kingdom and the adequacy of the old institutions to contain or convey what it brings.

9: 18–34 *Three Double Healings*

9: 18–26 (i) The ruler's daughter and the woman with the haemorrhage: Mk 5²¹⁻⁴³ (Held, pp. 178ff. and 215ff.)

Mt, as usual, strips these narratives down to bare essentials, but retains Mk's curious device of relating one inside the other. This makes it probable that he means the two to be seen, for purposes of arrangement, as a single miracle. Note that the emphasis on faith occurs only once in the two (it cannot, obviously, be required of the dead). (Held however [pp. 247ff.] makes the three of this group the woman with the haemorrhage, the ruler's daughter, and the two blind men).

18. *ruler:* Mk says of the synagogue; Mt is less explicit. *has just died:* in Mk she is at the point of death when the request is made, and is reported dead before Jesus can reach her. Mt heightens the effect by making the original request one for the raising of the dead.

20. *haemorrhage:* presumably some chronic menstrual disorder. This would have made the woman unclean according to the Torah (see Lev. $15^{25ff.}$); hence her secretive behaviour. *fringe* (Gk *kraspedon*): a detail introduced here by Mt (but cp. Mk 6^{56}); for the meaning see on 23^5. Jesus is represented as dressing as a pious Jew.

22. *your faith has made you well:* words found in Mk, but in Mt by the elimination of superfluous detail they stand out as the climax of the story.

23. *flute players:* Mt only; a normal accompaniment of a Palestinian funeral, the equivalent of the professional mourners at English funerals of the nineteenth century.

24. *the girl is not dead but sleeping:* this is no contradiction of the statement (both in Mk and Mt) that the girl was dead, but the expression of a particular belief about the state of the departed; cp. Is. 57^2, Dan. 12^2. This belief continued to distinguish Christians from their Jewish and pagan neighbours; numerous early Christian burial inscriptions have been found with the words IN PACE or their equivalent.

9: 27–31 (ii) Two blind men: (Held, pp. 223ff.)

Mk records two healings of blind men, the healing in two stages at Bethsaida (Mk $8^{22ff.}$) and that of Bartimaeus at the gate of Jericho (Mk $10^{46ff.}$). In the latter context Mt has a conflated version involving two men (20^{29-34}); it is a variant of this that he introduces here, though one which he has carefully shaped to his purpose. The substance of the pericope is the little dialogue on the nature of faith, and its climax the saying '*According to your faith be it done to you*'.

27. *Son of David:* see on 1^1.

30. There is no obvious reason for the addition of an injunction to silence, other than the secrecy of Mk $8^{22ff.}$, which is conveyed in quite other terms.

9: 32–34 (iii) A man with a double complaint: the dumb demoniac

Since no dialogue is possible with the dumb, this episode lacks the formal characteristics of the other miracles of healing. Its function is rather to indicate how the mighty acts of the Christ were received by those who witnessed them. The uncommitted *crowds* (see on 13²) are impressed; the *Pharisees*, the official teachers of Israel, prefer to explain them away. This anticipates their challenge at 12²²ᶠᶠ·. *prince of demons:* the anticipation of 12²⁴ prepares the reader for 10²⁵.

5. THE MISSION OF THE CHRIST THROUGH HIS DISCIPLES (CHAPTERS 9:35–10:42)

Among the best attested data about Jesus in the material available to Mt were:

(a) He saw his own mission as restricted to Palestinian Jews; cp. 10⁶, Mk 7²⁷ (=Mt 15²⁶);

(b) He sent his disciples on a mission of their own in Galilee during the period of his ministry there; cp. 10⁹⁻¹⁴ and parallels (see notes).

Mt seems to have viewed these facts of the tradition in the light of two further facts of Christian experience nearer to his own time:

(c) A prolonged Christian campaign, probably in the period after A.D. 70 (see Introduction pp. 29, 31), to win Jews to the faith had met not only with rejection but with persecution of the missionaries. See Hare, *JPC*, pp. 146ff, for the view that Mt had come to see this mission as an error, foredoomed to failure in view of the earlier Jewish rejection of Christ and the judgement it brought upon the nation (cp. especially 23³⁴⁻⁹, 27²⁵).

(d) The mission of the Church was not thereby halted, but enlarged to include Gentiles, and there continued with it an awareness of Christ's presence and activity in it (cp. 28²⁰).

Mt could not imply that the mission to Israel was concluded, or that to the Gentiles begun, in Jesus' own lifetime. But he leaves his readers with the thoughts (a) that the former will be of limited duration (cp. 10²³), (b) that the mission of Jesus through his disciples will continue beyond it, as an integral aspect of discipleship. The mission discourse (10⁵⁻⁴²) falls into two halves concerned with these two themes.

9: 35–38 The setting

35. This reproduces 4²³ almost word for word; either because both introduce one of the 'five discourses' of Jesus, or else, possibly, because the two verses, as it were, frame between them the two sections dealing respectively with the teaching and the mighty acts of the Christ, and the disciples in the section following are commissioned to reproduce both (cp. 10⁷ᶠ·).

36. *harassed and helpless:* Mt's own words, lit. 'mangled and cast down'. They suggest the sheep abandoned to the attacks of wild beasts in Ezek. 34³ᶠᶠ·. *sheep without a shepherd* confirms this, though the wording (taken over from a different context at Mk 6³⁴) is closer to Nu. 27¹⁷. Cp. 10⁶.

38–39. The idea of the kingdom of God as a harvest certainly goes back to Jesus himself (e.g. the parable of the sower, see 13³ᶠᶠ·), but the thought of apostles or other Christian disciples helping to gather it in is likely to be post-resurrection; cp. Jn 4³⁵ᶠᶠ·. At 13³⁹ the reapers of the final harvest are angels.

10: 1–4 The missionaries

Mt's commissioning of the Twelve conflates two Marcan passages, the appointment of the Twelve at Mk 3¹³⁻⁹ and the sending of them on a mission at Mk 6⁷ᶠᶠ·.

2. *the twelve apostles:* Jesus undoubtedly gathered around himself an inner circle of disciples whose number twelve signified that they were to form the nucleus of the new Israel (cp. 19²⁸). Attempts to deny the twelve any historical existence during the ministry of Jesus founder, as Bornkamm has shown (*Jesus of Nazareth*, p. 150), on the awkward fact, recorded by all four evangelists, that the betrayer of Jesus was 'one of the twelve' (10⁴, Mk 3¹⁹, Lk 6¹⁶, Jn 6⁷¹).

'Apostle' possibly represents the Heb. *shaliach* ('sent'), a technical term for a delegate who, within certain carefully defined limits, represents in his own person the authority of his superior (e.g. Abraham's steward in Gen. 24) (see K. H. Rengstorf in *TDNT* i. 398ff.). In earliest Christian usage it seems to have had both the wider connotation of 'missionary' (cp. 1 Cor. 9⁵, Rom. 16⁷), and a more specialized use to denote one who had received a direct commission from the risen Christ; this narrower meaning included, but was not restricted to, the Twelve (cp. 1 Cor. 15⁵⁻⁷). Mk only calls the Twelve 'apostles' once, on their return from their mission (Mk 6³⁰), i.e. as missionaries. Mt does not reproduce this in its Marcan context, and himself uses the word only here, elsewhere preferring 'disciple'. But his expression *the twelve apostles* is a stage nearer to the identification of the two groups generally assumed by Lk in both his volumes.

Mk 6⁷ says that Jesus sent out the Twelve (already named) in pairs; Mt, who conflates the naming and the sending, names them in pairs. Mk 3^{16-9} is apparently the basis for all subsequent lists of the names; there is complete agreement on the first nine, but considerable discrepancy about the last three; an indication of the small part played by them in the later history of the Church.

3. *Bartholomew:* i.e. son of Tolmai; otherwise unknown. *Thomas:* 'the twin' (cp. Jn 11^{16}); presumably a nickname. *the tax collector:* added by Mt in view of 9^9. *Thaddaeus:* other MSS. have 'Lebbaeus', and a similar variation of readings is found in Mk. Lk substitutes 'Judas the son of James'.

4. *Simon the Cananaean:* no connexion with Canaan. The name is derived from the Heb. root *qn'* ('to be zealous'), as Lk 6^{15}, Acts 1^{13} make explicit; it may either be descriptive of Simon's personal character or, more probably, of organized activities with which he was associated. For the difficulties involved in identifying these with the policy of all-out resistance to the Romans (rather than, say, zeal for the observance of the law) see Introduction, p. 25. *Iscariot:* Mk retains a Semitic form for this (*Iskarioth*); the fact the Mt Grecizes it (*Iskariōtēs*) shows that he regarded it simply as a proper name (cp. Jn 6^{71}, 13^2) and had no interest in its origin or meaning. Its derivation remains obscure. It may simply mean 'man of Kerioth' (a village in Judaea). The proposal to derive it from *sicarius* (see Introduction, p. 26) is very unlikely for the lifetime of Jesus, though Judas nevertheless may well have been an extremist. Torrey derived it from *ish karya* ('the false'); if this is right, *who betrayed him* may be a translation rather than a comment.

10: 5-42 *The Mission Discourse*

This may be analyzed as follows:

A. The mission to Israel: 10^{5-23}

    (1) Destination and programme: vv. 5-8

    (2) Instructions for behaviour on mission: vv. 9-15

    (3) Warnings of persecution: vv. 16-23

B. The disciple represents his Lord: 10^{24-42} (heading vv. 24-5)

    (1) He speaks for Christ: vv. 26-33

    (2) He suffers with Christ: vv. 34-9

    (3) He is received as Christ: vv. 40-2

10: 5-23 A. The mission to Israel

5-8. (1) Destination and programme

5. *Go nowhere . . . Samaritans:* it is conceivable that Jesus limited the mission of his disciples with a prohibition of this sort, but it is much

more likely that the saying derives from the exclusive standpoint of early Jewish Christianity. In that case Mt has neutralized its original force by the context in which he has placed it. See further on v. 23. Acts 8¹⁴ᶠᶠ· represents the mission to Samaritans as developing only after the persecution of Christians in Judaea. *go rather to the lost sheep of the house of Israel*: this saying accurately represents Jesus' view of his own mission, but the wording is probably Mt's own, like that of 9³⁶ which it takes up. He also introduces it into his version of the episode of the Canaanite woman (15²⁴). For its OT antecedents, cp. Jer. 50⁶, Ezek. 34⁴, Is. 53⁴, Ps. 119¹⁷⁶.

7. cp. 3², 4¹⁷. The mission of the disciples, and its message, is essentially one with that of the Lord himself, anticipated by the Baptist.

8.. A summary of the miracles of Chaps. 8–9 (done to Israel, cp. v. 5). What disciples have themselves received they must pass on to others. *raise the dead*: missing in some MSS., but necessary to the balanced rhythm of the passage. *give without pay*: this leads on to the next section.

9–15 (2) Instructions for behaviour on mission

This 'mission charge' is found in the synoptic gospels in no fewer than four versions. This makes the mission of the disciples during Jesus' ministry 'one of the best attested facts of the gospel' (Manson), and suggests that the instructions given for it were carefully preserved and acted upon in the situation of the post-resurrection Church, at any rate in Palestinian conditions (see on 6²⁵ᶠᶠ·). The two basic versions are Mk 6⁸⁻¹¹ (in indirect speech) (followed by Lk 9²⁻⁵) and Lk 10⁴⁻¹². Mt has conflated what he found in Mk with a tradition similar to that represented by Lk.

(a) vv. 9–10 The missionary must travel light and live by the gospel

9. *take no gold*: lit. 'do not procure', i.e. as provision. *copper in your belts*: the usual place for carrying small change.

10. *bag*: i.e. a begging bag. *two tunics*: as change of clothing. *no sandals*: so Lk 10⁴; Mk 6⁹ expressly directs that they be worn. W. L. Knox argues the impracticability of performing the gesture of v. 14 with bare feet (*Sources of the Synoptic Gospels*, ii. (Cambridge, 1957), 49). *the laborer deserves his food*: probably the commandment of the Lord referred to by Paul (1 Cor. 9¹⁴), which he has to excuse himself for not taking advantage of.

(b) vv. 11–15 The gospel is for those who will hear it

12. *salute*: Lk 10⁵ has 'say, "Peace be to this house!"'', and what follows in v. 13 suggests that this is the original wording.

13. *if the house is worthy*: cp. Lk 10⁶ 'if a son of peace is there', a Semitic expression likely to be original. The evangelist's 'peace' was regarded as having concrete existence, like a curse; it would settle on a house which was receptive of it, otherwise it would return to him and be available for future use.

14. *shake off the dust . . . :* implying that it is to be treated in future as if it was Gentile territory; evidence of use of the saying in a Jewish–Christian context.

15. This seems to be a quotation from the stanzas at 11[20-4].

16–23 (3) Warnings of persecution

vv. 17–22 are taken over from Mk 13[9-13], where they form part of the apocalyptic discourse (see notes on Chap. 24). For Mk, persecution is a sign of the approaching end, part of the 'Messianic woes' which precede it; for Mt it is an inevitable accompaniment of missionary work, and specifically of the mission to Jews (hence all references at this point to Gentiles as objects of mission are eliminated). See Hare, *JPC*, pp. 99ff.

16. *wise . . . doves:* probably a proverbial expression, paralleled in rabbinic writings.

17. *councils:* The Gk *sunedria* has suggested to some commentators the 'lesser sanhedrins' of Palestinian Judaism, which tried capital cases. But a word which is found already in Mk with little to suggest that the courts are necessarily Jewish is unlikely to have a technical significance in Mt; nor is there evidence that Jewish authorities treated Christian profession as a capital offence. See Hare, *JPC*, pp. 102f., cp. pp. 25ff. *flog you in their synagogues:* the Gk word (altered from Mk) denotes judicial flogging. Hare argues that it was imposed not for deviation from the Torah but for causing a breach of the peace, i.e. by missionary activity (see *JPC*, pp. 104ff., cp. pp. 45f.).

18. *to bear testimony before them:* that this is primarily 'speaking to convince' (the unconverted) rather than 'speaking to convict' (one's opponents) is clear from the reference to Gentiles and from 24[14]. Cp. Hare, *JPC*, pp. 100n, 106f. *and the Gentiles:* added by Mt as a substitute for the more explicit reference to the Gentile mission in Mk 13[10], which would be inappropriate in this context.

20. *the Spirit:* mention of this (also in Mk) clearly reflects the later experience of the Church. References to the Spirit in the synoptic sayings of Jesus are very few; see C. K. Barrett, *The Holy Spirit and the Gospel Tradition* (London, 1947).

21–22. This saying reads like a paraphrase of that in vv. 35f.

23. It is best to begin the interpretation of this difficult verse with an account of what it means to Mt in its present context. It is here addressed to missionaries, and directs them not to stay in a town to be persecuted, even if this means leaving it unevangelized; for the *parousia* (see note on 24[3]) will not wait for the conversion of all Jewry (whereas it will for the preaching of the gospel to all nations, cp. 24[14]). There is here at least a hint that the mission to Jews may be broken off if it meets with rejection.

Something needs to be said, however, about the antecedents of the verse. Much depends on whether it is taken as a unity or as the conflation of two originally independent sayings. Supporters of the unity of the verse have included (i) A. Schweitzer (*The Quest of the Historical Jesus* (ET London, 1910), pp. 357ff.), who argued from it that Jesus did not expect his disciples to return from their mission; that they did so was the first disappointment of his hope of an early appearance of the Son of man. Schweitzer attributed the whole mission charge as it stands in this chapter to Jesus himself, and his theory is too bound up with this critically naive position to carry much weight now; (ii) J. A. T. Robinson (*Jesus and his Coming* (London, 1957), p. 76), who connects the saying with the decision of the Christian community in Jerusalem during the siege of A.D. 67–70 to take refuge in the Greek city of Pella (see Introduction, p. 28); he takes it as a warning not to leave the holy city, or, if compelled, to settle in the nearest Jewish one. This interpretation puts a lot of weight on the expression *one town* (lit. 'this city'); and some scholars have rejected the flight to Pella as unhistorical.

The interpretation is less complicated if 23b is divided from 23a. 23a on this view presents little difficulty; it could have originated either as an authentic prediction of flight in the end-time (cp. Mk 13$^{14ff.}$), or in the later experiences of Christian missionaries hounded from one Jewish community to another (cp. Hare, *JPC*, pp. 110f.). Some scholars (e.g. W. G. Kümmel, *Promise and Fulfilment* (ET London, 1951), p. 63) regard 23b as an authentic saying of Jesus, showing that he expected the *parousia* in the lifetime of his disciples. But it reads more like an argument of conservative Jewish Christianity against any mission to non-Jews on the grounds of the imminence of the *parousia*. On this view its affinity with 10^{5b} (already pointed out by Streeter, *The Primitive Church* (London, 1929), p. 35) is striking. Put end to end, they read: 'Go nowhere among the Gentiles, and enter no town of the Samaritans; for . . . you will not have gone through the towns of Israel before the Son of man comes'. If this is sound, Mt has neutralized the original force of the saying, which he could hardly have assimilated, by using the two halves to enclose a missionary programme with a limited historical scope. Compare his method at 5$^{17ff.}$.

10: 24–42 B. The disciple represents his Lord

24–25. The first saying here serves as the heading of the whole section. For variants of it, cp. Lk 6^{40}, Jn 13^{16}, 15^{20}.

25. *Beelzebub:* cp. 9^{34} (where the devil is not named), 12$^{24ff.}$. *those of his household:* a play on the meaning of the name ('Lord of the house'); see on 12^{24}.

26–33 (1) He speaks for Christ
     A single extended logion of which an independent version is found
at Lk 12²⁻⁹ (in part also at Mk 4²², 8³⁸). The content of Lk's version
seems generally closer to the original, though Mt may be right in
connecting it with the mission of the disciples.

27. Mt contrasts the privacy of Jesus' teachings with the openness of
     their proclamation to the world; Lk (and probably his exemplar)
     emphasizes rather that the final judgement will reveal any timidity
     or half-heartedness in speaking up for Jesus however secret it has been.
     The whole passage is really about this, the need to fear God rather
     than men. Mt's version reflects, though it also combats, the esoteric
     character of much rabbinic teaching.

28. The body-soul distinction has been imported into this context by Mt
     or his source (contrast Lk 12⁵), surprisingly in view of his basically
     Jewish background; but Greek-speaking Jews (and Jewish–Christians)
     could not help being influenced by the assumptions of the Hellenistic
     world.

29. *penny:* a different coin from that at 5²⁶. The *as* (Mt uses the Gk
     diminutive form *assarion*) was 1/16 of a *denarius* (see on 20²). An edict
     of the emperor Diocletian in the late third century A.D. fixed the
     price of sparrows at 7 *assa* for 10—little more than this.

32–33. Mt's version of these verses assumes that the subject of them is
     Jesus himself, in line with his role as judge at 13⁴¹ᶠ·, 25³¹ᶠᶠ·. In Mk 8³⁸
     and Lk 12⁸ Jesus refers obliquely to 'the Son of man', from which
     many scholars infer that he spoke of this figure as distinct from
     himself (see Note B, p. 239). Lk 12⁹ however has the passive 'shall
     be denied', and Perrin (*Rediscovering the Teaching of Jesus*, p. 189)
     suggests that this reverential circumlocution for the action of God was
     the original form in Lk 12⁸ also.

34–39 (2) He suffers with Christ
     There are three distinct sayings here:
     (a) 34–36. Cp. Lk 12⁵¹⁻³. Mal. 4⁶ represents the work of Elijah,
the forerunner of the Messiah (see 11¹⁴, 17¹⁰ᶠᶠ·) as one of reconciliation.
Jesus seems to have disclaimed this with a reference to Mic. 7⁶, which
is embedded in the saying in a form not close to any known text. For
Mt the saying conveys that the gospel is unavoidably divisive of
families; the disciples must not shrink from the unpopularity that this
brings, any more than Jesus did, and for them, as for him (cp. 12⁴⁹ᶠ·)
it begins at home. This leads on to the following saying.
     (b) 37–38. The thought of putting Christ before father or mother
leads naturally enough into that of putting him before self, but it is
likely that the saying about taking up the cross was originally
independent. See note on 16²⁴ (another version) for the meaning of
the metaphor. The version of Lk 14²⁶ which speaks of 'hating' father

and mother etc. preserves the authentic Semitic idiom, which Mt or his source has paraphrased at this point (though not at 6^{24}) for the benefit of Greek-speaking readers.

(c) 39. The words about losing one's life to find it are the most quoted of all Jesus' sayings—six times altogether in the gospels—doubtless because it summed up, in words from his own lips, that aspect of him with which his later followers were particularly drawn to identify themselves.

40–42 (3) He is received as Christ

The sayings reproduced here are used by Mt as a kind of obverse of those at vv. 24f. There the disciple is to expect the same treatment as his Lord received; here service to him is reckoned as service to his Lord.

40. Another much quoted saying (cp. 18^5, Mk 9^{37}, Lk 10^{16}, Jn 13^{20}). Behind it lies the institution of *shaliach* (see on 10^2); according to the rabbis 'a man's agent (*shaliach*) is like himself' (Mishnah *Berakoth* v. 5; Danby, p. 6). The disciples are to represent Jesus as he himself represents the Father (cp. Jn 17^{18}, 20^{21}).

41–42. V. 42 is an altered version of Mk 9^{41}, but Mt has prefixed to it two other lines not found elsewhere in the tradition. 13^{17} confirms that *prophet* and *righteous man* denote OT figures; 1 Ki. $17^{8ff.}$ and 2 Ki. $4^{8ff.}$ are examples of what is meant by receiving *a prophet because he is a prophet*, and suggest that *a prophet's reward* means not a share in the reward the prophet receives but a reward from the prophet (cp. 2 Ki. 4^{13}). This fits the meaning of v. 42. Christ himself will reward those who do him service, in the persons of those whom he has sent (v. 40). The implications of this are spelled out at $25^{31ff.}$.

PART II: THE CHRIST REJECTED AND VINDICATED

I. REJECTION AND ITS PLACE IN THE DIVINE PURPOSE (CHAPTERS 11:1–13:52)

For the reasons for placing the major break in the gospel at this point, see Introduction, pp. 16f. The foregoing chapters have viewed the person and mission of the Christ from a number of angles with little action; from here onwards the narrative moves towards a rejection of him that will finally be total. Central to this first phase of it is the explicit repudiation of Jesus' dynamic healing activity by the official leaders of Israel (see 12²²ᶠᶠ·); Chap. 11 and the parables discourse of Chap. 13, each in its different style, find a place and a meaning for this setback in the ongoing purpose of God.

11: 1–30 *Jesus' Witness to Himself*

This chapter links the two parts of the gospel; it both recapitulates what has gone before and serves as a heading for what is to follow, not only in the present section but throughout the second half. Its contents reproduce in miniature the argument of the whole work:

(1) Jesus is 'he who is to come', the fulfilment of Israel's hope; a fulfilment which the greatest of the prophets recognizes and in which he has therefore his rightful though lowly place (vv. 2–15);

(2) 'this generation', contemporary Israel, has rejected the fulfilment offered, and has consequently forfeited its inheritance; the judgement on it will be severer than on Sodom (vv. 16–24);

(3) God's purpose for his people is not thereby frustrated; the little band of disciples has received the revelation which 'this generation' rejected, and the invitation to join it is open to all (vv. 25–30).

The contents of the chapter thus form a coherent whole. Almost all of it is reproduced in two separate contexts in Lk, and is therefore usually assigned to the source Q (see Introduction, p. 5). Readers not committed to that hypothesis are invited to recognize in the way in which individual sayings are built up into a unity, here as in the 'five discourses', the characteristic literary gift of Mt himself.

1. The regular formula for a new beginning after a discourse; cp. on 7²⁸.

11: 2–15 (1) The fulfilment of Israel's hope: cp. Lk 7¹⁸⁻²⁸

2–6 (a) The answer to the Baptist's question

2. *in prison*: cp. 3¹²; but there is no biographical interest. The Baptist's question is asked not so much on his own account as in the name of the old Israel. *the deeds of the Christ*: those related in Chaps. 8–9.

3. *he who is to come:* this, on the lips of John, recalls 'he who is coming after me' in 3[11], but there are also scattered indications (for which see F. Hahn, *The Titles of Jesus in Christology* [ET London, 1969], pp. 359ff.) that the words could be a designation for the 'eschatological prophet', the counterpart to Moses promised at Dt. 18[15ff.], whose role is very close to Messiahship as Mt understands it. Cp. the acclamation at 21[9], followed by the recognition of Jesus as prophet at 21[11].

4–6. The healing miracles here summarized (see 8[1–4], 9[1–8,18–34]) are seen as the fulfilment of prophecy, especially Is. 61[1], 35[5f.]. N.B. Is. 61[1] 'the Spirit of the Lord God is upon me, because the Lord has *anointed* me . . .'; i.e. the speaker is both prophet and Messiah ('anointed').

4. *the blind . . . sight:* the LXX of Is. 61[1] has 'restoration of sight to the blind' where Heb. has 'opening of the prison' (so RSV), probably an indication that this reply was not first composed in Aramaic.

5. *the poor . . . preached to them:* omitted by a few authorities, but the rhythm of the verse demands its retention. Chap. 10 records a preaching mission to 'the lost sheep of the house of Israel', i.e. the poor, in the OT sense; see on 5[3].

6. *takes no offence at me:* NEB 'does not find me a stumbling-block', i.e. an obstacle to faith. For the meaning and background of the image, see on 13[41], 15[12], 16[23], 18[6].

7–15 (b) The greatness and littleness of John the Baptist

The acknowledgement of Jesus' Messiahship calls for a definition of the true position of his great predecessor. In relation to the old dispensation John is the prophet *par excellence*, the culmination of 'law and prophets'; in relation to the new he is simply the forerunner, the role assigned to Elijah at Mal. 4[5]. Mt builds up this contrast from a series of sayings originally transmitted independently of each other.

7–9. A difficult but probably authentic saying has here received explanatory additions (e.g. v. 8b) and had its punctuation disturbed in the process. The original may have run something like this:

> What did you go into the wilderness to see?
> A reed shaken by the wind?
> But what did you go out to see?
> One clothed in soft raiment?
> But what did you go out to see?
> A prophet, and more than a prophet.

Cp. Mk 11[27ff.] (par. Mt 21[23ff.]) for a challenge by Jesus to his opponents on the subject of John the Baptist. *A reed shaken by the wind:* i.e. something that bends to every wind that blows; contrast the rabbinic saying quoted by Manson (*SJ*, p. 68): 'man should strive to be tender like the wind and not hard like the cedar', the opposite of what is expected of a prophet.

10. To Mt John is more than a prophet because he is also the fore-runner. Except for his last two words, Mt reproduces word for word the citation at Mk 1² (where it is wrongly ascribed to Isaiah). As it is not a straightforward quotation but a composite one which expands Mal. 3¹ with wording from Ex. 23²⁰, and we know that he was familiar with Mk, the presumption is (if it be allowed that Lk 7²⁷ could have derived it from Mt; see Introduction, p. 6) that he took it from Mk.

11. This saying reflects Christian controversy over the relative positions of John and Jesus. It has been suggested that the original sense of v. 11b was 'he who is less' (or 'younger'), i.e. the disciple (Jesus; see on 3¹¹) 'is greater than he in the kingdom'. This however is hardly an acceptable construction for the present word-order in Mt, for whom in any case 'least in the kingdom of heaven' has come to denote the Christian who is not fully approved of (cp. 5¹⁹, 18¹⁻⁴). The words need not imply John's personal exclusion from the kingdom.

12. The interpretation of this very difficult verse turns on the question whether the Gk verb *biazetai* is (i) passive ('has suffered violence'; so RSV text) or (ii) middle (with active sense: 'has been coming violently'; so RSVmg). If (i), it must mean violence offered to the kingdom, either in the sense of fierce opposition or obstruction, such as the mission of Jesus encountered from the Jewish authorities (and that of the Church of Mt's day from resurgent Judaism), or, less probably, in that of pursuit by violent means. If (ii), the kingdom is itself the source of the violence and evokes a correspondingly violent response from those to whom it comes. This is clearly the meaning of the paraphrase at Lk 16¹⁶. But the rare Gk word *biastēs* used by Mt is apparently always taken in a bad sense, and his *men of violence* can therefore be neither the preachers of the kingdom nor those who hear the message. (i) is the only interpretation of *biazetai* compatible with this fact. For Mt the response appropriate to the kingdom is in any case meekness rather than violence (cp. 5⁵, 11²⁹, 21⁵, etc.); and at 14¹ᶠᶠ· he relates the end of the Baptist in a context which suggests that he and Jesus are at one in the fate they suffer at the hands of official Israel.

It may be, however, that *men of violence take it by force* originated in the tradition as a gloss on the obscure *biazetai* (see Black, *AA*, p. 211n), and in that case, sense (ii), or something like it, is a possibility for the original Aramaic form of the saying (for further discussion of it see Kümmel, *Promise and Fulfilment*, pp. 121ff., and Perrin, *Rediscovering the Teaching of Jesus*, pp. 74–7).

13–14. These verses set the saying of v. 12 in a longer time-perspective than was possible in or near the Baptist's lifetime; their present form is probably due to Mt himself (v. 14 seems to be a summary of 17¹⁰⁻²). John, as the last of the prophets, is the end-term of the OT dispensation, and, at the same time, as Elijah *redivivus*, he is the precursor of the new age, the opening of which is marked by the trials suffered by God's elect. *all the prophets and the law prophesied: the law* is here inserted by Mt into a saying about prophecy, as at 5^{17} the prophets were introduced into a passage about law. Both contexts for Mt are concerned with the OT revelation as a whole; in 5^{17} the prophets have the same continuing validity in this age as the law, here the law is transcended by the coming of the kingdom in the same way as the prophets. But Mt may also wish to make clear (possibly against the original force of the saying) that it is the OT prophets, rather than prophecy as such, that are transcended; prophecy continued as a Christian activity, and Mt holds it in high esteem (see on 5^{12}, $23^{29,34}$).

15. A formula intended to draw attention to hidden meaning in the preceding words (cp. $13^{9,43}$), in this case the reference is to Mal. 4^5.

11: 16–24 (2) Rejection by this generation

16–19 (a) The perverse children: cp. Lk 7^{31-5}

See Perrin, *Rediscovering the Teaching of Jesus*, pp. 119–21, for a vindication of the unity and authenticity of the whole passage, on the following grounds: (i) the words translate back easily into Aramaic; (ii) they take a high view of the status of John the Baptist, which controversy in the later Church tended to depreciate; (iii) the practice of table-fellowship with the disreputable, and the charge of gluttony which it evoked from detractors, belong unmistakably to the ministry of Jesus himself.

The meaning of the parable is elucidated from first-hand know-ledge of Palestinian conditions by E. F. F. Bishop, *Jesus of Palestine* (1955), p. 104; cp. Jeremias, *PJ*, pp. 160ff.; summary in Perrin, p. 85. The scene is a children's game of 'weddings and funerals'.

17. *we piped . . . you did not dance:* dancing at weddings was the men's job, so these are the boys. *we wailed . . . you did not mourn:* breast-beating at funerals was the women's business, so these are the girls. Part of the group is not prepared to join in actively (N.B. *sitting*), but only to demand activity from the others (hence piping and wailing); they then blame the others for not responding to their invitations and so spoiling the game they had never really meant to join in.

18–19. Similarly (in the interpretation) the Jewish people have never really meant to take the kingdom seriously; they will neither repent with John because it is near, nor rejoice with Jesus because it is here, but, for perversely contrary reasons, find fault with both.

Because the parable brackets John and Jesus as equally rejected by their own people, Mt uses it to illustrate his own view of sacred history. The Jews have rejected not only their Messiah, but along with him the authentic representative of the old Israel. Hence their own rejection by God (vv. 20–4, and cp. 13⁵³–14¹², and Chaps. 21–3, *passim*).

19. *a glutton . . . a friend of . . . sinners*: Perrin (pp. 105f.) argues convincingly that both complaints concern a single feature of Jesus' ministry which his orthodox contemporaries found offensive, the table-fellowship to which tax-collectors and other excluded persons were invited (see 9¹⁰ᶠᶠ·). *wisdom is justified by her deeds*: a final comment (Mt's?) on the parable in its context. The *deeds* are 'the deeds of the Christ' (v. 2) and the *wisdom* that of God which was at work in them (and which will confound that of the professionally 'wise'; see on vv. 25f., and cp. 1 Cor. 1¹⁸ᶠᶠ·. But there is no explicit identification of Jesus with the personified Wisdom of the OT Wisdom literature here any more than in St Paul. The meaning is that the compelling evidence of what Jesus has done is not impaired by the perversity of its reception.

The variant reading 'children' for *deeds* has crept into some MSS. of Mt through assimilation to Lk 7³⁵. It looks secondary even in Lk, a not very felicitous attempt to tie up the conclusion of the parable with the children with whom it begins.

20–24 (b) The unrepentant towns: cp. Lk 10¹³⁻⁵

The transition is a little abrupt since, apart from a note at 9³⁴, no general reaction to Jesus' miracles has so far been recorded. This suggests that in placing the sayings here Mt is really looking forward rather than back. The call to repentance, explicit in John's preaching (3²), is also implicit in Jesus' miracles. The towns of Galilee, by their lack of repentance, forfeit God's mercy, and can now only expect his judgement; they foreshadow the rejection of Jesus by contemporary Judaism which is the theme of the later chapters.

The logia used by Mt in this context have a close formal correspondence with that at 12⁴¹ᶠ·. There is no good reason for not regarding either as authentic (Bultmann [*HST*, p. 113] himself admits this for 12⁴¹ᶠ·). Few would question that Jesus and his disciples conducted a preaching mission in Galilee, and it may well have been its final rejection which turned his thoughts towards Jerusalem. This implies a point at which he recognized that it had failed (see on 13¹⁸ᶠᶠ·), and with which these denunciations can be credibly connected.

21. *Chorazin*: known only from this passage and a single reference in the Talmud, but conjecturally identified with Khirbet Kerazeh, some two miles north of Capernaum. There are no good grounds for seeing here an anagram of 'Nazareth'. *Bethsaida*: cp. Mk 6⁴⁵, 8²² and Jn 1⁴⁴ (where it is said, quite credibly, to have been the home of Peter, Andrew and Philip). *Tyre and Sidon*: cities denounced by the prophets for their worldliness and paganism; cp. Is. 23, Ezek. 23, 28, Am. 1⁹. If Mt was in fact composed in that region (see Introduction, p. 32), the

evangelist may have seen in this saying a hint of the later Christian mission to Gentiles consequent on the rejection of the gospel by Jews.

23. *Capernaum:* the centre of Jesus' Galilean ministry and possibly his home during it. This fact will not save it from the general judgement on the unrepentant towns of Galilee. For other contexts in which the plea of close relationship with Jesus is rejected cp. 12⁴⁶ᶠᶠ·, Lk 13²⁶ᶠ·. *Sodom:* a byword for human wickedness (see Gen. 18–19), applied to Israel itself at Is. 1⁹ᶠ·.

11: 25–30 (3) The revelation of the Father: cp. Lk 10²¹⁻³

This great passage, called by Lagrange 'Matthew's pearl of great price', is the climax not only of its chapter but the whole presentation of the figure of the Christ which occupies the first part of the gospel; so far from being, as it has also been called, 'a thunderbolt fallen from the Johannine sky', it is integral to Mt and to its context. Its high Christology has encouraged, on the one hand, strenuous efforts to vindicate it *in toto* as an authentic saying of the Lord (for a recent example see A. M. Hunter, in *NTS* viii (1963), 241ff.), and, on the other, the theories of Scandinavian scholars in particular (notably E. Norden, *Agnostos Theos* [Leipzig, 1913] and T. Arvedson, *Das Mysterium Christi* [Uppsala, 1937]) which would derive it ultimately from the ritual and speculative elements of diffused oriental religion. Neither approach does justice to the wealth of biblical allusion in the text as a whole (impossible if its core was pre-scriptural, and un-paralleled in the authentic sayings of Jesus), and in particular to the close formal correspondence (recognized by Norden, though he drew the wrong conclusion from it) with the concluding chapter of Sirach, which, like this much shorter passage, is constructed as a sequence of thanksgiving—soliloquy—invitation. It is probably not accidental, given Mt's known methods of handling scripture, that he here takes as his model a passage spoken by an earlier bearer of the name Jesus (ben-Sirach; see on vv. 28–30).

It remains to consider the materials from which the text in its three sections has been built up.

25–26 (a) The thanksgiving

The form of these verses is known as a *berākāh*, or blessing addressed to God and naming the mercies for which he is to be thanked. This was a commonplace of contemporary Jewish liturgical practice (see, e.g., L. Bouyer, *Eucharist* [ET Notre Dame, 1968]), and there is nothing inherently improbable, as Bultmann admits (cp. *HST*, p. 160) in the use of such a form by Jesus himself, However, the Gk word used for *thank* (lit. 'acknowledge') occurs four times in the corresponding section of Sirach (51¹⁻¹²), and there are further indications of an OT background. The matter for which the Father is thanked, the hiding of the mystery from the wise and its revelation to the simple, is also the subject of 1 Cor. 1¹⁸ᶠᶠ⁻. From this it has been argued that Paul was familiar with this text as a saying of Jesus. But the basis of Paul's argument, which he actually quotes, is in fact Is. 29¹⁴; if he and Mt have a common starting-point it is the hostility of this text to the 'wise and understanding'. Since at 15⁸ Mt (here following Mk) quotes Is. 29¹³ *in extenso* in a passage in which he is attacking the 'tradition of the elders', it can be inferred that the whole context had associations of that kind for him. *these things:* probably a reference back to the 'deeds of the Christ' (vv. 2, 19), understood as the fulfilment of Messianic prophecy; the revelation is thus not of timeless truth but of divine purpose brought to fruition (cp. Davies, *COJ*, p. 142). *wise and understanding:* in addition to Is. 29¹⁴, cp. Dan. 2²⁰⁻³,²⁸. For the contemporary associations of 'wise', see Introduction, p. 24. *and revealed them to babes:* a reminiscence of Sir. 3¹⁹ 'to the meek he reveals his secrets' (relegated to mg by RSV, but found in the Heb. original). *babes* may be a deliberate alteration by Mt to distinguish the persons referred to from Jesus, who calls himself 'meek' (Gk *praüs*) at 11²⁹. The reference is to Christian disciples (called 'little ones' at 18⁶,¹⁰⁻⁴); they are contrasted not, as at 1 Cor. 3¹, with the mature, but with the *wise and understanding*, i.e. the scribes. Though inferior in equipment, they have yet received, gratuitously (v. 26), a revelation far beyond the wisdom which the latter have attained through much study. *thy gracious will* (mg 'well-pleasing before thee'): cp. 3¹⁷ where (as already noted) the good pleasure of the Father in the Son is something revealed by the heavenly voice to the witnesses.

27 (b) The soliloquy

There is a change of key in this verse. In v. 25 it is the Father who reveals hidden mysteries to babes; here it is the Son who reveals the Father to whom he will. Apart from the awkwardness of the transition, the new section, unlike the other, contains no reminiscence of the OT. Here, if anywhere in the text, we should look for sources; but there are two obstacles to attributing the words to Jesus himself: (i) 'The Son' used absolutely as a title is not really possible in Aramaic; (ii) the passage at first sight expresses the mutual personal knowledge of Father and Son in terms that are familiar from the language of 'Gnosis' (in the sense of that general preoccupation with esoteric 'knowledge' which pervaded the more sophisticated layers of Hellenistic religious thinking; see R. McL. Wilson, *Gnosis and the NT* [Oxford, 1968]).

Jeremias (*PrJ*, pp. 45ff.), following Dalman, argues that the two inner lines should be construed not as a directly theological statement but as an analogy:

'Just as only a father really knows his son,
So only a son really knows his father.'

This bold attempt to turn the force of the objections to authenticity meets with certain difficulties of its own:

(i) there is no real parallel in the recognized authentic sayings of Jesus in the synoptic tradition; Jn 5[19f.] (interpreted by C. H. Dodd on similar lines) and 10[15] are hardly substitutes for this;

(ii) the meaning suggested is inappropriate to the first and last lines of the verse; it is not obvious that fathers in general can only be known to others by what their sons reveal of them;

(iii) it is clear that Mt himself takes the words in their full theological sense, as does Lk.

Must we therefore conclude with Bultmann (*HST*, p. 159) that the passage is a 'Hellenistic revelation saying'? Clearly it was originally formulated in Greek, but certain scholars deeply versed in Hellenistic religious literature (e.g. W. L. Knox, *Some Hellenistic Elements in Primitive Christianity* [London, 1942], p. 8; R. M. Grant, *Gnosticism and Early Christianity* [New York, 1959], pp. 151ff.) have resisted the suggestion that this is the category to which it belongs; and Kilpatrick (*Origins*, pp. 105f.) warns against 'identifying the linguistic frontier between the Greek and Semitic worlds with the cultural frontier between Hellenism and Judaism'. And clearly it is in some sense a 'revelation saying'; the question is whether it is such in the esoteric sense characteristic of gnostic speculation. Davies (*COJ*, pp. 119ff.), in a close examination of the concept of knowledge in the DSS, finds there knowledge as associated with the law, secret knowledge, personal or intimate knowledge, and knowledge of the eschatological future—all of them relevant to this verse or its context —but no trace of the 'mystical' knowledge of a wholly transcendent God and the accompanying self-knowledge which are the hall-marks of Hellenistic Gnosis. He goes on to claim that Mt 11[25–30] 'was formulated in circles which in many ways were similar to those reflected in the DSS' (ib. p. 141), and that both sources speak of a revelation which is primarily eschatological. If this argument is accepted, it is possible to suggest, from the source which Mt is known to have had before him, a passage which could have served as the starting-point for v. 27. Mk 13[32] speaks of 'the Son' absolutely, in relation to the Father, in a context concerned with revelation; in this case, of the time of the end (for Mt's direct use of it see on 24[28]). Mt has extended its scope to cover the whole divine purpose, and he has thought more deeply about the relation of Son and Father; but all the elements in his version are present in germ in Mk. *no one knows the Son except the Father:* a number of scholars, including Bultmann (*HST*, p. 159) and Manson (*SJ*, p. 80), have argued that this line does not belong to the original form of the verse. The suggestion is attractive, because the whole thrust of the passage is towards the revelation of the Father by the Son, and this line seems to arrest it;

and if Mt has incorporated an already existing saying it could well be true of the form in which it reached him. But (i) there is an equivalent to this line in Lk (ii) no MS. totally omits it, (iii) the four lines in v. 27 correspond to the four in vv. 25–6, (iv) v. 26 refers to the good pleasure of the Father in the Son; and therefore it is overwhelmingly probable that the text of Mt has always stood in its present form.

28–30 (c) The invitation

In these verses, which form a self-contained strophe with a recognizable rhythm, Mt returns to his model in Sirach. Their absence from Lk is no obstacle to regarding them as part of the original composition, even on the Q hypothesis; Lk omitted them because they were inappropriate to the context in which he had placed his version of Mt 11²⁵⁻⁷ (see J. M. Creed, *Luke* (London, 1930), ad loc.). The correspondence with Sir. 51²³⁻⁷ is very striking both in form and language; other scriptures have contributed (see below), but there is no need to postulate any more immediate source. As Jesus ben-Sirach invites his readers to be instructed by him in the divine wisdom which he has received, so Jesus the Christ invites his audience to learn from him the meaning of the mysteries he has received from the Father.

The three parts of 11²⁵⁻³⁰ are thus bound together by the theme of 'revelation', and this serves also to fix the whole passage in its context (see introduction to the chapter).

28. *labor and are heavy-laden:* cp. 23⁴ for the heavy burdens laid on their people by the representatives of the scribal tradition. *I will give you rest:* cp. Jer. 31²⁵ (Heb.).

29. *take my yoke upon you:* i.e. become my disciple (cp. Sir. 51²³). In the OT 'yoke' means the service of God in general (cp. Lam. 3²⁷, Jer. 5⁵), and the rabbis identified the 'yoke of the kingdom of heaven' with the Torah. For Mt Jesus has fulfilled the Torah by his new interpretation of it (5¹⁷), and it is to this that aspirants to the kingdom must now submit. They will find it a light weight by comparison (v. 30). *learn from me:* i.e. from his example as well as his teaching; explained by the following words. *gentle and lowly in heart:* for the combination of adjectives cp. Sir. 3¹⁷. *gentle* represents the same Gk word as 'meek' in 5³. Jesus exhibits in his person what he enjoins on others. *you will find rest for your souls:* parallel to Sir. 51²⁷, but the wording is closer (especially in Heb.) to Jer. 6¹⁶, which continues 'but they said "We will not walk in it"'. It thus points forward to the rejection of the message in the rest of the gospel, beginning with the next section.

12: 1–50 *Jewish Opposition and its Consequences*

Mt now returns to the sequence of Mk's narrative, at a point where its emphasis is on the mounting hostility to Jesus' message, an emphasis which he intensifies by the omission of material (chiefly miracles and the appointment of the Twelve) already used by him in Chaps. 8–10. The theme comes to a climax in the Beelzebul slander of 12^{22ff}, and is carried over into the parables discourse of Chap. 13, for which a necessary consequence of the gospel is the polarization of its audience.

12: 1–14 *Jesus and the sabbath: two challenges to the Jews*

The two opening episodes illustrate the 'easy yoke' of 11.30, understand it in terms of the law, and offer a challenge to the Pharisees on that issue.

1–8 (i) The plucking of the ears of corn: cp. Mk 2^{23-8})

Mk's version reaches its climax in the saying (as authentic as anything in the gospel tradition) 'the sabbath was made for man, not man for the sabbath' (Mk 2^{27}). This can hardly mean less than the abrogation of the law of sabbath as a universally binding precept. Mt omits this saying; he adds (v. 1) the detail that the disciples 'were hungry' (and therefore there were extenuating circumstances); he includes a further illustration, not in Mk, from the claims of urgent temple duty for priests—something recognized by the rabbis—and he throws in the injunction from Hos. 6^6 to prefer mercy to sacrifice, i.e. to put the needs of persons before exact observance of the ceremonial law. It would seem that for Mt Jesus' attitude to the law of sabbath is not one of abrogation but of liberal casuistry, though vv. 6 and 8 clearly reserve for him the right to go beyond the existing tradition.

1. *pluck ears of grain:* Dt. 23^{25} permits the plucking of corn in another man's field, but the rabbis forbade it on the sabbath, as a form of reaping.

2. *David:* see 1 Sam. 21^{1-6}.

4. *bread of the Presence:* see Lev. 24^{5-9}.

5–6. The example added by Mt is technically a better argument because (a) it actually mentions the sabbath; (b) it rests on a definite legal precept (Nu. $28^{9f\cdot}$, cp. Nu. 28^{24-7}) and is therefore *halakah*, whereas David's action, being a historical event, belongs to *haggadah* and could not serve as a precedent; (c) it was recognized by the rabbis themselves; cp. Daube, *NTRJ*, pp. 67ff.

6. added by Mt, on the analogy of $12^{41f\cdot}$. See next note.

7. Hos. 6^6, already used, though with a somewhat different application, at 9^{13}. Hummel finds here an echo of the rabbinic debate about ways of atonement for sin which could be substituted for sacrifice after the

destruction of the temple. For Mt, however, Christ is not an alternative to the temple and its rites; he has transcended them.

8. Originally (in Mk) an interpretative comment on Mk 2²⁷. Mt's retention of it without the latter indicates that for him, too, the final authority is not the Mosaic law as it stands, but as reinterpreted by Jesus. It is on the scope of the practical application of this principle that he appears to be more Jewish than Mk.

9–14 (ii) The healing of the withered hand: cp. Mk 3¹⁻⁶

Mt alters Mk's wording slightly, and inserts from another source a challenge about works of mercy on the sabbath, to produce a more direct confrontation between the law of sabbath and the law of love. Barth (*TIM*, p. 79) concludes that he is offering guidance to a Christian congregation in which sabbath observance is still taken for granted.

10. *they asked him:* Mt, as usual, alters Mk to give greater emphasis to the dialogue between Jesus and his opponents.

11. This appeal to compassion and commonsense is paralleled at Lk 14⁵ (cp. Lk 13¹⁶f.). It would not by any means have met with universal agreement in Judaism either in Jesus' time or Mt's (an extreme example is the Qumran prohibition of the rescue of even a new-born calf or kid from a ditch or cistern on the sabbath; see CD xi. 9 (V, p. 113), etc.). But later Jewish opinion came round to the view that any case of danger to life took precedence over the sabbath (Mishnah *Yomah* viii. 6; Danby, p. 172).

12: 15–21 *Jesus' response to opposition:* cp. Mk 3⁷⁻¹²

Mt greatly abbreviates Mk's summary of Jesus' healing activity of which he has said enough elsewhere; here he is only interested in the injunction to secrecy (see next note).

16. *ordered them not to make him known:* the injunction to secrecy is relatively common in Mk where it appears to be linked with the concealment of Jesus' Messiahship, though scholars are not agreed on whether this 'Messianic secret' had some foundation in fact or was imposed by the evangelist on his material (see Nineham, *Mark*, pp. 31f.). Mt may himself have been puzzled by it, since on his view of Messiahship there could have been no motive for concealing it; in any case he re-interprets it as a fulfilment of the text which follows.

18–21. Is. 42¹⁻⁴—the longest of the formula quotations in Mt and the most divergent from traditional texts, both Heb. and Gk. Lindars (*NTA*, pp. 147ff.) attributes the alterations to a long history of apologetic use in the Church; Stendahl (*School*, pp. 107ff.) to the work of the 'school' of interpretation behind Mt; Barth (*TIM*, pp. 125ff.) to the editorial work of Mt himself. The connexion between these alterations and themes treated elsewhere in the gospel makes the latter the most likely.

18. *my servant whom I have chosen:* contrast RSV of Is. 42¹. *chosen* has been transferred from the second half of the verse to make way there for a more explicitly Messianic expression. *my beloved with whom my soul is well pleased:* for the wording cp. 3¹⁷, 17⁵. Jesus is not merely the Servant but the Son of God and Messiah. A play on the ambiguity of the word *pais* (son/servant, see on 8⁶) may be intended.

19. *He will not wrangle* does not really correspond to anything in the Isaiah text. It interprets Jesus' withdrawal from controversy at 12¹⁵ as an acting out of the attitude of gentleness and humility attributed to him at 11²⁹.

20. *bruised reed . . . smoldering wick:* i.e. a person of low vigour or vitality. The saving work of the Servant will not be at the expense of the weak. *till he brings justice to victory: to victory* may have been suggested by Hab. 1⁴, but this is less significant than the meaning of the word. The role of the Servant is to execute the judgement of God upon Israel and to do so with power (see Barth, *TIM*, p. 141).

21. *and in his name . . . hope:* at this point only is Mt in accord with LXX.

The quotation is thus used to express in miniature Mt's conception of the role of the Christ which is spelt out in the gospel as a whole. He is God's chosen instrument, and his vocation is to declare God's righteousness to all mankind. But his mission is accomplished in obscurity (see on 2²³); he is the agent of God's judgement of his people, and only when that is effected—again by his submission—can the message be taken to the Gentiles.

12: 22–32 *Exorcism through Beelzebul: the Jews' Challenge to Jesus*

There is no question that Jesus not only shared the attitude of his contemporaries which attributed various symptoms of mental disturbance to demoniac possession, but himself attracted attention by his effectiveness as an exorcist. It was this aspect of his ministry that his opponents attempted to discredit by ascribing his success to his being in league with the devil. Jesus' reply to this charge (see vv. 25–8) reveals what was distinctive in his own attitude; for him the manifestations of evil have a single source or principle ('Satan'), and it is this which in individual exorcisms is really under attack (see Jeremias, *NT Theology i*, pp. 93f.).

Belief in possession survives in pre-scientific cultures to the present day, and has tended to revive especially in those

Christian circles where a renewed experience of charismatic gifts has been interpreted along fundamentalist lines. But, as an authoritative student of these has observed, 'most of the phenomena of possession can be explained within the framework of modern psychiatric knowledge, even if they cannot be healed'; and though he inclines, as do many missionaries, to the view that there is nevertheless an 'inexplicable remnant', this 'does not point to the existence of demons, but to the inaccuracy, perhaps only temporary, of our explanation of reality' (W. J. Hollenweger, *The Pentecostals* (ET London, 1972), pp. 380f.). The reality of evil and of its effects upon human beings, on which our Lord insisted, does not stand or fall by the mythology in which he found it natural to express it.

The 'Beelzebul controversy' was clearly the great challenge to Jesus' personal authority during his ministry, and the sayings which have been grouped together in this section all seem ultimately to derive from it; see Barrett, *Holy Spirit and the Gospel Tradition*, pp. 59ff. Mt's presentation of it is based on Mk, but he sets it in much bolder relief in the total context. He introduces it with a variant of the miracle related at 9^{32-4}, and he conflates Mk's rather confused version of the saying about Satan casting out Satan with a fuller one which is probably nearer to the original.

22–28 (i) Can Satan cast out Satan?: cp. Mk 3^{22-6}, Lk 11^{14-20}

22. *blind and dumb demoniac:* blindness is added to the condition described at 9^{32}, and the miracle is thus represented as a comprehensive and compelling exercise of spiritual power.

23. *people:* lit. 'crowds', the uncommitted masses, who are contrasted with their leaders (*Pharisees*, v. 24). See on 7^{28}, 13^2, 23^1. *Can this be the Son of David?:* i.e. the possibility is entertained (cp. Jn 4^{29}). The Messiahship of Jesus as a controversial issue with Jews is focused on this title (cp. 1^{1-17}).

24. *Beelzebul* (some good authorities have 'Beezebul'): a name familiar in contemporary demonology; the context makes it clear that it is used synonymously with 'Satan', of the ruler of the demonic order. The evidence of the sayings at vv. 25, 28, and especially 10^{25} suggests that it was interpreted by Jesus himself to mean 'lord of the house'; but since this takes the name as a hybrid between the Aramaic *be'el* and

the Heb. *zebul* (see Jeremias, *NT Theology* i, p. 7) it can hardly be the original etymology (cp. the interpretation of the name 'Barnabas' at Acts 4[36]). Translators from Jerome onwards confused the appellation with 'Baal-zebub' ('lord of flies'), the derisive nickname given to the god of Ekron in 2 Ki. 1[2].

25. *house:* see previous note.

26. *if Satan casts out Satan:* the crucial point in the argument (hence its position in Mk at the head of the saying). If Jesus' exorcisms show him to be in league with the devil, he is using Satan's power against Satan's own agents, and this is a situation that cannot continue.

27. *by whom do your sons cast them out?:* exorcism was a common practice in the Jewish and surrounding world; the objection raised to Jesus' exorcisms applies equally to other practitioners. *therefore shall they be your judges:* probably a glossing comment on the previous question.

28. *by the Spirit of God:* cp. v. 18. Lk 11[20] has 'finger of God' (cp. Ex. 8[19]). The arguments for the two versions are fairly evenly balanced, but the contrast between Beelzebul the spirit of evil and the Spirit of God is slightly in favour of Mt. (But for the opposite view see Manson, *Teaching of Jesus* (Cambridge, 1935), pp. 82f., and Barrett, op. cit., pp. 62f.). *kingdom of God:* Mt, for once, does not alter his source and write 'kingdom of heaven'. To do so would have obscured the connection between the activity of the Spirit of God and the presence of the kingdom of God. *has come upon you:* the Gk *ephthasen* has a ring of anticipation ('has burst in upon you'), though it is disputed how far it retained this force in the first century A.D. In any case, if the work of Jesus is not rejected as diabolical, it can only mean that the kingdom of God is present, proleptically at least, in power.

29–30 (ii) Binding the strong man: cp. Mk 3[27], Lk 11[21–3]

A separate logion, as is shown by the fact that Mt here reverts to following Mk (except for v. 30, found also at Lk 11[23]); but its connection with the Beelzebul controversy is obvious, especially in its repetition of the theme of the *house* (cp. vv. 24f.). The common Jewish expectation was that Satan would be bound in the last day.

31–32 (iii) The sin against the Holy Spirit: cp. Mk 3[28–30], Lk 12[10]

A third distinct saying deriving from the Beelzebul controversy and originally aimed at the perversity which attributed the work of Jesus not to the Spirit of God but to the power of evil. This was not only to call white black but to reject the offer of the forgiveness of God contained in the proclamation of Jesus. The original force of the saying was inseparable from this life-situation; after that had passed, the unforgiveable sin came to be identified with apostasy after baptism (cp. Heb. 6[4–6], and see Barrett, pp. 103–7). Mt's version may show traces of this, but the apostasy he has particularly in mind is that of the Jewish people in rejecting their Messiah.

Mt appears to quote two versions of the saying in succession; he may be simply conflating, as he often does, but he may be correcting an ambiguity in Mk's expression 'sons of men'; men, who need forgiveness, are to be distinguished from the Son of man, who bestows it. The distinction is repeated at 16¹³.

32. *either in this age or in the age to come*: Mt's wording. The rabbis excluded certain categories of persons (including 'heretics') from the world to come; see Mishnah *Sanhedrin* x. 1 (Danby, p. 397), and cp. 23¹³.

12: 33-45 *A People Delivered to Satan*

The verses which Mt has added to this context draw out the nature of Israel's apostasy and underline its diabolical origin. There may even be a deliberate contrast with the temptation story (4¹⁻¹¹), since (i) the words that issue from apostate Israel are patently not those that 'proceed from the mouth of God' (contrast 4⁴), (ii) 'this generation' demands a sign, which Jesus refused to give (cp. 4⁷), (iii) whereas he refused the apostasy of receiving from Satan what was his to give (4¹⁰), they by their apostasy have left open for Satan's occupation a kingdom that was previously God's own. Thus where Jesus in the wilderness acted as the true Israel, they have now become false Israel. See on 27⁴⁰ᶠᶠ.

33-37. (i) A cluster of sayings from different sources (*brood of vipers* and the image of the unfruitful tree have already been used against the Pharisees at 3⁷,¹⁰; for the latter cp. also 7¹⁶⁻²⁰), centred on the thought that what a man says necessarily reveals what he is.

34-35. *heart . . . treasure*: cp. 6²¹.

36. *careless word*: cp. Ex. 20⁷. The saying is probably connected with Jesus' attitude to swearing; see on 5³³ᶠᶠ.

38-42 (ii) The demand for a sign: cp. Mk 8¹¹ᶠ·, Lk 11²⁹⁻³².

The Pharisees' demand for a sign at Mk 8¹¹ᶠ· is met with a categorical refusal. In Mt (16⁴, the Marcan context, and here) they are allowed only *the sign of Jonah*. The following verses offer two alternative interpretations of this. The second of these (v. 41), which interprets it as a sign of repentance, makes the more straightforward connexion (though the fact that the second half of the double logion [v. 42] has nothing to do with Jonah or repentance shows that it is nevertheless an editorial one); the first (v. 40), which makes Jonah a type of the resurrection, belongs to a later stage of Christian reflection, familiar to us from early Christian art. Certainly the gospel shows no further interest in the typology of resurrection, and its introduction here is out of line with the context as a whole, which is concerned with the impiety of the Pharisees in seeking a sign, not with supplying one. Stendahl (*School*, pp. 132f.) shows reason for thinking that it was missing from Justin Martyr's text of Mt; in which case it can be regarded as an early expansion of the original text, which would have approximated to that at Lk 11³⁰. ('for as Jonah became a sign to the men of Nineveh, so will the Son of man be to this generation'). If this is right, the sign of Jonah is no new sign, but one always available to Israel in its own scriptures and already acted out in Jesus' own preaching. Those who have rejected it can expect no other (cp. Lk 16²⁹ᶠᶠ·).

40. *three days and three nights:* an assimilation of the interval between Jesus' death and resurrection to the text it is seen as fulfilling (Jon. 1¹⁷).

41. See Jon. 3⁵ᶠᶠ·.

42. See 1 Ki. 10¹⁻¹⁰.

43–45 (iii) The house swept and put in order: cp. Lk 11²⁴⁻⁶

This little parable, which is really a warning of the void left by an act of exorcism and the danger of relapse if it is not filled (see Jeremias, *PJ*, pp. 197f.), is apparently applied by Mt to the state of the Jewish people after, and despite, the mission of Jesus; see v. 45b.

waterless places: the desert, the natural habitation of a demon; but a human *house* (see v. 25) to which he can do damage is what he prefers.

12: 46–50 *Conclusion: Jesus' True Kin;* cp. Mk 3³¹⁻⁵

The divisive effect of Jesus' mission extends even to the heart of his own family (cp. 10³⁴ᶠᶠ·). The demands that he makes on others he accepts for himself; the gospel has priority over claims of kinship, and those whom it brings to him are to stand to him in place of a family. For Mt this probably carried overtones of the displacement of the 'sons of the kingdom' (8¹²) by converts from the Gentiles.

50. *does the will:* cp. 7²¹.

13: 1–52 *Parables of the Kingdom*

This chapter must be read in its context in the unfolding action of this part of the gospel. Israel has refused to recognize the significance of Jesus' acts of power (11²⁰⁻⁴), and its leaders have rejected them as diabolical (12²⁴), a rejection which Mt treats as itself diabolical, the final and unpardonable blasphemy. From this point Jesus has no positive message (though much by way of reproach and counter-argument) for official Israel. The real recipients of his teaching are now the disciples, as the nucleus of the future Church.

This of course was hindsight; Mt knew that no abrupt separation of the two took place in Jesus' own ministry, or indeed for a considerable time afterwards, and that no clear statement of it could be extracted from his received sayings. He had before him, however, in Mk 4$^{1-34}$ a collection of our Lord's parables understood as concealing a secret meaning from their audience. This was not strictly the way that the parable was used by Jesus himself (modern study has disclosed how many of his parables were originally addressed controversially to his opponents, in terms which they would have had no difficulty in grasping; cp. Jeremias, *PJ*, pp. 33ff., 115ff. *passim*). But 'enigmatic saying' was a possible meaning of the Heb. *māshāl* (see on 13^3 below); and it was common practice for a rabbi engaged in controversy to offer a veiled answer to his questioner in public and to elucidate it privately to his disciples afterwards (see Daube, *NTRJ*, pp. 141ff.). Mk uses this device as a clue to the unreceptiveness of those to whom the gospel was originally addressed, and Mt takes it over from him, though he applies it rather differently. In Mk the disciples themselves do not understand the parables until they are explained to them; in Mt the capacity to understand parables is what distinguishes disciples from the rest (cp. 13$^{11ff.}$), and the need for interpretation is not due to their incomprehension but to their changed situation, which is foreshadowed in the parables of growth, and addressed in the parables of the end. Mt's interpretations are thus directed to the Church of his own day; the parables themselves are correspondingly expanded from Mk's three to a series of seven, in a beautiful and characteristic formal arrangement:

The scene set: vv. 1–3
The model demonstrated: (1) the sower: vv. 4–9
The model justified: purpose of parabolic teaching: vv. 10–7
The model explained: interpretation of the sower: vv. 18–23

The model extended: three parables of growth:
    (2) the tares: vv. 24–30
    (3) the mustard seed: vv. 31–2
    (4) the leaven: v. 33
Break, with change of audience: vv. 34–6
The tares interpreted as a parable of the end: vv. 37–43
Three parables of the end:
    (5) the treasure trove: vv. 44–5
    (6) the pearl: v. 46
    (7) the dragnet (with interpretation): vv. 47–50
Conclusion: things new and old: vv. 51–2

On the whole chapter, see J. D. Kingsbury, *The Parables of Jesus in Matthew 13* (London, 1968).

13: 1–3 The setting

1. *house:* a significant detail introduced by Mt, its point being that the crowds on the shore (v. 2) are outside it. At v. 36 Jesus takes the disciples inside for further instruction. Probably, as at 9^{10}, it stands for the Church.

2. *crowds:* used by Mt to denote the mass of the Jewish people as distinct from their hostile leaders (cp. 7^{28}, 9^{35}, 12^{23}). They occupy a neutral position between the old Israel which, as such, is past recovery, and the Church to which they will be an object of missionary concern. See Kingsbury, pp. 24ff. *boat:* taken over from Mk. If there is a symbolic reference it cannot, in view of v. 1, be simply to the Church, as in $8^{23ff.}$; rather it suggests its missionary activity (cp. v. 47).

3. *parables:* the Gk word represents (as in LXX) the Heb. *māshāl* (from a root meaning 'to be like'). In the OT it covers a wide range of forms from simple comparisons and traditional proverbs to enigmatic oracles (e.g. Balaam's, Nu. 22–4) and full-dress allegories; and though it is not expressly used of stories carrying a single pointed comparison (like Nathan's in 2 Sam. 12, which is very close to our Lord's own use of the parable) the close connexion of these would be generally admitted. A similar range of usage is found in the rabbinic literature (which contains many parallels to the gospel parables), and —with reservations about deliberate obscurity and the use of allegory (see on vv. 18ff.)—in the practice of Jesus himself.

The word is only used five times in Mt outside this chapter, and not at all before this point. By avoiding the word (though not the thing) elsewhere, Mt is able to use it consistently here to denote 'an enigmatic form of speech directed primarily at outsiders' (Kingsbury, p. 31).

13: 4–9 The sower: cp. Mk 4²⁻⁹

The opening parable is not introduced, like the rest, by 'the kingdom of heaven is like'. Rather it serves as (i) a specimen parable, a model of how the method is used; (ii) the basic 'parable of growth', of which those of vv. 24–33, which are more directly to Mt's purpose, are developments or variations.

The details presuppose an understanding of Palestinian agricultural methods, in which sowing preceded ploughing, and there was inevitable waste of seed before it could be ploughed in (see Jeremias, *PJ*, pp. 11f.).

4. *along the path:* i.e. that already trodden across the field, which will finally be ploughed in with the rest.

5. *on rocky ground:* i.e. where the soil is shallow, but the rock underneath not visible before ploughing.

7. *upon thorns:* these are ploughed in with the rest of the field, but liable to grow up again with the corn.

9. *some a hundredfold, some sixty, some thirty:* inverting Mk's order (cp. 25¹⁴⁻³⁰). The figures represent a miraculously abundant yield (tenfold was reckoned good and seven and a half average), symbolic of the age to come.

13: 10–17 The purpose of parabolic teaching: cp. Mk 4¹⁰⁻¹²

Jesus now, without any explicit change of position, addresses not the crowds but the disciples, since the message of these verses (and the section following) is for their ears alone. Mt is not troubled by the dramatic improbability of this.

11. *secrets of the kingdom of heaven:* the plural (contrast Mk 4¹¹) is probably Mt's inclusive expression for the whole revelation of God through Jesus. For the disciples (i.e. the Church) as recipients of this, cp. 11²⁵ᶠ·.

12. This verse (introduced at a different point from Mk) is probably to be interpreted in terms not of growth in understanding but of reward; cp. its use as comment on the parable of the talents (25²⁹). What will be given to him who has and taken from him who has not (its present holder) is the kingdom itself (cp. 21⁴³).

13. *because:* contrast Mk 4¹², 'so that'. For Mk parables are expressly designed, in the mysterious providence of God, to produce incomprehension in their audience, the disciples included; for Mt they are simply a consequence of the incomprehension that already exists, and thus serve to distinguish disciples from the rest. Mt is less 'predestinarian' than Mk (cp. on v. 38). *seeing . . . understanding:* an abbreviated form of Mk's quotation from Is. 6⁹ᶠ·, which is taken up by Mt at vv. 16f. But this connexion is interrupted by vv. 14f. which cite the Isaiah text in full. The wording of the formula introducing it is unique and un-Matthaean in its vocabulary, and the quotation itself

is unusual in following LXX virtually word for word, and in being introduced not as a reflection of the evangelist but of Jesus himself. Stendahl (*School*, pp. 132f.) suspects an early interpolation into the text of Mt, and Kingsbury (pp. 38f.) supports him with further arguments.

13: 18–23 Interpretation of the sower: cp. Mk 4$^{13-20}$

Mt takes this over from Mk; it may be earlier than Mk, but few scholars will allow that it can have come from Jesus himself. Modern work on the parables of Jesus from Jülicher onwards (and notably Dodd, *Parables of the Kingdom*; Jeremias, *PJ*) has tended to discount the presence of allegory (i.e. a non-literal meaning for single details in the picture or story, as in Bunyan's *Pilgrim's Progress*) altogether. This is possibly too sweeping (E. J. Tinsley argues for an element of oblique allegory in them in A. T. Hanson (ed.), *Vindications* (London, 1966), pp. 153ff.); but it is hardly possible that this rather clumsy 'key', which identifies the hearers of the word with the seed sown rather than the soil that receives it, came from the creator of the original parable. The point of the latter lies in the contrast between the obscurity and uncertainty of the beginnings of the kingdom and the miraculous abundance of the harvest, and may well have been connected, as N. A. Dahl has suggested, with the disappointment in which Jesus' Galilean mission ended. To interpret it of the reception of the gospel preaching by individuals was the work of a later, missionary, Christianity. Reinterpretation of this sort was inevitable as the original point of the parables was forgotten; it frequently resorted to allegorization, and Mt contributes his share of this both in the present chapter and elsewhere.

19. *hears . . . does not understand*: taking up v. 13b. In Mt's vocabulary of belief, 'understanding' denotes the inner counterpart of hearing the spoken word, the process by which a man makes it his own.

21. *falls away*: see mg ('stumbles'), and cp. 18^6, 24^{10}.

22. *delight in riches*: Mt takes these words from Mk, but they clearly point to a problem of his own church; cp. on 6$^{19ff.}$, 19$^{16ff.}$.

13: 24–30 The tares

This, Mt's first explicit 'parable of the kingdom', replaces Mk's parable of the seed growing secretly (Mk 4$^{26-9}$) and is regarded by some (e.g. Manson, *SJ*, p. 192) as an expansion of it; but it may just as well have formed a pair originally with the dragnet (vv. 47ff.), both being parables of the separation of good from bad in the judgement. Possibly Mt has conflated two parables; this could explain how the end-product comes to be narrated as a parable of growth, but interpreted as a parable of judgement. In any case the interpretation at vv. 36ff., as Kingsbury points out, cannot exhaust the meaning of the parable in its context, since that is concerned primarily not with the final harvest but with what happens in the interim. It seems to be an allegory of the present kingdom as *corpus mixtum*, a community in which good and bad are found side by side until separated by the judgement (cp. Bornkamm, *TIM*, p. 19); this certainly covers the original situation of Christians and Jews before they formed two distinct communities (the whole meaning for Kingsbury), but is no less applicable to that of a later church containing nominal adherents.

24. *them:* i.e. the crowds; cp. v. 34 and contrast v. 36.

25. *weeds* (Gk *zizania*): not any sort of weed, but that known as 'darnel' (*lolium temulentum*), which, botanically, is closely related to bearded wheat and in the early stages of growth hard to distinguish from it (so Jeremias, *PJ*, p. 224).

28. *an enemy:* the devil, as the interpretation shows; not St Paul, as has been implausibly suggested (most recently by Brandon, *Fall of Jerusalem*, pp. 234f.). Mt is not writing for a conservative Jewish–Christian community, and the allegory as we have it is a literary construction, unlikely to have come from such a source. *gather them:* this, according to Jeremias (*PJ*, p. 225), was normal practice.

29. *root up the wheat:* it is the quantity of darnel that makes uprooting dangerous, as its roots become entangled with those of the wheat.

30. *to be burned:* i.e. as fuel.

13: 31–33 The mustard seed and the leaven: cp. Mk 4$^{30-2}$, Lk 13$^{18-21}$

These clearly formed a pair from the first, as in Lk (though *Thomas* breaks them up [see *NTAp i*, pp. 513, 520]). Mk has only the mustard seed, and Mt characteristically conflates his version of it with that found also in Lk.

The original point of both parables, as of that of the sower, is the contrast between the insignificant beginnings of the kingdom and the magnitude of its final fulfilment. Mustard is proverbially the smallest of all seeds, yet the plant reaches, under Palestinian conditions, a height of 8–10 feet, and the parable calls it a tree for birds to nest in. A little yeast will leaven far more than enough bread for a household's needs (the amount indicated is approximately 20 kilograms). The deliberate exaggeration conveys that the expected fulfilment will be not natural but God-given.

Both parables are so worded as to convey a hint of the inclusion of Gentiles in the kingdom (cp. vv. 32f.), a further development of the thought underlying the parable of the tares.

31. *field:* repeated from v. 24, to show that this parable continues the theme of the previous one—the progress of the kingdom through the mission of the Church.

32. *a tree:* a familiar OT image for a kingdom affording shelter to all its subjects: cp. Ezek. 17^{23}, 31$^{3ff.}$, Dan. 4$^{11f.}$. *make nests:* the Gk word

had become a technical term for the incorporation of Gentiles into the people of God (see Jeremias, *PJ*, p. 147).

33. *leaven*: abstained from by Jews at Passover time, and therefore seen by them as a symbol of pervasive wickedness (cp. 1 Cor. 5[6]). The parable keeps the thought of pervasiveness, but in a good sense; the new community is to be inclusive, not exclusive. *measures*: the Gk *saton* was equivalent to 13·3 litres.

13: 34–36 Break, with change of audience

There is now a change of audience, of scene, and of emphasis. Everything so far, apart from vv. 10–23, has been addressed to the crowds on the shore. Vv. 34–5 conclude this section; all that follows is addressed to the disciple in the house. Jesus is not only, like a good rabbi, explaining to his followers the inner meaning of his more reserved public utterances; he is also addressing through them the Church of Mt's own day. The note of gradualness implicit in the parables of growth (and in the progress of the kingdom to which they refer) gives way to the note of urgency in the face of the coming judgement. The time has been long, but it will be short, and Christians are urged to concentrate on the one thing needful.

There is no need to see the break in this chapter, with Fenton, as a major division in the whole gospel. Both the previous discourses, the Sermon on the Mount and the Mission discourse, have final sections addressed specially to Mt's contemporaries (7[13ff.], 10[24ff.]), and this one continues the practice.

35. Quoted from Ps. 78[2] in a free version of the Heb. text. Mt's understanding of the function of the parable as obscuring truth is thus given scriptural justification from a text in which the word can only mean a 'dark saying'. *prophet*: unusual in references to the Psalter. A few MSS. add 'Isaiah', perhaps to fill the gap; the reading 'Asaph' which was known to Jerome, could have the same explanation. The heading of this psalm ascribes it to Asaph, who is called a 'seer' at 2 Chr. 29[30] (see also on 1[8]). More probably the word derives from the general tendency to treat the psalms as prophetic utterances (cp. Lk 24[44]). Jesus' revelation of hidden mysteries, and his use of parables for the purpose, are seen as a 'fulfilment' of the prophets (cp. 5[17]).

36. *house*: the function of this in the discourse (cp. v. 1) is now made clear.

13: 37–43 The tares interpreted as a parable of the end

This interpretation is offered, on the face of it, as a key to the entire parable, and it says nothing to cancel what has already been found in it. But its whole emphasis is on the final harvest, as an image of the judgement. It thus serves as a kind of bridge between the two halves of the chapter. The vocabulary strongly suggests that it is Mt's own composition (see Jeremias, *PJ*, pp. 81ff.).

37. *Son of man:* Jesus in his glorified state (as revealed in 28[16-20]); see Note B, p. 241.

38. *the world* (Gk *kosmos*): the extension of this term turns on that of *his kingdom* in v. 41. Those who identify the kingdom of Christ with the Church (e.g. Bornkamm, *TIM*, p. 44; Tödt, *Son of Man* (ET London, 1965), pp. 69ff.) are obliged to put the same construction on *world*. But there is nothing elsewhere in Mt to suggest that he would understand the word in this restricted sense, and 25[31ff.] indicates that the judgement will not be of Christians only. See on v. 41. *sons of the kingdom:* those who should inherit it; used negatively at 8[12] of Jews excluded from the Messianic banquet, here of Christians (and others?) who pass the test. 21[43] gives warning that the kingdom is to change hands. *sons of the evil one:* these are to be found even in the Church. Despite the mythological language, it does not seem to be meant that individuals are predestined to this role, only that the response of some to the gospel is corrupted (cp. v. 19), and that a man is known by his deeds (cp. 7[21]).

39. *close of the age:* Mt's characteristic expression for the end; see on 24[3], and cp. 28[20].

41. *angels:* contrast 9[35] where the mission harvest is to be gathered by disciples. For angels at attendants of the Son of man at the judgement, cp. 16[27] (contrast Mk 8[38]), 24[31], 25[31]. *his kingdom:* 28[18] assigns 'all authority in heaven and on earth' to the risen Christ, and this is obviously not confined to the Church, though 28[19] implies that it is through the mission of the Church that he will claim it for his own. There appears to be an explicit contrast between the kingdom of Christ, progressively realized in this way, and 'the kingdom of the Father' (v. 43) which the righteous will enter as their reward. With this cp. 1 Cor. 15[24-8]. *causes of sin:* a correct paraphrase, in this context, of the Gk *skandala* (lit. 'stumbling-blocks'), elsewhere obstacles to faith (cp. 11[6], 13[57]) or perseverance (cp. 18[6], 24[10]). See on 15[12] for the OT background of the image. The reference is clearly to persons, as the following words and the parallel usage at 16[23] make clear (see also on 7[13ff.]). *evildoers:* lit. 'doers of lawlessness', possibly with a hint of antinomianism as at 7[23].

43. A clear allusion to Dan. 12[3]; the formula *he who has ears . . . hear* may either draw attention to this (as at 11[15]), or warn the hearers to apply the parable as interpreted to themselves (cp. v. 9).

13: 44-46 The treasure trove and the pearl

Formally, this little pair of parables is the counterpart in the second half of the discourse to the mustard seed and the leaven in the first half, and it is possible that Mt sees a parallel between the smallness of the mustard seed and that of the pearl, and between the hiddenness of the leaven and that of the treasure until it is claimed (a *chiasmus*).

But whereas the first pair are concerned with the way the kingdom comes, the second pair is concerned with the priorities required of those who set their hearts on entering it.

44. According to Jewish law, treasure found belonged to the person who could 'lift', i.e. take formal possession of, it irrespective of the ownership of the land. But the finder, if not himself the owner, would be likely to be working for him in some capacity, in which case his 'lifting' of it would normally be treated as work done for his employer, who would thereby acquire the treasure for himself. The only way for the finder to get undisputed right to the treasure is to have clear legal access to the land, i.e. to buy it, however incongruous this may be with his way of life hitherto. But he is under no obligation to inform the present owner, who prior to 'lifting' has no more right to it than the finder himself. Hence the action of covering it up. See Derrett, *LNT*, pp. 1ff.

45–46. The case of the merchant, though obviously parallel to that of the finder of the treasure, is not quite the same, since the acquisition of pearls is his business, whereas the treasure was found by accident. Thus the attainment of the kingdom may either require a sudden change of heart, or crown a lifetime of search and application; but the end-result is the same.

13: 47–50 The dragnet, and its interpretation

This is, as already noted, in some sense a pair to the parable of the tares, even if not in all particulars to the present form of it, and the parallelism obviously plays a part in Mt's formal arrangement. The harvest of the sea corresponds to the harvest of the field, and the same separation of good and bad follows both. The parable thus recapitulates the theme of the present activity of the kingdom in the mission of the Church (developed in vv. 24–30), and the interpretation that of its future fulfilment in the judgement (developed in vv. 37–43).

47. *net*: a large seine-net, placed by a boat (cp. v. 2) and then hauled back to shore by ropes (see Jeremias, *PJ*, pp. 225f.). For fishing as an image of missionary activity, cp. 4¹⁹, and for the net as an image of the universal Church ('every kind'), Jn 21¹¹.

48. *the bad*: some fish were regarded as unclean (cp. Lev. 11¹⁰f·), others as inedible; see Jeremias, *PJ*, p. 226.

49–50. The imagery corresponds closely to that of vv. 41f.

13: 51–52 The conclusion

51. *Have you understood all this?*: it is assumed that disciples can, without further elucidation; cp. vv. 18f.

52. *Therefore*: introduces the conclusion to the whole discourse; cp. 18²³. Jesus' final remark is itself a parable of the disciples' under-

standing. *every scribe . . . heaven:* von Dobschütz's conjecture that this is the concealed signature of the evangelist as a converted rabbi (see Introduction, p. 31) assumes that *scribe* is used here in its developed rabbinic sense, of a teacher of the law. The difficulty about this is that the exegesis practised in this chapter has nothing to do with the law and hardly more with the OT as a whole; it is concerned with the parabolic teaching of Jesus. This would have required the work of 'scribes', in the humbler sense of copyists, for its preservation, and it is relevant that the (evidently Christian) 'scribes' of 23³⁴ (see commentary ad loc.) are distinguished from 'wise men', the earlier designation for professional exegetes (see Introduction, p. 24). The form of the saying here suggests nevertheless that those referred to will have been scholars by training or aptitude before they became Christians. For Christian scribes see also Stendahl, *School,* pp. 20ff. *been trained for:* lit. 'become a disciple of' (cp. NEB 'become a learner in'). 23⁸⁻¹⁰ insists that all Christians remain in this category, whatever their qualifications. *what is new* (as a disciple) *and what is old* (as a scribe): note the *chiasmus*. In the context of this chapter the 'old' would appear to mean not the Torah but the original teachings of Jesus, as preserved and studied by the 'scribe', and the 'new' the application of them to fresh situations in the Church, the task of the instructed disciple, as illustrated in vv. 36–50.

2. REJECTION IN GALILEE: THE CHURCH FORESHADOWED (CHAPTERS 13:53–18:35)

The formula at 13⁵³, occurring as usual after a discourse, recalls the reader from the concerns of the later Church to the story of Jesus, and opens a new division in it. The stage is set for this by the opening section 13⁵³⁻⁸ (cp. Mk 6¹⁻⁶), the story of the rejection of Jesus in his own country. Neither Mk not Mt specifies this as Nazareth (contrast Lk 4¹⁶ff·); rather it is taken as symbolic of the whole rejecting people, the old Israel. But for Mt it is significant that the rejection takes place in 'Galilee of the Gentiles' (4¹⁵); in this part of the gospel there are some implicit indications that the future of the gospel lies with the Gentiles (see on 15²⁴ff·, ²⁹⁻³¹, ³²ff·), and some explicit instructions for the Church in which that future is to be embodied (16¹⁸f·, Chap. 18 *passim*).

13: 54 *their synagogue:* as at 4²³· 9³⁵ etc., this dissociates the Christian community from the Jewish. This is Mt's last reference to the presence of Jesus in a synagogue; from this point on he is separated from his people.

55. *brothers*: though these are nowhere explicitly stated to have been the children of either Joseph or Mary, there is no sign that either Mt or his source questioned that they were actually the children of both. Ancient Christian writers from at least the early third century, and unanimously from the fifth, took the view that the divine motherhood of Mary implied her perpetual virginity, and regarded the 'brothers' either as the sons of Joseph by a previous marriage or as cousins of Jesus. *James*, later the presiding figure of the church of Jerusalem (Gal. 2⁹, Acts 12¹⁷, 15¹³, 21¹⁸), and put to death by order of the Sanhedrin in A.D. 62, is the only brother of whom there is any subsequent record.

57. *took offence*: lit. 'were caused to stumble', in the same sense as at 11⁶; they found his claims incredible. *a prophet . . . country*: apparently a proverbial saying, like 9¹².

58. *he did not do many mighty works there*: Mk says roundly that he could do none, though he immediately qualifies this. Mt is not prepared to attribute incapacity to Jesus.

14: 1–12 *The Death of John the Baptist*: cp̄. Mk 6¹⁴⁻²⁹

Jesus is not the only prophet to whom the saying at 13⁵⁷ applies. It is characteristic of faithless Israel that it 'slays the prophets' (cp. especially 23²⁹⁻³⁶), and the martyrdom of John recorded at this point both is an indication of the fate that awaits Jesus from the same quarter and serves to associate the two in the purpose of God (cp. 11¹⁸ᶠ·). See Wink, *John the Baptist*, pp. 27f.

Mk's version, which Mt adapts to his own purposes, rests on popular tradition, not to say bazaar gossip, and is no more reliable in its details than such sources generally are. A more sophisticated account, but considerably later in date, is given by Josephus, *Ant.* xviii. 109ff. On the whole episode and the problems raised by it, see Nineham, *Mark*, pp. 172ff.; from another angle, Derrett, *LNT*, pp. 339ff.

1. Mt, following Mk, does not suppose that the death of the Baptist took place at this point, but only that Herod was reminded of it. By v. 13, however, he has forgotten this. *Herod*: Herod Antipas, son of Herod the Great (cp. on 2¹ᶠᶠ·), tetrarch of Galilee and Perea from his father's death in 4 B.C. till his own banishment in A.D. 39.

3. *Herodias:* actually the wife not of Philip but of his half-brother (and her own uncle), also called Herod and long resident in Rome; *Philip,* tetrarch of Iturea and Trachonitis, married her daughter Salome. Lev. 18[16], 20[21] condemn sexual relations with a brother's wife as incestuous; the special case of the levirate (Dt. 25[5f.]) concerned a dead brother's widow and is irrelevant here. Josephus suggests a political motive for Herod's action, arising out of John's popularity and the fear that it might lead to rebellion.

5. The hostility of Herodias in Mk is transferred to Herod by Mt. John and Jesus are at one in attracting the enmity of the Herods (who stand, here as in Chap. 2, for 'Israel after the flesh').

6. *danced:* see Nineham, loc. cit., on the improbability of a king's daughter performing an oriental dance in the presence of men.

10. *prison:* Josephus says that John was imprisoned in the fortress of Machaerus near the Dead Sea; as there was a palace attached to this it is not impossible that some episode of the sort described took place there.

12. *and they went and told Jesus:* by altering a statement in Mk (6[30]) about the disciples of Jesus, to make it refer to those of John, Mt has made his own connexion between John's death and Jesus' withdrawal to 'a lonely place'.

14: 13–21 *First Feeding of the Multitude:* cp. Mk. 6[32–44]

Mk's account (see Nineham, pp. 177ff.) relates (i) a nature miracle, in which a very large number of people are fed, and satisfied, from a very small store of provisions; (ii) a quasi-sacramental meal, described in terms reminiscent of the Christian eucharist; (iii) a feeding of people with bread in the wilderness, which recalls the episode of the manna (Ex. 16, Nu. 11), and is at the same time an anticipation of the Messianic banquet (cp. 8[11]). It is likely that the tradition developed in the inverse order to this, and that Schweitzer was right in describing the original episode as 'a veiled eschatological sacrament'; but it is obviously impossible to penetrate behind the narrative to the details of what actually happened.

Mt alters Mk in two ways. First, the disciples' puzzled question, where they are to get sufficient food, is suppressed; in Mt the disciples understand at once what is expected of them, but lack confidence in the power of Jesus to enable them to carry it out—hence their reply in v. 17. They are seen as the exemplars of later Christian disciples whose faith falters, and this will be continued in the following section. Secondly, the role of the disciples in the distributions of food is emphasized; see especially the concluding words of v. 19. What Jesus gives to hungry men (the thought is of Mt's contemporaries) he gives at the hands of his disciples. Cp. 10⁴⁰, and see Held, *TIM*, pp. 181ff.

17. *two fish:* fish (especially dried) was regularly in the Mediterranean world eaten with bread as a relish. Under the influence of this story fish became a common eucharistic symbol in early Christian art, often in association with baskets of loaves.
19. *blessed . . . broke . . . gave:* the actions familiar to Mt's readers from the eucharist; cp. 26²⁶.
21. *besides women and children:* So again at 15³⁸. If Mt is here trying to heighten the miraculous effect, his way of doing so is rather pedantic. Possibly he is concerned about the universal appeal of the gospel of Christ, in whom 'there is neither male nor female' (Gal. 3²⁸). But there may be simply a verbal reminiscence of Ex. 12³⁷.

14: 22–33 *The Walking on the Water:* cp. Mk 6⁴⁵⁻⁵²

This follows the first feeding in Mk, and the two were probably linked already in the oral tradition (cp. Jn 6¹⁶ᶠᶠ·). Once again it is impossible to recover what originally happened; very possibly this story and that of the storm on the lake derive from a single episode. This form of it has clearly been influenced by OT passages which speak of the path of Yahweh through the waters, especially Ps. 77¹⁹, Is. 43¹⁶; it is an epiphany of Jesus to the disciples, in the same category as the Transfiguration (17¹ᶠᶠ·).

Mt follows Mk fairly closely, but adds the further incident of Peter's attempt to imitate his Master. This can hardly have existed independently of the story in Mk, and its vocabulary and the deliberate parallels with his version of the stilling of the storm (8²³ᶠᶠ·) indicate that Mt was the first to set it down in writing (see Held, *TIM*, pp. 204ff.); rather than longstanding oral tradition about Peter (Mt's interest in Peter is not biographical), this suggests later Christian reflection on the story of the walking on the water. Peter is here the typical Christian disciple. He sets out in faith, in response to the command of Jesus, and thus is able to be 'as his master' (10^{25}), for all things are possible to one who has faith (17^{20}, 21^{21}). But in time of danger his faith falters, until the Lord intervenes in response to his prayer and restores it. The interest has thus shifted from the figure of Jesus in isolation to that of the disciple in dependence on Jesus. It is not to be supposed that Mt expected his readers to take the Lord's prescription literally; it is rather a pictorial representation of the way of discipleship, and a striking illustration of the devotional use to which at least one group of primitive Christians put the reported incidents of the life of Jesus.

25. *in the fourth watch:* between 3 and 6 a.m. Mt takes over Mk's Roman time unaltered.
30. *Lord, save me:* as in 8^{25}.
31. *O man of little faith:* see on 8^{26}.
33. *Truly you are the Son of God:* the presence of the Lord in the boat and his reassurance of the disciples evokes from them an explicit confession of faith. Mt substitutes this for Mk's account of their astonishment and incomprehension; he does not wait, as Mk does, for Peter's confession at 16^{17}. Mt is not concerned about the dramatic aspects of the disclosure of Jesus' identity; the first half of his gospel has made it abundantly clear what his claims are, and the remainder of it is occupied with the acceptance or rejection of those claims.
34–36. A summary account of healings, taken over from Mk without significant alteration.

15: 1–20 *The Dispute about Ceremonial Purity:* cp. Mk 7^{1-23}

See Nineham, *Mark*, pp. 188ff., for the problems raised by the Marcan section which is the basis of Mt. Briefly, it falls into two parts: (1) a question about eating with unwashed hands, which Jesus answers with a denunciation of the Pharisees for observing the oral tradition (of interpretation and observance of the law) in such a way as to nullify the provisions of the law itself. The specific case attached (see below) raises problems, since later rabbinic tradition, as represented by the Mishnah and Talmud, was as severe on the kind of casuistry implied as Jesus shows himself here; possibly what was originally a single *cause célèbre* has been turned into a generalizing statement in the course of transmission. The

denunciation has certain obvious parallels with those collected in Mt 23. (2) A further answer, loosely connected with
the original question and obviously belonging to a different
question now lost, since it is not concerned with uncleanness of
hands (which, at any rate originally, could not be transmitted
to food handled by them) but with uncleanness of food itself—
a matter not of the oral tradition but of the written law (see
Lev. 11). This answer is, in the regular rabbinic manner,
first offered to the crowds as a parable, i.e. a saying with a
concealed meaning (cp. p. 130), and then explained privately
to the disciples. It is probable that this explanation has been
modified in the course of its transmission to, and use by, a
Gentile Christian church (cp. that on divorce at Mk 10[11f.]),
since it contains an abrogation of the food laws so explicit that
if it had come from Jesus himself it would be impossible to
understand the later controversy in the Church over the terms
on which Gentiles were to be admitted to it. But it seems in-
contestable that in this matter, as on sabbath observance,
Jesus, though without rejecting the scriptural prescription as
such, was prepared in practice to apply it with a freedom which
was finally incompatible with contemporary Jewish attitudes.

Mt not only tidies up the passage to make for smoother
reading, but modifies it in the following ways:

(a) He suppresses details in Mk's account of Jewish practice
which reflect, at best, a second-hand understanding of what
Jews actually did, and which, where accurate, would be
sufficiently familiar to his readership.

(b) All the emphasis is now laid on the initial dispute with
the Pharisees, thus making it clear that the ground of the
attack is not the written Torah but the oral tradition.

(c) In line with this, Mk's crucial aside 'Thus he declared
all foods clean' (Mk 7[19]) is omitted, and the whole dispute is
made to turn on the issue of eating with unwashed hands (cp.
the conclusion at 15[20]). He thus avoids a head-on collision
with the provisions of the law, but in doing so implies that,
for the scribal tradition, to eat with unwashed hands transmitted ritual uncleanness to the food. Possibly this was after

144

all the rationale of the Pharisaic insistence on the practice, in a period of intensified emphasis on the separation of the Jew.

Did the Christians for whom Mt wrote continue to observe the food laws, as they apparently observed the sabbath (see on 12[1ff.]), in spite of their commitment to the Gentile mission? The decree of the so-called council of Jerusalem prescribed abstinence from 'what has been sacrificed to idols and from blood and from what is strangled' (Acts 15[29]). The letters of St. Paul betray no hint that this prescription was known to the churches to which he wrote (food offered to idols is for him a matter of respecting the conscientious scruples of others, not of a formal and universal prohibition; cp. 1 Cor. 8[4ff.]), but it need not therefore be dismissed as wholly fictitious. Possibly what Lk ascribed to the council was in reality a later ruling with a more restricted circulation, and the formerly Jewish-Christian communities of Palestine and Syria were those originally affected by it (for evidence of the continued observance of it see R. P. C. Hanson, *Acts* (Oxford, 1967, in this series), p. 155n). Certainly Mt's reshaping of Mk in this section does not suggest that the food laws were an issue in the community for which he wrote. His main purpose, as with the sabbath, is to present the teaching of Jesus as not undermining the written law, but fulfilling it in a more radical way.

2. *tradition of the elders:* the interpretation of the law and its application to particular cases was still a matter of oral tradition in the time of Jesus and indeed in that of Mt, though the tradition in some form goes back at least to the time of Ezra (c. 400 B.C.) and came to be ascribed, like the written Torah, to the authority of Moses himself (see Introduction, p. 23). It is this tradition that Jesus is represented, probably correctly, as holding himself free to attack. *wash their hands when they eat:* this was obligatory only for priests in Jesus' time, and was not imposed generally until the second century. But this general imposition is likely to have been preceded by a period of controversial pressure for it, with the Pharisees strongly in favour of strictness; there is no reason why this should not have gone back to the time of Jesus, and the fact that Mt reproduces it in his version is itself evidence that it was the practice of those Jewish circles with which he was in controversial contact.

4. *God commanded:* Mt substitutes *God* for Mk's 'Moses'; either because

the quotation is from the Decalogue which Ex. 20[1] represents as the *ipsissima verba* of God, or to emphasize that though the 'tradition of the elders' may (in Jewish thought) go back to Moses, the Torah is the word of God himself.

5. *given to God:* Mk has 'Corban' representing a Heb. word, which could be used either literally to denote something offered or devoted to God, or in a non-literal sense as a formula for a specially solemn vow or oath. The first meaning would imply that the man in the case withheld money from the support of his parents by vowing it to the temple treasury (without, presumably, relinquishing the use of it); the second that he swore not to support his parents. In the latter case the conflict would not be between the law and the tradition but between two different prescriptions of the law, since the Torah is extremely severe on breaches of vows (see, e.g., Dt. 23[21–3]).

It is quite possible that the original case which evoked the protest of Jesus was one in which a man used a technical conflict between points of the law as an excuse for evading elementary human (as well as religious) obligations to parents, and a protest of this kind would have been very much in line with his recorded attitude, e.g., to those who objected to his healing on the sabbath (see 12[1ff.]). But Mk seems to have intended the word to be taken literally, since he translates it and represents the whole case as an instance of observance of the oral tradition at the expense of the law itself, and Mt simply makes this interpretation more explicit. Apart from the priority of the law over the tradition, his attitude to a passage involving the inviolability of oaths would have been complicated by his emphasis on Jesus' direction to avoid swearing altogether (5[33ff.], cp. 23[16ff.]).

Jewish scholars have objected to the whole attack on Jewish traditional casuistry on the grounds that its real object was dispensation from, rather than the upholding of, vows. This undoubtedly holds good for the written form of the tradition, which is later than the NT, but does not preclude an earlier stage at which the position was, in some quarters at least, less clearly understood.

8–9. A compressed version of Is. 29[13] (LXX), taken over almost verbatim from Mk.

12–14. A direct attack on the Pharisees, introduced into this context by Mt. *offended:* lit. (as usual) 'caused to stumble'. The OT background of this image is Lev. 19[14] 'You shall not . . . put a stumbling-block before the blind', i.e. to prevent him continuing on his way; cp. also Dt. 27[18]. It is here used to furnish a debating-point. If the Pharisees have been 'tripped up' (i.e. put off, hindered from accepting him) by Jesus' teaching, that means that they are blind; what becomes then of the pride of the orthodox Jew in being a 'guide to the blind' (cp. Rom. 2[19])? The saying about the blind leading the blind is obviously proverbial.

17. RSV has evaded rendering the crude directness of the Gk; mg ('is evacuated') is slightly preferable.
19. Mk has at this point a long list of 'Gentile' vices reminiscent of St Paul (cp. Gal. 5[19f.]). Mt substitutes a much shorter list of offences against the Ten Commandments. *out of the heart:* the inward contrasted with the outward; cp. 5[8].
20. *to eat . . . man:* Mt adds this clause to tie up the dispute about food with that over ceremonial purity; i.e. he avoids a frontal attack on the Torah (of which the food laws formed part) by assimilating the substance of the passage to the preceding dispute about ceremonial purity, which was only a matter of the tradition.

15: 21–28 *The Canaanite Woman:* cp. Mk 7[24–30]

Mt has rehandled Mk's version more drastically than usual, so much so that some scholars have suspected that he is relying on an older tradition than our present Mk. This conclusion is unnecessary if it is recognized that Mt normally reduces healing narratives to dialogues designed to elicit faith (see p. 98 above), and that in this particular case he has assimilated Mk's story of the Syrophenician woman to his own story of the centurion (8[5ff.]). In both episodes a Gentile parent wins healing for a sick child (performed at a distance) by a striking retort which is commended for the faith that prompts it; and in both the future attitude of the Church to Gentiles is prefigured. Mt himself fully accepts the Gentile mission (cp. 28[19] etc.), and there is no reason to suppose either that he knew Mk's story in a more 'Jewish' form or that he has 're-judaized' it. His alterations emphasize that Jesus' personal mission was to his own people, and that the turning to the Gentiles was a consequence of its rejection.

21. *Tyre and Sidon:* Kilpatrick (*Origins*, pp. 131ff.) gives reasons for connecting the gospel with this region.
22. *Canaanite:* Mk calls her a 'Syrophenician'. Kilpatrick suggests that Mt has diverted the reference of the story, which is not complimentary, from the Greek-speaking people of the great ports (for whom he was writing) to the Semitic inhabitants of the villages. But the name may also have a theological reference, since for much of the OT the Canaanites whom the Israelites displaced are the heathen *par excellence*, with all the overtones of uncleanness that this carried. *from that region:* the Gk word denotes the border country. Mt alters

Mk to make clear that Jesus did not enter Gentile territory, but the woman crossed the frontier to speak with him. *O Lord, Son of David*: the Messianic form of address (strange on the lips of a Gentile, but it expresses a faith which is later commended, and in terms which Jesus' own people will afterwards reject; cp. 21[15f.]) is for Mt almost a stereotyped opening for a petition for healing.

23–27. The stages of the dialogue which Mt has built up here underline the woman's persistence. She responds to Jesus' silence by continuing to call to him (v. 23), to his explicit limitation of his mission (v. 24) by an appeal to his compassion (v. 25), and to his offensive reference to her as a Gentile (v. 26) by a witty deflection of it (v. 27). Her refusal to be put off is the measure of her faith.

24. *I was sent only . . . Israel*: the wording here is Mt's own; cp. 10[6].

26. *It is not fair . . . dogs*: Mt here rejoins Mk, but omits Mk's 'Let the children be fed first'. Mk, like Paul (see Rom. 1[16]), views the Gentile mission as something additional to the original mission to Jews; Mt sees the Jews as having rejected the gospel so decisively that the Gentiles are evangelized in their place. *dogs*: a common Jewish term of abuse for Gentiles. Some commentators have attempted to soften the offensiveness of this on the lips of Jesus by pointing out that the Gk word here (as already in Mk) is a diminutive, used of the puppies in the house rather than the pariahs in the streets. There is something of this in the woman's reply, but it is still to an abusive remark that she is replying. And it seems that by this period the word had lost its diminutive force, to which in any case there is no equivalent in Aramaic.

27. *Yes*: i.e., 'Yes, it *is* fair'. This requires 'for' as the sense of the following conjunction, and *yet* is in fact a mistranslation. *crumbs*: actually the scraps of bread with which the diners wiped their mouths.

28. *great is your faith*: introduced by Mt; cp. 8[10].

15: 29–39 *Second Feeding of the Multitude*: cp. Mk 8[1–10]

The two feedings in Mk are evidently variant accounts of the same event, and that he has chosen to record both with the less interesting placed second is a fact calling for explanation. The answer given will vary with the overall view of Mk's literary method, but a growing body of opinion would take seriously the view first advanced in patristic times, that he means the first feeding to be taken as a symbolic feeding of Jews, and the second (which is preceded by a section implying abrogation of the food laws, and by two healings in Gentile territory) as a corresponding feeding of Gentiles (see, e.g., A. Richardson, *The Miracle Stories of the Gospels* (London, 1941), p. 98). If this was in fact in Mk's mind, it is fully possible that Mt picked up the allusion, and there are scattered indications that he has (see next note, and the following section, 16¹⁻¹²).

29–31. *the Sea of Galilee:* previously only at 4¹⁸, where it follows the Isaiah text associating Galilee with Gentiles. *into the hills:* the Gk words are identical with those rendered 'on the mountain' at 5¹, the setting of the Sermon on the Mount. The general summary of healings which follows in place of Mk's healing of the deaf-mute (Mk 7³¹ᶠᶠ·) is recapitulated in v. 31 in terms very similar to those used at 11⁵ of the healings reported in Chaps. 8–9. These details are all peculiar to Mt and suggest that by introducing them here he is hinting at an extension to Gentiles of the teaching and saving acts offered to Israel in the first part of the gospel. Mt, by making the same crowd (v. 32) the recipients of the feeding, at once avoids the abruptness of Mk's opening and underlines the Gentile reference.

39. *Magadan:* this, like Mk's 'Dalmanutha' which it replaces, is wholly unknown. Megiddo has been suggested, but this is more than twenty miles from the lake. The variant 'Magdala' in some late MSS. is simply a case of substituting the known for the unknown.

16: 1–12 *Warning against the Pharisees:* cp. Mk 8¹¹⁻²¹

The demand of the Pharisees and others for a sign, with which the section opens, is introduced very abruptly, and indeed in its geographical context oddly, both in Mk and Mt. In Mk Jesus' answer is an unqualified refusal; here he offers only the sign of Jonah, as at 12⁴¹ where Mt has interpreted it as a demand for repentance. So long as they fail to respond to that sign they need expect no other. In this context, however, it may also point forward to 'Simon Bar-Jona' at 16¹⁷.

The passage which follows in Mk is the most enigmatic in his whole gospel, and it is more than likely that Mt himself has not fully understood it. In it Jesus warns the disciples in the boat against the leaven of the Pharisees and of Herod (Pharisees and Herodians have already been found conspiring against Jesus at Mk 3⁶, after an episode which showed up the hardness of heart—i.e. obtuseness—of the Jewish leaders, 3⁵), and then complains of their own obtuseness in failing to discern the significance of the two feedings and particularly of the numbers fed. Since ancient writers saw great mystical significance in numbers, it is probable that Mk's play on them in this section covers a mystery to which we have lost the key. Any attempt at a solution, such as those of Richardson, loc. cit., and A. Farrer, *A Study in St. Mark* (London, 1951), pp. 294ff., can be no more than conjectural.

Mt may be supposed to have understood Mk's play on the numbers, since he is careful to reproduce it. But besides, as usual, correcting Mk's references to obtuseness in the disciples (which would imply an initial absence of faith) to 'little faith' (v. 8), he substitutes Sadducees for the now unfamiliar Herodians, and the leaven which can no longer stand for obtuseness is instead referred, somewhat lamely, to the teaching of the two groups, as if it were the same. The whole incident now takes place not in the boat but on the far shore. This appears to continue the symbolism noted at 15^{29-31}, and to be warning disciples that the mission to Gentiles adumbrated there means a break with the official Jewish leadership and with its teaching, and thus prepares the way for the following section, in which the Church founded on Peter emerges as the true successor to the old Israel.

1. *Pharisees and Sadducees:* previously linked at 3^7, in a sharp warning to the combined Jewish leadership about repentance.

2–3. '*When it is evening . . . times:* these verses are usually regarded as an interpolation, both on textual grounds (see mg) and because the weather-indication they contain, unlike that of Lk 12^{54-6}, is not known to hold good for Palestine. See Manson, *SJ*, p. 201.

16: 13–20 *Peter's Confession and Christ's Promise to him:* cp. Mk 8^{27-30}

In this passage Mt's gospel reaches one of its high peaks. It is not a turning-point in his narrative of the ministry (nor indeed necessarily in Mk's, though many have so regarded it). Nor is it the dramatic disclosure of a great Christological secret; Jesus himself has spoken at $11^{25\text{ff.}}$ of his divine significance as something 'revealed to babes', and the disciples have already acknowledged it at 14^{33}. It is concerned not so much with the content of the revelation as with its recipient. The truth about Jesus in his relation to God, and its rejection by the representatives of the old Israel (emphasized once again in the preceding section), together require a new beginning for the people of God; this is the Church, and Peter who makes the representative confession of faith is its foundation.

In Mk the response of Jesus to Peter's attribution of Messiahship to him is an injunction to silence; and the rebuke 'Get behind me, Satan' a few verses later indicates that though Peter has made the formal confession of faith correctly he has quite misunderstood its inner meaning. (Some scholars believe that in the earliest form of the story 'Get behind me, Satan' was Jesus' immediate response to the suggestion that he was the Messiah, presumably in view of its political implications). Mt has altered the whole significance of the episode by his two alterations: (i) he has made Peter's confession an unambiguously religious affirmation by the addition of words qualifying the title 'Christ'; (ii) he has introduced into the context a reply of Jesus, vv. 17-9, which accepts Peter's designation of him as God-given, and bestows a corresponding recognition on him in return. This must now be examined. It falls into three rhythmical strophes:

17. Blessed are you, Simon Bar-Jonah!	18. (And I tell you) You are Peter,	19. I will give you the keys of the kingdom of heaven,
For flesh and blood has not revealed this to you,	And on this rock I will build my church,	And whatever you bind on earth shall be bound in heaven,
But my Father who is in heaven.	And the gates of Hades (cp. mg) shall not prevail against it	And whatever you loose on earth shall be loosed in heaven.

The passage is comparable with 11²⁵⁻³⁰, both in its tripartite formal structure and in the way it has been built up from OT texts handled along midrashic lines, sayings ascribed to Jesus in the tradition, and constructions of the evangelist's own. Verse 17 is inseparable from its context here and so can hardly have been transmitted separately; its theme of the mystery revealed by the Father to a disciple clearly echoes 11²⁵ᶠ·, itself in its present form probably a construction of Mt (see ad loc.). The last two lines of v. 19 reappear by themselves. addressed to all the disciples, at 18¹⁸ (cp. Jn 20²³ for a related version), and it is thus open to question whether they originally formed part of a logion addressed specifically to Peter. If then there is any traditional core to the promise to Peter, it is to be looked for in v. 18. The origins of this verse, and its relation to what is historically known of Peter are discussed in Note C, p. 242.

13. *Caesarea Philippi:* a town lying at the foot of Mount Hermon on the extreme north border of Galilee, formerly named Paneas and renamed by Herod the Great, who rebuilt it, after his son Philip. *Son of man:* Mt's substitution of this for Mk's 'I' repeats the contrast between 'men' and 'Son of man' found already at 12³², and makes it parallel to that between 'you' and 'I' in v. 15. It is improbable that it makes any distinction between the figure of the Son of man and Jesus himself; cp. Note B, p. 241.

14. *Jeremiah:* Jewish apocalyptic writings foretold the appearance of the famous dead before the coming of the Messiah, and Jeremiah is specifically mentioned at 2 Esdr. 2¹⁸·, 2 Mc. 15¹⁴ᶠ·

But he is also for Mt the typical prophet, partly at least because he anticipates Mt's own theme of the doom of Jerusalem (cp. 2¹⁷ᶠ·, 23³⁸, 27⁹·²⁵), and it is probably for this reason that Mt has introduced his name into Mk's unspecified reference to 'the prophets'.

16. *the Son of the living God:* Mt's addition carefully defines the sense in which Jesus' Messiahship is to be understood, in line with Mt's general Christology (cp. 4³·⁶, 11²⁷, 14³³, etc.).

17. *Simon Bar-Jona:* the solemn address may imply that Mt regards the title 'Rock' as having been conferred at this point; unlike Mk he has no previous reference to the naming, though he has not scrupled to use the name 'Peter' in the foregoing parts of the gospel. Jn 21¹⁵⁻⁷ calls him 'Simon, son of John'; Mt is almost certain to be nearer to the original tradition. O. Cullmann mentions, but is cautious about, a suggestion that the patronymic conceals an Aramaic designation for a terrorist (*Peter, Disciple, Apostle, Martyr* [ET² London, 1962], p. 23). *flesh and blood:* i.e. natural human powers; a Semitism, as

natural for Mt as for Paul (cp. 1 Cor. 15⁵⁰, Gal. 1¹⁶), and therefore not necessarily indicative of a source.

18. *Peter . . . on this rock* (Gk *Petros . . . petra*): the play on the words is fully effective only in Aramaic (*kēpha . . . kēpha*) where there is no distinction of gender. The first Greek-speaking Christians including Paul (1 Cor. 1¹², etc.; Gal. 1¹⁸, etc.) continued to use the Aramaic form of the name.

Does the word denote solid ground, as at 7²⁴, or a foundation-stone laid upon it, as in Is. 28¹⁶? In Jewish speculation the two images tended to merge. On the one hand Is. 51¹ (Abraham as the rock from which Israel was quarried) was interpreted in the light of the rock on which the world was founded (a widespread theme of oriental religious literature); cp. the text quoted by Strack–Billerbeck, i. 733: 'When God looked upon Abraham who was to appear, he said: Behold, I have found a rock on which I can build and base the world. Therefore he called Abraham a rock'. On the other hand rabbinic exegesis of Is. 28¹⁶ identified the same rock with the foundation-stone in the centre of the temple at Jerusalem which was further regarded both as the topmost part of the earth (and thus the point of entry into heaven) and as sealing off the waters of the abyss, which were always threatening to rise and overwhelm the earth (see R. J. McKelvey, *The New Temple* [Oxford, 1969], pp. 188ff., and references cited there). Both images have contributed to the saying here. Peter is to be to the new covenant what Abraham was to the old, the man of faith (cp. Rom. 4); but what is built on him, the Church, is the counterpart of the temple at the world's centre rather than of the world as a whole.

I will build my church: church (Gk *ekklēsia*) is found in the gospels only here and at 18¹⁷, where it clearly derives from the post-resurrection situation. In LXX it renders the Heb. *qahal*, the word used for the elect people of God; in the NT its meaning oscillates between this theological conception, understood by Christians as the reconstituted people of God, the new Israel, and the local communities in which it is concretely embodied. The latter is plainly the meaning at 18¹⁷ (though it is conceivable that the text goes back to the primitive Jerusalem church, which would originally have seen itself, as the Qumran community also did, as a separate group within the still continuing old Israel). Here, however, it is used in its 'universal' and theological sense. The notion of 'building' the Church is sufficiently explained here (as at Eph. 2²⁰ᶠ·) by the addition of the image of the temple (cp. Zech. 6¹² for the part played by Joshua [=Jesus] in connection with this). K. L. Schmidt's argument (*TDNT* iii. 524f.) that the word represents the Aramaic *kenishta* (which can mean both the people of God, a separate 'synagogue', and the building in which it meets) is only called for if an Aramaic origin for the whole saying is insisted on. See further Note C, pp. 244ff. *powers of death*: lit. 'gates of

Hades' (so mg; 'Hades' is the equivalent of the Heb. *Sheol*, used both of the abyss and the place of the departed). The foundation-stone of Is. 28[16] is laid down to withstand the onslaughts of death and Sheol (see Is. 28[15,18]), and this is the main theme here. The actual wording however is found at Is. 38[10] (cp. Job 38[17], Ps. 9[13], 107[18]), and prepares the reader for *keys* in the following line.

19. *the keys of the kingdom of heaven*: Is. 22[22] says of Eliakim, steward-elect of the royal household: 'I will place on his shoulder the key of the house of David; he shall open, and none shall shut; and he shall shut, and none shall open' (applied to Christ himself at Rev. 3[7]). The point of the allusion is that Eliakim is to be made steward in the place of Shebna whose conduct was unworthy of his office. The latter dismissal has its counterpart in the present context in the rejection of the Pharisees and Sadducees at v. 12. Note that at 23[13] the scribes and Pharisees are accused of shutting the kingdom of heaven against men.

Peter is thus addressed as the steward of the kingdom of heaven, chosen to be his master's vicegerent in the place of those who were not worthy. Since the kingdom is not the same as the Church, the passage is probably speaking of the function of the Church, as founded on and represented by Peter, in relation to the kingdom, rather than of that of Peter, or the apostles whom he represents, within the Church. *bind . . . loose*: in rabbinic literature these words are normally used in connexion with a rabbi's ruling on a point of the law, to mean 'forbid' and 'allow'. But, as Jeremias points out (*TDNT* iii. 751), this usage is only a particular application of language which belongs originally to a judge's verdict, to 'bind' meaning to imprison or to excommunicate, to 'loose' meaning to acquit or to forgive. The rabbinic usage need not be wholly excluded here, though Peter is not, as Streeter thought, 'the supreme rabbi'; that position is reserved in Mt for Jesus himself as the Messianic interpreter of the Torah (cp. 23[8,10]). But the association of the authority, even though awkwardly, with keys, and the repetition of the same formula at 18[18] in a context explicitly concerned with church discipline and forgiveness, mean that the disciplinary thought is primary; those whom the earthly Church excludes from the kingdom will be so excluded (i.e. by God) in the final judgement, and those whom it admits will be admitted. Jn 20[23] translates the imagery into plain language.

20. *that he was the Christ*: Mt restricts Mk's general injunction to silence to the Messianic (and therefore political) aspects of Peter's confession, which his own treatment has entirely transcended.

16: 21–28 *Passion and Discipleship*: cp. Mk 8[31]–9[1]

The first prediction of the Passion recalls Mt from his

glimpse of the future Church centred on Peter to Mk's dominant theme that Messiahship involves suffering and that
disciples are called to share it. He follows Mk with small but
significant variations.

21. *Jerusalem:* Mt emphasizes the part played by the holy city in the
rejection of Christ. This is to become a major theme of Chaps. 21–3,
culminating in 23³⁷⁻⁹. *the third day:* a correction of Mk's 'after three
days' which brings it in line with the wording of Hos. 6².

23. *Get behind me, Satan:* Mt takes this from Mk, but for his readers it
unmistakably echoes the temptation story of 4¹⁰. *you are a hindrance
to me:* Mt only; *hindrance* represents the Gk *skandalon*, a stone to trip
over (see on 15¹²). The linking of the idea of the foundation-rock
(Is. 28¹⁶) with that of the stone of stumbling (Is. 8¹⁴) was a familiar
feature of early Christian exegesis (e.g. 1 Pet. 2⁶⁻⁸). Usually both are
applied to Christ. By making both apply to Peter, Mt is able to in-
tegrate his own theme of Christ's promise to Peter with Mk's theme
of the Satanic in Peter.

27. This verse expands Mk into a summary of what is depicted in full at
25³¹ᶠᶠ·. *he will repay . . . done:* quoted from Ps. 62¹², cp. Sir. 35¹⁹.

28. *the Son of man coming in his kingdom:* Mk has 'the kingdom of God come
with power', an unambiguous reference to the *parousia* (see on 24³)
which it was still possible when Mk was written to expect within the
lifetime of Jesus' own audience. For Mt, writing some twenty years
later, this is no longer feasible, and he has therefore to modify Mk's
prediction so that it refers to the intermediate kingdom of Christ in
and through his Church (see on 13⁴¹). The Transfiguration which
follows immediately is an anticipation rather than the fulfilment of
this; probably Mt sees the promise as fulfilled at 28¹⁶⁻²⁰ (cp. especially
28¹⁸).

17: 1–13 *The Transfiguration:* cp. Mk 9²⁻¹⁰

It is probably not now possible to distinguish the original
circumstances of this experience of the disciples, sometimes
regarded as a post-resurrection one, from the rich overlay of
OT imagery and theological interpretation with which, like
the baptism, it is presented by the evangelists. For a full study
see A. M. Ramsey, *The Glory of God and the Transfiguration of
Christ* (London, 1949.).

Mk's version of it is (i) a confirmation of the truth of Peter's
confession, with which it is linked by the very unusual

chronological note 'after six days'; (ii) a recapitulation to the chosen disciples of the divine Sonship revealed to Jesus (and the reader) at the baptism; (iii) a symbolic statement that this implies the fulfilment of law and prophets; (iv) a visionary anticipation of Jesus' glorified state after the resurrection or at his return. For Mt the truth of Peter's confession has already been confirmed in the responsive promise to him, and he is in any case not interested in a progressive disclosure of the person of Christ which he has presented unambiguously to his readers from the start. And though his post-resurrection 'Christophany' at 28$^{16-20}$, itself an anticipation of the *parousia*, may be anticipated here, it is not much emphasized. Mt's emphasis is on the Christological implication of the story, which he assimilates more closely than Mk with the baptism (itself already in Mt a revelation to the witnesses rather than to Jesus; cp. 3^{17}), and on its presentation of Jesus as the new Moses. Once again Mt reveals his concern for the continuity of the new covenant with the old.

1. *after six days*: at Ex. 14$^{13-8}$ Moses is six days on Sinai before God calls to him from the cloud.
2. *his face shone like the sun*: Mt's addition; cp. Ex. 34^{29,35}.
3. *Moses and Elijah*: Mt, by putting them in this order (inverted in Mk), makes it explicit that they stand for the law and the prophets (cp. 5^{17}, 7^{12}, 11^{13}, 22^{40}).
5. *a bright cloud*: i.e. the Shekinah or cloud of glory, the visible sign of the presence of God; cp. Ex. 24$^{15-8}$, 40$^{34ff.}$, and the Exodus narratives generally. *my beloved Son . . . pleased*: virtually as in the baptism narrative, 3^{17}. *listen to him*: Jewish expectation identified the prophet 'like' Moses promised in Dt. 18$^{15ff.}$ with the Messiah who would give a new interpretation of the Torah (cp. 11^{3}).
6–7. The note of the disciples' fear and Jesus' reassurance of it, introduced here by Mt, is characteristic of him (cp. 14$^{26ff.}$) and designed to reassure Christian disciples of his own day.
9. Only in its fulfilment in the resurrection will the meaning of the transfiguration become plain.
10. *Elijah*: his appearance in the vision could be interpreted as a reason for publishing the news of the latter, since his return was widely expected as a sign of the imminent end (see Mal. 4^{5}). Jesus' reply is that the real return of Elijah was in the person of John the Baptist (see on 11^{14}). Mk leaves this to be inferred; Mt makes it explicit (v. 13).

17: 14–21 *The Epileptic Boy:* cp. Mk 9[14–29]

As Held has shown (*TIM*, pp. 187ff.), Mk's version of this story contains two discrepant elements: a rebuke to the disciples for the lack of faith which made them unable to heal in the absence of Jesus, and a dialogue eliciting faith from the child's father as a basis for healing. Mt has not only, as usual, reduced the healing narrative to its bare bones, but, by transferring the instruction about faith to the conversation with the disciples after it and omitting altogether the moving dialogue with the child's father, has made it clear that the faith he is concerned with here is not that of the person healed (or his proxy), but that of the disciple healing in the name of Jesus.

17. *O faithless and perverse generation:* an echo of Dt. 32[5]; to whom is it addressed? Not to the father, whose problem of belief (see Mk 9[22–4]) plays no part in Mt's version; nor to the crowd, who are wholly outside the action. Nor, at first sight, to the disciples, since their failing, as always in Mt, is not unbelief but 'little faith' (v. 20). Yet the saying is Jesus' response to the disciples' failure to heal; it must therefore attribute their 'little faith' to their involvement in a people hostile to Jesus and to what he stands for.

18. *instantly:* lit. 'from that hour'; cp. 8[13], 15[28].

20. The saying about faith is introduced into this context by Mt (cp. 21[21] for another version; also Lk 17[6]). The humorous exaggeration is characteristic of Jesus' own personal style; by inserting the saying here Mt insists that the miraculous power of Jesus is available to any disciple with sufficient faith in him. *mustard seed:* cp. 13[31f.]; not 'little faith', but great faith from small beginnings.

17: 22–23 *Second Prediction of the Passion:* cp. Mk 9[30–2]

Son of man . . . men: cp. 12[31f.], 16[13]. This prediction, unlike the others, makes no allusion to the part played in the passion by the Jewish authorities. By placing it here Mt may imply that there are other ways of betraying Christ besides that which actually brought him to his death. See on 18[6].

17: 24–27 *The Temple Tax*

In accordance with the provisions of Ex. 30[13], 38[26], every adult Jewish male was required to contribute an annual tax of half a shekel towards the expenses of the sanctuary. Down to

A.D. 70 this was paid into the temple funds; after the destruction of the temple it was not simply suppressed but diverted by the Romans to the treasury of the God Jupiter Capitolinus, in token of the subjection of Israel's national god to Rome's, and in this form, as the *fiscus Iudaicus*, it continued to be levied on all Jews who maintained their national practices. Many, as can be imagined, tried strenuously to avoid payment. See further Ehrhardt, *Framework of the NT Stories*, pp. 116f.; Derrett, *LNT*, pp. 260–2; H. Montefiore in *NTS* (1964), pp. 60ff.

Although considerations of vocabulary (for which see Kilpatrick, *Origins*, pp. 41f.) indicate that Mt was the first to set down the tradition in writing, it is not to be assumed that the Roman form of the tax is the situation to which it was addressed. For v. 27 implies that it is non-payment rather than payment which will give scandal to others. This must mean that the story has been transmitted orally from the period when the temple still stood, when the issues for Christian casuistry would have been rather different from those raised by the *fiscus Iudaicus*. Derrett (*LNT*, pp. 247ff.) argues cogently for a Palestinian background, though his confidence that the episode can be situated in the ministry of Jesus is not widely shared.

Whatever its derivation, the starting-point of the passage is Jesus' own admitted payment of the tax, which would imply on the face of it both obedience to the law and recognition of the claims of the temple. Using once again the rabbinic device of private elucidation of a public answer, Jesus explains to his disciples that the tax is paid not because the collectors have a right to claim it from him, but to avoid 'giving scandal'. Payment is an expression of pastoral concern, of readiness to be all things to all men, which does not count against the claim that in Jesus 'something greater than the temple is here' (12⁶). The discourse on pastoral care in the Church (Chap. 18) forms an appropriate sequel.

24. *half-shekel*: Gk *didrachma*, a coin of the Syrian coinages accepted as the equivalent of half a temple shekel.
25. *tribute*: lit. 'census' (poll-tax); see on 22¹⁷. *from their sons or from*

others?: better 'from their sons or from other men's?'. *sons* in this context cannot mean 'subjects', as some translators suppose; it should be obvious that a king's subjects are not exempt from taxation. But his immediate kin have traditionally been exempt, and so normally in the ancient world were the members of his household and others directly employed by him, who were not uncommonly spoken of as his 'sons'. If this episode derives from the ministry of Jesus or from the earliest Palestinian Church, his answer could imply, as Derrett argues, that the disciples are the 'family' of God, employed on his business and wholly dependent on him for their livelihood (see on $6^{25ff.}$). But since the point at issue is Jesus' own freedom in the matter of payment, it is more probable that 'sons' is to be taken literally here, and that the plural conceals a reference to Jesus' own sonship to God as his followers came to understand it.

27. *not to give offence to them:* whom? If 'sons' in v. 25 is taken to mean disciples, it would be possible to regard these as the objects of the pastoral concern urged here, with emphasis presumably on those as yet unemancipated from Jewish legal scruples. If, however, it is taken literally, as recommended above, *them* can only refer to the collectors (assuming these to be Jews still, and not agents of the Romans, as by Mt's day they had become), and *give it to them* below supports this interpretation. *give offence:* lit. 'scandalize'; the precise sense of this word has as usual to be settled by the context. According to Derrett (*LNT*, pp. 256f.), refusal to pay could involve the collectors in the guilt of unlawful exaction; this would be 'causing them to sin'. On the other hand those who witnessed non-payment without understanding the underlying motive might be hindered thereby from grasping the truth about Jesus, 'put off' as at 15^{12}. *shekel:* Gk *stater*, the Syrian coin taken as equivalent of the temple shekel. *for me and for yourself:* payment of a single stater on behalf of two people was in the days of the temple more convenient, and apparently more profitable, than to find a separate equivalent, of exact weight, to the half-shekel payable by a single person.

It is only at this point that the question of payment by disciples is raised, and then only indirectly. Peter, who has confessed the divine sonship of Jesus (16^{17}), and been associated with him in the foundation of the Church which is to supersede the temple (16^{18-9}), shares in the exemption proper to sons. It is not stated that he did as he was instructed; the interest of the story for Mt lies not in the presumed miracle (to which there are numerous parallels in rabbinic and other literatures) but in the interpretation of the law for Christians.

18: 1-35 *Pastoral Care and Forgiveness in the Church*

Mt has amplified a paragraph of loosely connected sayings which lay before him in Mk and built it up into the fourth of

his formal discourses (note the characteristic formula at 19¹).
It is most usefully compared with the second, that at 10⁵⁻⁴², of
which it seems to be a kind of mirror-image. There a programme for a mission to Jews of limited duration (10⁵⁻²³) is
followed by instructions on apostolic attitudes for which no
such time-limit holds good (10²⁴⁻⁴²); here directions for the
practice of community discipline which presupposes the
existence of the later Christian Church (vv. 15–35) are preceded by instructions about the nature and implications of
discipleship (vv. 1–14) which were as applicable in the
ministry of Jesus and in the period of transition to a separate
Church as they are to Mt's own contemporaries (cp. the
double application of the parable of the tares, 13²⁴⁻³⁰, ³⁶⁻⁴³).

The persons addressed in this chapter are in some way contrasted with the 'little ones', a designation that Mt is anxious
to vindicate as applicable to all disciples, which probably
implies that the people he is addressing have been using it
disparagingly of others (like 'weak' in Rom. 14¹ff·, 1 Cor.
8⁷ff, 9²²). Who are these 'little ones', and on what grounds are
they despised? They have so far been mentioned only at
10⁴², where the expression is evidently used of disciples in
general, but a possible clue to the meaning may be discovered in 5¹⁹, which says that 'whoever . . . relaxes one of the
least of these commandments . . . shall be called least in the
kingdom of heaven'. It seems that Mt has neutralized the
original force of this saying by applying it to the commandments of Jesus, but its original reference was clearly to those of
the OT law. Probably a saying which had originated in the
controversy in the early Christian community over the terms
on which non-Jews were to be admitted, came afterwards to
be used by the Judaizing section in a mixed congregation to
disparage those (whether emancipated former Jews or
Gentiles) who sat loosely to individual precepts. That the
meaning of 'little ones' is connected with this text is supported
both by the fact that the present chapter starts from a discussion of 'greatness in the kingdom of heaven' and by the
use of 'least' with the same meaning at 25⁴⁰,⁴⁵.

The disciples are warned against 'scandalizing' the 'little ones' (vv. 6–8). In the predominantly Gentile churches for which St. Paul wrote this would have meant the 'liberated' leading the 'unliberated' into what for them is still sin. But the presence of the two parables used by Mt in this section suggests that here it is the other way round; it is the 'little ones' who are going astray and the established disciples who are allowing them to be lost. This could apply equally to a failure in mission (the sin of earlier Jewish Christianity, as of Judaism before it; cp. 9³⁶, 10⁵) and to a failure in pastoral concern and responsibility (the sin of certain of Mt's contemporary Christians). In the latter case the persons concerned are assumed to have some sort of responsibility for other Christians, but whether this forms part of the general obligations of discipleship, or arises out of seniority in the Church, or is the task of a formally constituted ministry, it is impossible to say with confidence. 23⁸⁻¹⁰ warns against the use of honorific titles, but that is in a context of controversy with the Pharisees, and it is not safe to conclude that Mt is combating the beginnings of prestige attaching to office in the Church.

Mt does not necessarily approve of the conduct of the 'little ones'; indeed the strong warning of 7¹⁵ᶠᶠ· may be directed against following their example. But he insists that the proper attitude to them is not premature condemnation, but reclamation of the backslider and a readiness to forgive.

18: 1–14 A. The worth of the disciple

18: 1–4 (i) The disciple in his own estimation: 'littleness': cp. Mk 9³³⁻⁶

1. Mk's dispute between the disciples about precedence, which would be pointless for Mt in view of 16¹⁸ᶠ·, is turned by him into a general question put to Jesus about spiritual greatness.
3. Introduced by Mt from Mk 10¹⁵; but whereas the saying in Mk emphasizes the essential newness of life in the kingdom (cp. the familiar Jewish comparison of a proselyte to a newly-born child), Mt characteristically applies it to the moral qualities expected of disciples, as is shown by the plural *children* in his own version. *become:* in spite of the word *turn*, the emphasis is less on the change involved than on the attitude to which it leads; cp. 5⁴⁵, 10¹⁶,²⁵, where the Gk uses the same verb.

4. Mt only. The quality of the child which the disciple is to exhibit is defined as humility (inculcated by Jesus in the beatitude at 5⁵, and exemplified by himself at 3¹⁵, 11²⁹, 12¹⁸⁻²¹, 21⁵). The 'littleness' of the disciple (cp. 10⁴², and 'babes' at 11²⁵) is to be understood in this sense, and it applies to all alike.

18: 5–9 (ii) The disciple in relation to Christ: cp. Mk 9³⁷,⁴²⁻⁸

5. Mt now reverts to the Marcan context with which he started. Having adapted Mk10¹⁵ to show that disciples are to see themselves as children, he now uses Mk 9³⁷ to show that they are to look on other disciples as on Christ himself. The very abruptness of the transition suggests that it is deliberate, and that it is addressed to Christians who have tended to see the others as children and themselves in the place of Christ.

6. The converse of what is said of the disciple in v. 5; that to be the cause of another disciple's downfall (the consequence of not receiving him as Christ) is a matter of infinite gravity. *causes . . . to sin:* a paraphrase rather than a translation of *skandalizō*, and probably too restrictive. For the image of the stumbling-block see on 15¹², and cp. 11⁶, 13²¹,⁴¹,⁵⁷, 16²³.

  To fall into serious sin, to fail to arrive at faith, to lose faith and to lapse from membership, are all instances of what is meant by 'stumbling-block', and it is not clear that the first is to be preferred; indeed the parable at vv. 12–4, the discipline outlined at vv. 15–8, the injunction to personal forgiveness at vv. 21f., and the final parable which clinches it all point to the conclusion that the disciples addressed are not leading their fellow-Christians into sin, but discouraging them by being too severe on their failings. *great millstone . . . drowned:* not unknown to Galileans as a rough and ready method of execution; cp. Jos., *Ant.* xiv. 450.

7. Mt only. There is a striking parallel between the language of this verse and that used of the treachery of Judas in 26²⁴. This may simply mean that Judas is the archetypal example of what this verse is saying: that the presence of 'stumbling-blocks' is inevitable, since they are part of the mystery of evil, deriving from the devil (cp. 13³⁹,⁴¹); yet that does not absolve those who present them from personal responsibility in the matter, for which they will have to bear the total consequences. But it may also convey that as to receive a disciple in Christ's name is to receive Christ (v. 5), so to 'scandalize' such a one is to betray Christ. *temptations to sin:* mg ('stumbling-blocks') is better (see on previous verse).

8–9. These verses, both in Mk and Mt, fit only loosely into their context, to which they are linked by the catchword *skandalizō*. Clearly their original reference was to parts of the body as occasions of sin, and they are used with this meaning at 5²⁹⁻³⁰. Here however the parts of the body seem to be used figuratively (as in 1 Cor. 12; is there some indirect dependence here?) of members of the Church, in this case of those who endanger the salvation of others, for whom no means of eradication are held to be too ruthless.

18: 10–14 (iii) The disciple in the sight of God: cp. Lk 15³⁻⁷

A fresh angle on the worth of the individual disciple, which is to be seen not only in the light of his relation to Christ, but of his share in the providence and the mercy of God.

10. *their angels:* i.e. guardian angels. Jewish popular belief in these personal embodiments of the divine providence developed greatly in the inter-testamental period, probably out of reflection on Ps. 91¹¹. Their principal functions of guidance on journeys, protection from danger (especially from demons), and care for the correct observance of the law are illustrated by the role of Raphael in the book of Tobit. They would also be called upon to testify for or against their *protégés* in the judgement. But there was general agreement in Jewish tradition that angels cannot look upon the face of God (cp. Is. 6²), and that only the most exalted of them are to be found in his dwelling-place. That the traditional view can be reversed here shows the degree to which early Christian teaching about the Fatherhood of God has modified contemporary Jewish notions of divine transcendence. In this context it is a vivid expression of the value in God's sight of even the humblest disciple.

11. 'For the Son of man came to save the lost' (mg) has crept into some MSS. from Lk 19¹⁰.

12–13. On this parable see Linnemann, *Parables*, pp. 65ff. She rightly shows that whereas Lk preserves the original application (to Jewish outcasts, not backsliding Christians), Mt is nearer to the original form of the parable as an analogy from real life, since he does not assume that the sheep will be found (*if he finds it*), and has not been influenced, as has Lk, by the image of the Good Shepherd. The shepherd's valuation of his sheep is conveyed by his sense of loss when it strays (in that moment he cares more for the one that is lost than for the ninety-nine that are safe) and by his corresponding joy at finding it. So also the fact that the 'little one' has fallen into sin does not make God's care less for him, but more.

14. Mt's own conclusion to the parable distinguishes 'straying' from 'perishing'. That perdition must follow sin is no part of the declared will of God; that it does so in particular cases can be the fault of those who should be carrying that will out (cp. 7²¹), Christians with pastoral responsibility for others. This prepares the way for the next section.

18: 15–35 B. Sin and forgiveness in the Christian community

18: 15–20 (i) The purpose of church discipline

The pastoral attitudes urged so far invite the question: how is concern for the individual to be balanced with responsibility for the church as a whole—at what point does pastoral care pass into judgement? Mt introduces at this point what is in itself a procedure for excommunication (vv. 15–7); its disparaging reference to 'a Gentile and a tax-collector' (v. 17) betrays its strict Jewish–Christian antecedents. Dodd (*NT Studies*, pp. 57ff.) points out parallels in Paul (Gal. 6¹ for the effort at reclamation; 1 Cor. 5¹⁻⁸ for the excommunication), and the DSS have revealed a similar practice of admonishing the sinner in the presence of witnesses before bringing charges in the open assembly (see 1 QS 5²⁶–6¹ [V. p. 80]; cp. CD 9¹⁻⁴,¹⁶⁻²² [V. pp. 110f.]). Despite the absence of rabbinic parallels, this must be presumed to be a discipline which early Christianity took over from its Jewish background. See H. von Campenhausen, *Ecclesiastical Authority and Spiritual Power in the First Three Centuries* (ET London, 1969), pp. 124ff.; S. E. Johnson in *SNT*, p. 139.

That Mt is familiar with this text and reproduces it means that the discipline still operated in his community. Nevertheless, like all his Jewish–Christian material, it must be read with an eye on the context he has constructed for it; he is not merely recording, but interpreting. It is not only preceded by v. 14, but followed by the separate saying at v. 18 which speaks of 'binding' and 'loosing' in that order (contrast Jn 20²³). Mt does not deny the appropriateness of excommunication for the obstinately impenitent, but he seems to be suggesting that the overall aim of the exercise is forgiveness of the sinner (contrast 1 Cor. 5⁵, where it appears to be his death). That God has given authority for this has already been stated at 9⁸; and the danger of premature judgement in a Church in which good and bad continue to exist side by side has been illustrated by the parable of the tares (13²⁴ff·). The addition of the further saying at vv. 19f. seems to imply that even if efforts at reconciliation fail, the sinner is still not beyond the reach of the prayers of his fellow-Christians; if Christ was present in the assembly which had to excommunicate (cp. 1 Cor. 5⁴), he is present also in the small prayer circle, and prayer in his name will not be rejected.

15. *your brother*: see on 5²³f·. *against you*: important MSS. omit these words, and the context implies that the discipline here has to do with conduct calling for the public censure of the church, rather than with the settlement of personal grievances, for which see vv. 21f. *gained*: almost a technical term in the early Church for conversion (cp. 1 Cor. 9¹⁹⁻²², 1 Pet. 3¹), here extended to the reclamation of the erring Christian. Jas. 5¹⁹f· envisages a similar situation.

16. *two or three witnesses*: a reference to Dt. 19¹⁵, which lies behind the

procedure common to DSS and early Christian practice, and which widely influenced the discipline of the early Church; cp. 2 Cor. 13[1], 1 Tim. 5[19].

17. *church:* elsewhere in the gospels only at 16[19]. Though Mt presumably found the word, or its equivalent, in his Jewish–Christian source, the fact that the present existence of local churches is here presupposed (whereas in 16[19] the establishment of the universal Church is still something promised for the future) is a clear pointer to the real audience of this section. *a Gentile and a tax collector:* i.e. (in Jewish eyes) a 'notorious sinner'. For traces of this way of speaking elsewhere in the gospel cp. 5[46f.], 7[6]; for Mt's own attitude, 8[11f.], 9[9–13], etc.

18. For the possible meanings of *bind* and *loose* see on 16[19b], which this verse virtually duplicates. Both in the immediate context of the disciplinary procedure and in the total context of this chapter's emphasis on the necessity of forgiveness, the reference here must be to excommunication and release from it. Is the saying addressed to a restricted circle, or to the disciples as representative of the whole church (as appears to be the case with the related version at Jn 20[23])? Probably the final responsibility of the assembled church for the sentence of excommunication (v. 17) extends to 'loosing' also, though that does not necessarily exclude a presiding role for an individual or group within it (cp. the role played—even *in absentia!*—by the apostle in 1 Cor. 5[4]).

19–20. A further distinct saying (note the introductory formula). The role of 'two or three' (cp. v. 16) is not confined to witness against the sinner; it can extend to intercession on his behalf. For similar sayings expressing confidence in prayer cp. Jn 14[12], 15[16], 16[13]. The ground of this confidence is the continuing presence of Christ in the midst of praying Christians conveyed by v. 20, a Christian variant on a well-known Jewish saying which is found in several forms, the most familiar being that ascribed to R. Hananiah b. Teradion (A.D. c. 135): 'If two sit together and words of law (are spoken) between them, the divine presence rests between them' (Mishnah *Aboth* iii. 2; Danby, p. 450). The Shekinah, or indwelling presence of God, is associated in the OT and Jewish tradition with the temple. It is presumably in consequence of the destruction of the latter that this saying transfers it to the synagogue (itself already understood—outside Palestine—as a means of spiritual communion with the worship of the temple) in its function as a place for the study of the Torah. Christian spiritualization of the meaning of the temple had begun earlier than this in some quarters; but Palestinian Christians apparently continued nevertheless to use it till its destruction. The fact that the Christian saying is so close to the Jewish, with Christ substituted for both Torah and Shekinah, is a sign that both communities were, in their different ways, reacting to the same situation. The thought of Christ as himself mediating the divine presence is important to Mt, since it is the note on which the gospel begins and ends (1^{23}, 28^{20}; cp. also Jn 1^{14}, 2^{21}, Rev. 21^3 NEB).

18: 21–22 (ii) Personal forgiveness

The existence of provisions for church discipline declares that there are limits to the church's public tolerance of scandalous conduct by its members. Where personal grievances between individuals are concerned, however, there is no point beyond which forgiveness ceases. *seventy times seven*: the Gk can equally well mean 'seventy-seven times' (so mg), and on this interpretation alludes to and reverses Gen. 4^{24}: 'If Cain is avenged sevenfold, truly Lamech seventy-sevenfold'.

18: 23–35 (iii) The judgement on the unforgiving: the unmerciful servant

The parable follows closely on the instruction on personal forgiveness, and its basic lesson, stated at v. 35, is that of the petition for forgiveness in the Lord's Prayer and the comment following it at 6^{14}; only those who have forgiven others can expect forgiveness for themselves. But it also forms the conclusion to the whole discourse, and this implies that the whole discourse has been about forgiveness, taking that to include mercy (cp. 5^7) and refraining from judgement (cp. $7^{1f.}$). The unmerciful servant was at fault not only in refusing to forgive his debtor, but in forgetting that the two of them stood in the same relation to the king, and in exacting strict justice where the king had waived it. Since all are equally under judgement, those who pass judgement on others are not only 'playing God' towards their fellow-men, but doing so in a way which ignores that his 'property is ever to have mercy and to forgive'.

On the details of the parable see Derrett, *LNT*, pp. 32ff.; Jeremias, *PJ*, pp. 210ff.

23. *settle accounts with his servants*: the servants have obviously (as in the parable of the talents, $25^{14ff.}$) been entrusted with big financial responsibilities, and the amounts quoted reveal that their business is tax-farming; i.e. they are not slaves but ministers of the king.

24. *ten thousand talents*: it is impracticable in a period of rapidly mounting inflation to offer a modern monetary equivalent; it will suffice to say that as one talent was equivalent to a little over 5000 *denarii* (a *denarius* being a day's wage; cp. on 20^2), the first servant owed the king more than 500,000 times as much as he was himself owed by the second. NEB 'whose debt ran into millions' conveys the general sense admirably. The figures are not for all that to be dismissed as fantastic. Josephus (*Ant.* xii. 176) mentions the case of a man who contracted

166

to raise 16,000 talents in taxation and defaulted, and the figure is not unparalleled; see Derrett, *LNT*, p. 36n, against Jeremias.

25. Selling up a man and his family for debt (like imprisonment for it in v. 30) was unknown in Jewish law, but was common practice in the non-Jewish systems under which most Jews had to live.

27. *debt*: the Gk really means 'loan', and the time to pay that the minister has asked for, really involves a loan of the sum owing from him, to be repaid with the following year's assessment.

28. It need not be assumed that what the second servant owed the first was a private and personal debt; it could equally well be a sum owed in taxation. In that case the determination of the first servant that the king's interests shall not suffer in consequence of his leniency is both psychologically plausible, and significant for the application of the parable.

34. *jailers*: lit. 'torturers' (see mg). Examination by torture was regularly practised in the ancient world in this sort of case, as a means of discovering a man's total assets and of putting pressure on his relatives and friends (who would be held morally responsible if he died in the process); cp. Jeremias, *PJ*, pp. 212f.

35. Mt's own conclusion, the converse of that at v. 14. The infinity of debt means an eternity of punishment (cp. 5^{26}, $25^{30,46}$); the only way out is forgiveness, and this is what the Father wills (v. 14), but the unforgiving have foreclosed it by their own action.

3. REJECTION IN JUDAEA: THE JUDGEMENT FORESHADOWED (CHAPTERS 19–25)

Mt's new section is marked by a change of scene. It begins with his move from Galilee into Judaea (19^1); the central part is concerned with the entry of the Son of David into Jerusalem, David's city; it will end with the lament over the city and the prediction of its desolation (23^{37-9}). The final phase of Israel's rejection of Christ is to take place on its home territory.

The section as thus defined is however controlled less by geographical interest than by its emphasis on Christ the teacher. The Sermon on the Mount has already shown Jesus teaching 'with authority and not as their scribes' (i.e. as Messiah, 7^{28}) a righteousness which is to 'exceed that of the scribes and Pharisees' (5^{20}). 19^1–20^{16} recapitulates some of the points in which he does so. His action in the central part (20^{17}–22^{46}) is a claim to authority (as Messiah and prophet) which is at once challenged by the religious authorities. The consequence of this is the great denunciation of scribes and Pharisees, the teachers of the old Israel, who are held responsible for its condemnation.

19: 1–20: 16 *The Greater Righteousness*

Mt has shaped the material which lay before him in Mk and the tradition into the following (chiastic) pattern:

(1) Public teaching on marriage: general prohibition of divorce; 19^{3-9}.

(2) Private teaching on marriage; renunciation for some; 19^{10-2}.

(3) The kingdom is for the childlike (i.e. the humble); 19^{13-5}.

(4) Private teaching on wealth: renunciation for some; 19^{16-22}.

(5) Public teaching on wealth: its dangers for all; 19^{23-6}.

Conclusion: the reward of a disciple; $19^{27}-20^{16}$.

19: 1–9 (1) Public teaching on marriage: general prohibition of divorce: cp. Mk 10^{2-12}.

The way in which Mt has modified the pattern of Mk is analysed by Daube (*NTRJ*, pp. 143ff.). Mk's sequence is the familiar rabbinic one of (i) public question, (ii) public answer (enigmatic), followed by (iii) private request for elucidation, (iv) private answer (explicit). Formally Mt follows this pattern also, but he has rearranged the content; the assertion that the marriage of divorced persons is adultery is now (with an exceptive clause added) made part of the public answer, and the saying about eunuchs is introduced as the private elucidation.

Why has Mt done this?

(a) Whereas Mk's version is a self-contained unit, Mt, as shown above, makes his part of a larger whole, which is concerned with the distinction between what the gospel explicitly requires from all and the specific demands which for reasons of personal vocation or sheer spiritual prudence it may make on individuals (see further on v. 21 below).

(b) The background to the dispute is the interpretation of Dt. 24^1, which allows (does not prescribe, though Jewish practice came to take it that way) divorce in the case of 'some indecency' being found in the wife. The rabbis disputed the scope of this. Shammai restricted

it to adultery; the more liberal Hillel allowed it to cover compara-
tively trivial matters like bad cooking. The attitude of Shammai was
dominant in the Palestine of Jesus' time, and Mk's account represents
Jesus as dissociating himself from both parties to the dispute and
going behind them to the positive teaching of the Torah about the
nature of marriage. But the neo-Pharisaic Judaism with which Mt
was familiar had come to be dominated by the views of Hillel, and in
that situation an adherence to the position of Shammai would have
sufficed to mark the righteousness of Christians as 'exceeding that of
the scribes and Pharisees'.

(c) We have seen that for Mt Jesus as Messiah offers not a new
Torah but a new interpretation of Torah, and that at 12¹ᶠᶠ·, 15¹ᶠᶠ·,
he modifies Marcan passages to avoid any suggestion of the abrogation of the written Torah or of contradiction between passages in it.
The same considerations appear to be at work here. Where Mk starts
with the Deuteronomy passage and implies that it is contradicted by
the Genesis passage, Mt starts with the Genesis passage as the basic
principle, and then emphasizes that the Deuteronomy passage is a
grudging permission and not a commandment.

(d) The distinctive position of the Christian Church on the subject of
divorce would by Mt's time have been well enough known to make a
special private counsel to disciples about it seem pointless.

(e) It is possible that pastoral considerations were in part responsible
for the introdution of the exceptive clause *except for unchastity*, but its
presence is better explained as a harmonization of the passage with
5³¹ᶠ·, which for him had equal authority as a saying of the Lord.

3. *and Pharisees came up to him:* most MSS. of Mk 10² have an equivalent
expression, but there is reason to suspect that it was not in the original
text of Mk. If it is Mt who has introduced it here (and the phrase is
characteristic of him), it is significant both for the scope of his discussion of divorce and for the context in which he has placed it (see
p. 166).

4–5. Gen. 1²⁷ followed by 2²⁴ (corrected by Mt in accordance with the
LXX text).

6. *man:* i.e. (in a Jewish situation) the husband.

7–8. Jesus' interlocutors here take Dt. 24¹⁻⁴ as a commandment of the
law. The point of Jesus' reply is that it is not really in the spirit of the
law, but an unwilling permission of which men would do better not
to avail themselves.

9. *except for unchastity:* Mt derives this exception from the form of the
saying preserved by him at 5³², but the wording in which he reproduces it here is more unambiguously a ground for the dissolution of
marriage. See on 5³² for the possible meanings of *unchastity;* the
background of the Shammai–Hillel dispute makes it probable that
Mt has understood it to mean (or, at any rate, include) adultery.

The addition in the mg 'and he who marries a divorced woman commits adultery' seems to have crept in in some MS. traditions from 5[32].

Jesus' own teaching on marriage, and the lines on which it was developed in the early Christian tradition, are discussed in Note D, p. 248.

19: 10–12 (2) Private teaching on marriage: renunciation for some

The public requirement on the Christian disciple is thus the *intimate* maintenance of the Lord's ruling on the permanence of marriage. The *knowing* private, interior demand on his heart is the subject of a further question and answer: it is a matter of personal calling and gift, but can involve for some a life of celibacy (cp. 1 Cor. 7[7]).

11. *this precept* (lit. 'this saying'): does this refer to the ruling at v. 9 or to the disciples' objection at v. 10? If the former, what follows must be understood either as restricting the application of that ruling to those who are capable of rising to it, or (with J. Dupont) as a severe assessment of the situation of those whose marriage has broken down; neither of these is at all probable. If, as seems more natural, the reference is to the comment *it is not expedient to marry*, Jesus' answer implies that there is truth in this, but that everything will depend upon the motive. In any case Mt has constructed an artificial setting for the saying at v. 12.

12. *eunuchs*: Dt. 23[1] excludes eunuchs from the community of Israel; but later Jewish teaching distinguished between those congenitally defective and those mutilated by men, and limited the application of the text to the latter. Jesus' answer maintains this distinction, but adds a third category, those who voluntarily refrain from marriage. *made themselves eunuchs*: the figurative use of the word is harsh and unexpected in view of the general Jewish contempt for eunuchs (cp. the paraphrase in NEB which avoids it altogether). J. Blinzler (see R. Schnackenburg, *Moral Teaching of the NT* (ET London, 1965), p. 49) argues that it was originally a term of abuse by Jesus' Jewish opponents (cp. those found at 11[19]) and that his own positive use of it was a retort to this. Jesus' own abstention (so far as the records, which cover only the period of his ministry, take us) from marriage, though not absolutely unknown for a rabbi (at least one remained unmarried in order to devote himself solely to the study of the Torah), certainly ran completely counter to the Hebrew tradition as a whole, which set the highest valuation on marriage and procreation (see Gen. 1[28]). The true reason for it, as the tenor of his demands on others shows, was the urgency of his mission to proclaim the kingdom; but such a departure from Jewish norms was bound to attract misunderstanding and abuse. Thus, while it is not impossible that the controversy which produced the saying was later than the time of Jesus, a setting within

his own ministry is quite as feasible. In addition to his own example and that of disciples who followed his lead, he could have pointed to the practice of celibacy in the Essene communities which was also eschatologically motivated (see Davies, *SSM*, pp. 393ff.). *for the sake of the kingdom of heaven:* not in order to attain to the kingdom (i.e. not as a form of asceticism), but either as a sign of its transcendence of earthly institutions (cp. 22³⁰) or as a committed response to the missionary demands that it makes. A negative fear of commitment to the obligations of marriage (see v. 10) is not an adequate motive for celibacy. *He who is able:* almost equivalent to 'the strong' (cp. Davies, *SSM*, p. 395). Does this imply a 'double standard' of Christian practice? See on v. 21 below.

19: 13–15 (3) The kingdom is for the childlike: cp. Mk 10¹³⁻⁶

The original situation of this story may well have been a conflict between the demands of the itinerant preaching ministry of Jesus and his followers and normal family life. Mt's insertion of the saying about eunuchs seems to recall his readers to the original point, but this is not necessarily his intention. A childlike attitude has already been demanded of disciples at 18³, and 18⁴ interprets this as humility (cp. 5⁵). 18³ is a variant of Mk 10¹⁵, which Mt accordingly omits from the present context, leaving v. 14b as its climax.

13. *lay his hands on them and pray:* Mt's alteration of Mk brings Jesus' action into line with the Jewish practice of taking children to a rabbi to have his hands laid on them, which was interpreted not as conferring a blessing, but as asking one from God.

19: 16–22 (4) Private teaching on wealth: renunciation for some: cp. Mk 10¹⁷⁻²²

The main question about wealth, in contrast to that about marriage, is asked not by a group but by a single individual privately; i.e. it is about personal vocation. This may be simply a matter of formal arrangement, or dictated by the order of the material in Mk; but it may also imply that whereas marriage is a divine institution and renunciation of it for the few to whom it is given, wealth is always a grave risk to discipleship, and renunciation of it may well be the most prudent course for the majority.

16–17. *what good deed:* in Mk's version Jesus himself is addressed as 'Good Teacher', to which he replies bluntly 'Why do you call me good? No one is good but God alone'. Mt finds this too ambivalent for his more explicit understanding of Jesus as divine; he therefore shifts the emphasis from the person of the teacher to the kind of action which merits salvation, a familiar subject of debate in Judaism.

19. *You shall love your neighbour as yourself:* Lev. 19¹⁸, added by Mt. At 22³⁹ᶠ· it is bracketed with the commandment to love God with the

whole heart as the two precepts on which the whole law depends.
Mt sees love of neighbour as belonging with nos. 5–9 of the Ten
Commandments. Love of God is, evidently, represented by the first
four. But Mt's list significantly stops short of the final commandment not to covet, which is a matter not of outward observance but
of interior conformity to the spirit of the law; this is part of what is
meant by purity of heart (see on 5⁸·²⁸). Thus the commandment to
love one's neighbour points beyond itself to the total love of God.

21. *If you would be perfect:* Mt omits Mk's statement that Jesus 'loved' the
man, which implies that the call to leave everything and follow him
was a mark of special favour, and instead makes him offer a spiritual
incentive. The meaning of *perfect* (Gk *teleios*) is determined by its
previous use at 5⁴⁸ (addressed to all disciples), where the expression is
virtually equivalent to 'pure in heart'. A formal observance of the
commandments of the law is here contrasted with single-hearted
devotion to the will of God.

Is a double standard of Christian practice implied here, one level
for the ordinary disciple and another for the *élite*, as later Christian
exegesis has often inferred? Mt seems to accept that there will be
differing levels of performance, but a double standard of demand is not
consistent with 5⁴⁸ or with the Sermon on the Mount as a whole.
The demand of Christ for radical conformity to the will of God is
addressed to all alike; it is recognized that many will settle for less,
and they are not therefore necessarily excluded from the kingdom, but
it does not follow that less was asked of them in the first place. Nor is it
implied that all who would be 'perfect' must sell their possessions; the
demand will take different forms with different individuals, and it was
because the young man's wealth was dividing his heart, as the sequel
shows, that he was called upon to give it up. Some can maintain
poverty of spirit without becoming materially poor; those who
cannot are only able to attain purity of heart by giving up what they
have.

(The command to be 'perfect' is thus directed to all, and does not
in itself express a double standard. Mt does envisage for some a special
call to celibacy, but this is not a matter of 'perfection', but of total
availability for the work of the kingdom.)

treasure in heaven: cp. 6²⁰.

22. *young man:* only Mt calls him this. The fact that Mt's additions
include both this word and 'perfect' in v. 21 suggests that he has in
mind Ps. 119⁹ᶠ·: 'How can a young man keep his way pure? By
guiding it according to thy word. With my whole heart I seek thee;
let me not wander from thy commandments!'

19: 23–26 (5) Public teaching on wealth: its dangers: cp. Mk 10²³⁻⁷

The preceding incident has made clear that for Jesus (as interpreted by Mt) wealth can be a grave obstacle to a man's spiritual progress and even a risk to his salvation. The lesson is now spelt out for disciples in general. For a rich man to keep his riches and enter the kingdom is not absolutely impossible, but it is the exception, possible only by the grace of God (and thus a kind of negative parallel to the renunciation of marriage at vv. 10–2).

Mt appears to be writing for a relatively affluent community; cp. 6[19–21,24ff.], 13[22].

24. *for a camel to go through the eye of a needle:* various attempts have been made to tone down the grotesqueness of this image; a few inferior MSS. have the reading *kamilon* ('a ship's cable') for *kamēlon* ('a camel'), and it has also been suggested that 'the needle's eye' was the name of a small wicket-gate in Jerusalem. On the other hand a Jewish proverbial reply to a tall story known to the rabbinic tradition runs: 'You clearly come from Pumbeditha, where an elephant can go through the eye of a needle' (quoted by Filson, ad loc.); and many of our Lord's illustrations have what G. K. Chesterton called this 'gigantesque' quality. *kingdom of God:* not altered by Mt (unusually for him) to 'kingdom of heaven' (contrast v. 23 above). Possibly this is in order to preserve the correspondence with v. 26. The kingdom is God's and not man's, and the decision about who are to be admitted to it rests finally with him and not on human achievement (see following parable).

19: 27–20:16 Conclusion: the reward of a disciple: cp. Mk 10[28–31]

Peter, on behalf of the twelve, enquires whether the call to give up 'everything' (i.e. both relationships and belongings) carries with it a differential in reward. Jesus replies (i) that those who make this response will share as assessors in his work of judgement (i.e., they will be judges instead of judged) (v. 28); (ii) that they will be compensated many times over for what they have given up (v. 29); (iii) that this must not be taken to imply that the original disciples have a privileged position over or against their successors (19[30]–20[16]).

28. Mt's addition, and in its present form probably constructed by him. Cp. Lk 22[30] for part of it. *new world:* the Gk *palingenesia* ('regeneration', 'new birth') is found in the NT only at Tit. 3[5], where it is used of baptism, and here, where the reference must be to the 'new era' of Jewish speculation; cp. Is. 65[17], 66[22], and see Manson, *SJ*, pp. 216f., for Jewish views of what might be expected. Stoicism, which taught a periodic reconstitution of the universe after its destruction by fire, may have contributed the word, but hardly the meaning. *Son of man . . . throne:* cp. I *Enoch* lxii. 5: 'When they shall see that Son of man sitting upon the throne of his glory' (it is uncertain which writer is dependent on the other). The words are repeated at 25[31] in the context of the great assize, which makes it clear that it is the

final judgement that Mt has in mind and not the day to day government of the Christian Church. *sit on twelve thrones:* Dan. 7⁹ speaks of
'thrones', and the rabbis interpreted this to mean that righteous
Israelites would share in the judgement. This is already part of the
Christian understanding of the return of Christ at 1 Cor. 6²ᶠ·. *twelve
tribes of Israel:* this for Mt must mean the new Israel, since he regards
the judgement of the old as already executed (cp. 23³⁷⁻⁹, 27²⁵). It
does not follow, for Mt at least, that because the tribes are twelve the
assessors are limited to the original twelve disciples.

29. Slightly altered from Mk 10²⁹ᶠ·. *an hundredfold:* 'manifold' (RSVmg)
is to be preferred.

19: 30–20:16 The labourers in the vineyard.

The starting-point for this concluding illustration is 19³⁰ (already in
Mk), which is repeated in an inverse form at 20¹⁶. The two verses serve
as parentheses to enclose a parable not constructed for this context,
which has as good a claim as any to be regarded as an authentic
parable of our Lord. There is an interesting rabbinic parallel:
  ' "And I shall be free for you". To make a comparison, what is this
like? It is like a king who hired many labourers, and there was one
labourer who worked for him a long while. The labourers came in to
get their pay, and that labourer came in with them. The king said to
him, "My son, I shall be free for you (in a moment)". These many
labourers are those who did little work for me, and I am giving them
little pay, but as for you, I have a large account to settle with you'.
(*Sifra* xxvi. 9; see Morton Smith, *Tannaitic Parallels to the Gospels*,
JBL Monograph Series, vi (Philadelphia, 1951), pp. 51ff.).
  Sifra goes on to interpret this of the Gentiles (the short-time
workers) and Israel (the large account), and this thought may be
present in Mt's inverted version also. But if the parable goes back to
Jesus himself, the original reference would have been rather to the
tax-collectors and other outcasts (cp. 21³¹ᶠ·). The differences between
the Jewish and the Christian parable are as significant as the correspondences, and, together with the fact that it is the Jewish version
which is true to the ways of the world, suggest that Jesus may have
been deliberately contradicting the teaching of the Pharisees by
reference to a parable which expressed it. For them the good observant
Jew had a right to preferential reward; for him the kingdom is
offered to all, whatever their past record, who will by repentance
receive it (cp. 18³).
  For Mt it conveys (a) the paradoxical character of reward in the
Christian scheme; (b) that Christians of his own day, and recent
converts, are on an equal footing with foundation members; there
are no grades of discipleship; and, possibly (c) the equality of Gentile
with Jew in the Christian Church.

20: 2 *denarius:* cp. RSVCEmg 'a day's wage for a labourer' (in our Lord's time its value was a generous day's pay). The point of the parable depends on this.

15. *do you begrudge my generosity:* lit. 'is your eye evil because I am good?' (so mg); cp. for the evil eye, 6²²ᶠ·, and for the impartial goodness of God, 5⁴⁵.

16. This verse, since it repeats 19³⁰, is an example of *inclusio*, and since it does so with the members in inverse order, of *chiasmus* as well.

20:17–22:46 *Jesus the Son of David*

20: 17–28 The passion foretold: cp. Mk 10³²⁻⁴⁵

The last of the three predictions of the passion in Mk, and the episode of the sons of Zebedee that goes with it, are used by Mt as the introduction to the entry of Jesus into Jerusalem. That he has chosen to open his account in this way is a reminder that though, symbolically, it was the coming of the Messiah to his own, in actual fact it was a journey that ended in his death, and that the true vindication and recognition of his Messiahship lie the other side of this.

17. *Jerusalem:* Mt's first reference to Jesus' destination, though he has been in Judaea from 19¹. From now on until 23³⁹, the holy city and its role in his rejection will be in the centre of the picture.

20. Mt has transferred the initiative of the opening request from the sons of Zebedee to their mother; probably in view of the preeminence conferred on Peter at 16¹⁸, which the other disciples could hardly be represented as not recognizing.

22. *Are you able . . . drink?:* Mt omits the further question found in Mk 'or to be baptized with the baptism with which I am baptized?' Both expressions are images of suffering, and Mt continues to interpret the cup in this way (cp. 26³⁹); but he feels obliged to interpret 'baptism' literally, and to distinguish Jesus' own baptism, which was 'to fulfil all righteousness' and unique, from that of Christian disciples, which is for forgiveness of sins. Mt is unfamiliar with the Pauline doctrine of baptism into Christ's death (Rom. 6³ᶠᶠ·).

23. *for those for whom it has been prepared:* who these are is revealed at 27³⁸.

28. *to give his life as a ransom for many:* the only clue to Mt's understanding of these words is his addition to the word over the cup at 26²⁸. *many:* see on 26²⁸.

20: 29–34 The two blind men: cp. Mk 10⁴⁶⁻⁵²

Mt substitutes two men for Mk's Bartimaeus, possibly because he has omitted the healing of the blind man at Bethsaida (Mk 8²²⁻⁶). He has already used a more abbreviated version at 9²⁷⁻³¹; in both cases his schematizing tendency is at work (cp. Held, *TIM*, pp. 219ff., 223ff., etc.).

30. *Son of David:* characteristic of Mt's healing narratives (cp. 9²⁷, 15²²); in this context it also points forward to the following section, in which Jesus is acclaimed as Son of David in David's capital city.

21: 1–22 *The Son of David comes to his own:* three prophetic signs

21: 1–11 (1) The entry into Jerusalem: cp. Mk 11¹⁻¹⁰, Jn 12¹²ᶠᶠ.

All four gospels record the symbolic action of Jesus in riding into Jerusalem, but it is unlikely that any of them relates it just as it happened. Mt is, as usual, dependent on Mk; for the Marcan account and problems connected with it, see Nineham, *Mark*, ad loc. It is possible that Jesus' acting out of a Messiahship he was unwilling to claim verbally was less allusive than later Christian reflection on it—in the light of OT texts—has made it look; at the same time, the fact that no immediate action appears to have been taken either by the Jewish or Roman authorities, seems to indicate that as a public act it was relatively insignificant, as the number of Jesus' disciples would in any case suggest. All the gospels place it a few days before the Passover feast at which Jesus suffered. It is possible, however, that his ministry in Jerusalem was more extended than this, and certain features of the episode, especially the cutting of branches from the trees and the acclamation from Ps. 118, suggest either the feast of Tabernacles or, as F. C. Burkitt was the first to suggest, that of Dedication, the ceremonies of which were modelled on those of Tabernacles.

Mt spells out the significance of the scriptural allusions in Mk, and by his additions considerably enhances it. For him, Jesus by the actions of this chapter revealed himself, and was acclaimed, as the Messiah of the house of David (cp. 1¹⁻¹⁷), the true king of Israel; it was with full knowledge of this that his people finally rejected him.

1. *Mount of Olives:* cp. Zech. 14⁴, which popular Jewish belief connected with the coming of the Messiah (see Jos., *Ant.* xx. 169, *BJ* ii. 261f.).

5. *Tell the daughter of Zion:* quoted from Is. 62¹¹ (LXX). The remainder of the verse is a free version of Zech. 9⁹, which clearly underlies Mk's narrative, though he does not quote it. Mt's shortened form of the text (still further abbreviated at Jn 12¹⁵) concentrates on the designation of the king as *humble;* cp. 5⁵, 11²⁹ for the word, 2²³ and 12¹⁸ᶠᶠ. for its implications for Messiahship. Here it may carry the further connotation of 'non-violent'; to enter on a donkey was a sign of coming in peace, and Mt has rearranged the equivalents for 'ass' in the versions before him (the Heb. has three different words) so as to emphasize this. (The second word rendered *ass* in RSV really means a 'beast of burden', lit. 'subject to the yoke' (found also in LXX, though in a different position), and this recalls the language of 11²⁹ᶠ·; see below).

On the whole text see Stendahl, *School*, pp. 118ff., Lindars, *NTA*, pp. 113ff.

7. The prophecy quoted at v. 5 is written with the characteristic parallelism of Hebrew verse; it does not speak of two animals, but of one twice over. Mt, however, though he is perfectly familiar with poetic parallelism and himself writes in it on occasion, has taken it as fulfilled in the most literal way possible, with both ass and colt. The presence of the two is sufficiently explained on the grounds (i) that the good disciple obeys his master's instructions to the letter, especially where they are concerned with prophecy; (ii) that the only way to recognize an unbroken colt (Mk 11²) was to find it still with its mother. But there is still the problem of this verse. RSV's *thereon* (the animals or the garments?) renders an ambiguity in the Gk which could well have been intentional. Mt will hardly have meant anything so grotesque as that Jesus literally rode both animals; but he may yet be hinting that, symbolically speaking, that was what he did. The thought developed by Justin (*Dialogue with Trypho*, p. 53), that 'the ass is a symbol of the Jews yoked to the law, the colt of the unharnessed Gentiles' (see Lindars, *NTA*, p. 115) is by no means foreign to Mt's way of thinking, and suggests an explanation for what must otherwise remain a puzzle. The ride into the holy city which took Jesus to his death may also prefigure his taking possession of the kingdom that is to belong to him by virtue of his death (cp. 28¹⁸ᶠᶠ·). He will do this through the mission of those who bear his 'easy yoke and light burden' (11³⁰) and these will be recruited from both Jews and Gentiles.

9. A free quotation from Ps. 118²⁵ᶠ·. Mt has altered Mk to convey a more personal recognition of Jesus as Son of David. There is clearly parallelism between *Hosanna to the Son of David* and *Blessed be he who comes in the name of the Lord*. *Hosanna*: the literal meaning of the word is 'save now'. Mk however treats it as a greeting, and Mt not only retains but duplicates this. As it is highly improbable that he did not himself understand Hebrew, we have to conclude that the word had become so familiarized in Christian liturgical use (cp. *Did.* x. 6) that its original Hebrew meaning could be disregarded.

11. *prophet:* Jesus, who fulfils the OT prophecies (5¹⁷, 11⁵, etc.), is himself hailed as a prophet; and like the earlier prophets he is to die in the city he has just entered; cp. 21³⁵⁻⁷, 23³⁴⁻⁷.

21: 12–17 (2) The cleansing of the temple: cp. Mk 11¹⁵⁻⁷, Jn 2¹³⁻⁷

If the records of this approximate to what actually happened (which, e.g., Nineham doubts), it must have been quite as significant an act as the entry into Jerusalem, and much more provocative to the authorities. It can be seen both as a prophet's symbolic action and as a pointed challenge to those who had responsibility for the temple (the Sadducees; see Introduction, p. 22), and the latter aspect of it at least could have been construed as an extreme nationalist gesture.

Mt appears to play down its significance as compared with Mk; this is probably because the action signified judgement on the old Israel, and Mt reserves that theme for the denunciation of Chap. 23, which also takes place in the temple.

12. *temple:* the traffic took place in the outer court of the Gentiles. *money-changers:* as the only legal tender in the temple was the Tyrian tetradrachm (taken as the equivalent of the biblical shekel) it was possible to make a profitable business of the exchange of currency. But I. Abrahams, *Studies in Pharisaism and the Gospels* (London, 1917), i. 82ff., maintains that the trading was strictly controlled and on the whole fair. *pigeons:* required by poor people for sacrifices of purification; cp. Lev. 1¹⁴, Lk 2²⁴.

13. *My house . . . prayer:* Is. 56⁷. Mt's omission of the words 'for all the nations' (Mk 11¹⁷) does not imply any hostility to the Christian mission to the Gentiles, but only an *ex post facto* awareness that this part of the prophecy is to remain unfulfilled, since the temple will have been destroyed before they are gathered in. It may even carry a rejoinder to those who looked forward to a restored temple. *but you . . . robbers:* Jer. 7¹¹.

14–16. An insertion by Mt on the basis of OT texts, developing the theme of Jesus as the Son of David and his rejection as such by the leaders of his own people. The LXX of 2 Sam. 5⁸ makes David demand the slaughter of the 'blind and lame', and predict that they will not come into the house of the Lord. The Son of David, on the other hand, is found by them in the temple, and heals them there. The children's acclamation is introduced in order that it may be interpreted as a fulfilment of Ps. 8³ (LXX), i.e. the prophecy of David.

17. Mt alters Mk 11¹¹ᵇ to convey a very pointed rejection of the city, the temple and the Jewish authorities.

21: 18–22 (3) The cursing of the fig-tree: cp. Mk 11¹²⁻⁴,²⁰⁻⁶

Mk appears to treat this as symbolic of the rejection of Israel, and therefore narrates it in a kind of counterpoint with the cleansing of the temple which for him symbolizes in some sense the redemption of Israel. For Mt the latter event symbolizes only the rejection, and the interposition of v. 17 indicates that the lesson of the fig-tree is directed exclusively to the disciples. It is here simply a miracle story introducing sayings on prayer and faith (found already, in a more subordinate position, in Mk). The story, which is hardly characteristic of Jesus as it stands, may originally have developed out of a parable (cp. Lk 13⁶⁻⁹), but Mt describes it like any other miracle. Note the immediate fulfilment of the curse (deferred by Mk until the following day, probably for symbolic reasons) in v. 19, and the way this is taken up in v. 20 as the starting-point for teaching on the power of faith.

21. Mt here follows Mk, but he has used another version of the saying at 17^{20}. It must therefore have been originally independent of this context.

22. Mt assimilates this saying to the logion at $7^{7ff.}$, and thereby eliminates the awkward implication in Mk that those who believe that they have already received what they pray for, receive it in fact.

21: 23–22: 14 *The authority of Jesus and its rejection:* three parables: cp. Mk 11^{27}–12^{12}

In vv. 23–7 Mt reproduces Mk's account of the Jewish leaders' trap question and Jesus' avoidance of it virtually unaltered, except that he drops 'scribes' from the list of the questioners; as the question is not about matters of the law, their presence would have been inappropriate. But where Mk follows Jesus' answer to the question with the parable of the wicked tenants, containing a thinly-veiled threat of the disinheritance of the old Israel, Mt adds two more, making an ascending series of three: (1) The parable of the two sons $21^{28–32}$) represents the situation of Israel at the time at which Jesus was speaking; (2) that of the wicked tenants ($21^{33–46}$) represents the judgement on Israel within history (externally fulfilled in the destruction of Jerusalem); (3) that of the great supper ($22^{1–14}$) represents the final eschatological fulfilment, from which the old Israel has been excluded, but in which members of the Church which has superseded it cannot take their participation for granted.

21: 28–32 (1) The two sons

Vv. 28–31, to quote Manson (*SJ*, p. 222), 'present a very complicated textual problem, for they have come down to us in no fewer than three forms, each form supported by important manuscripts or versions. The three forms are as follows:

  (i) The first son says "No" and repents; the second son says "Yes" and does nothing. Who did the will of his father? The first.

 (ii) The first son says "No" and repents; the second son says "Yes" and does nothing. Who did the will of his father? The second.

(iii) The first son says "Yes" and does nothing; the second son says "No" and repents. Who did the will of his father? The second.'

(i) is adopted by RSV following AV and RV; (iii) is adopted by NEB following Westcott and Hort. (ii) cannot be reconciled with the context in Mt, unless the leaders deliberately give the wrong answer and Jesus' rejoinder condemns them rather than applies the parable, which is probably too subtle. (i) and (iii) say essentially the same thing, but Mt's recurring theme of the rejection of the original recipients of God's promise in favour of others makes (iii) preferable on formal grounds.

30. *I go, sir:* the Gk is *Kyrie* (Lord), and the reminiscence of 7²¹ probably deliberate.

31. *will of his father:* for this cp. 7²¹, 12⁵⁰. *kingdom of God:* in this context not simply equivalent to 'kingdom of heaven', but to be understood in line with its use at v. 43. There the kingdom of God (i.e. the present relationship of Israel to God, along with the promise that accompanies it) is to be taken away from the old Israel and given to a new nation; here the tax collectors and prostitutes have a better claim to represent it, even as it is, than the Jewish leaders, since they at least responded to the voice of God through his prophets (vv. 26, 32).

32. The parallel with Lk 7²⁹ᶠ· is not really close and has been overstressed. *way of righteousness:* cp. 3³,⁷⁻¹⁰.

21: 33–46 (2) The wicked tenants: cp. Mk 12¹⁻¹²

As presented by Mk, this parable is already a thinly veiled allegory of God's dealings with his people, culminating in what was actually to happen to Jesus at the hands of his countrymen. In this form it is certainly a later Christian construction; but scholars are divided over the question whether this was a completely fresh creation or adapted from an authentic parable of Jesus (for the latter view see Dodd, *Parables of the Kingdom,* pp. 124ff.; Jeremias, *PJ,* pp. 70ff.; and especially Derrett, *LNT,* pp. 286ff.). The answer to this question does not bear directly on the interpretation of Mt, who starts with the Marcan version as it stands and modifies the conclusion which Mk draws from it. For Mk the point of the parable is not that the vineyard was unfruitful but that the tenants were wicked, and killed the owner's son. For Mt it is rather that those who originally worked the vineyard did not produce the fruit expected of them, no matter who came to demand it, and therefore it must be handed over to others who will. As usual, Mk's interest is Christological, Mt's ecclesiological.

33. There is a strong verbal echo of Is. 5¹ᶠ·. Later Christian interpretation of a story about a vineyard could hardly forget that 'the vineyard of the Lord of hosts is the house of Israel' (Is. 5⁷).

35. The wording here is clearly reminiscent of 23³⁷, 'killing the prophets and stoning those who are sent to you', and establishes that Mt interpreted *servants* as the prophets; cp. especially Jer. 7²⁵. Whether he went further and interpreted the two groups of the 'former' and 'latter' prophets is more debatable. Probably he is more concerned for numerical tidiness; he has (as against Mk) three missions in all, with that of the son as their climax.

38. The point in Jewish law is (i) that three successive failures on the part of the owner to collect his share of the annual harvest (Mk mentions

three missions of servants) gave the tenants a case for claiming the vineyard as their own; (ii) this case would be strengthened in practice, if not in law, if they could dispose of the heir for whose benefit the property was being developed (especially if the landlord was an absentee). See Derrett, loc. cit.

41. cp. NEB: 'he will bring those bad men to a bad end'. *who will give him the fruits in their seasons:* a verbal echo of Ps. 1³ (LXX).

42. The quotation is from Ps. 118²²ᶠ·. The history of the use of these verses in early Christian apologetic is discussed by Lindars, *NTA*, pp. 169ff.

43. Added by Mt to convey his interpretation of the parable. *nation:* the Gk word used is not *laos*, which Mt uses, in no specially hieratic sense, for the Jewish people, but *ethnos*, which he elsewhere uses in the plural for non-Jewish nations. Here the reference is clearly not to a single nation but to the supra-national (but basically non-Jewish) Christian Church. 1 Pet. 2⁹ ('a holy nation') comes close to his meaning. The choice of word suggests that we should be cautious about attributing to Mt an explicit conception of the Church as the 'new'; or the 'true' Israel (the latter expression would for him be more appropriate to Christ himself; see Hare, *JPC*, pp. 153ff.).

v. 44 (mg) follows awkwardly on v. 43 (which mentions no stone), and most textual critics regard it as an interpolation from Lk 20¹⁸.

46. *prophet:* there is irony here in view of the fate of the servants in vv. 35f.

22: 1–14 (3) The great supper: cp. Lk 14¹⁵⁻²⁴

The concluding parable of Mt's series is not in Mk, but a simpler form of it is found in a different context in Lk. Features common to the two versions are: the feast as an image of the kingdom (a commonplace of contemporary Jewish expectation repeatedly used by Jesus), the refusal of those originally invited to come, and the substitution of others previously regarded as unsuitable. Jesus himself was in the habit of inviting 'tax collectors and sinners' to his table in anticipation of this Messianic banquet (see on 9¹¹, 11¹⁸ᶠ·), and a challenge to him from observant Jews over this could well have been met with a counter-challenge to the latter about their own reluctance to respond to his preaching. See Jeremias, *PJ*, pp. 178f., for the suggestion of W. Salm that Jesus is actually adapting a Jewish story in which the host was himself a tax collector, who sought acceptance with the men of influence in his city by inviting them to a great banquet, and when they despised the invitation responded by summoning the poor in their place.

Mt's version, however, has passed through a number of stages to reach its present form, and the *midrash* on Zeph. 1⁷⁻⁹ (based on variations between the received text and that of the Targum) suggested by Derrett (*LNT*, pp. 126ff.), may well have been one of them, though it is hard to accept his argument that it was the original one. According to this the banquet will celebrate victory in the holy war against the enemies of God. On this view of the parable, the incident of the wedding garment can be shown to be integral to it (see note), and most of the other details are internally consistent and need not be regarded as allegorical in their origin. The war-motif demands that the host be a king, and Mt has in fact depicted him as a typical Syrian minor ruler—even the military campaign against those who despised the invitation, incongruous as it sounds, is just credible in the light of these potentates' susceptibility to insult. Only in the detail that the feast is for a wedding (irrelevant to the heart of the story), and in allowing the punishment of the guest who came unprepared to shade off into the language of eternal torment, is Mt indisputably, as Linnemann puts it (*Parables*, p. 97), 'letting the "reality" part press into the "picture" part'.

Nevertheless, in the context in which he places it, Mt means the parable to be interpreted, like the preceding one, allegorically. Because those to whom the gospel came (the Jews) despised its invitation and suffered the consequences (as predicted at 21^{43}), others (i.e. Gentiles) are summoned in their place; but these are 'both bad and good' (v. 10), and failure to prepare themselves for the occasion will mean rejection for them too.

2. *a marriage feast for his son*: cp. 25$^{1ff.}$, Rev. 19^9.

7. *his troops*: does Mt mean this to be taken allegorically? If so, the Roman armies of A.D. 67–70 are regarded as the instrument of God; for OT parallels cp. Is. 10$^{5ff.}$, 44^{28}, Jer. 27^6.

11–14. The episode of the man without a wedding garment is usually regarded (as by Jeremias, *PJ*, pp. 187ff., Linnemann, *Parables*, p. 169) as a separate parable introduced into this context by Mt. But if there is a *midrash* on Zeph. 1$^{7–9}$, this incident is an integral part of it; cp. Zeph. 1^8: 'I will punish (lit. "visit") the officials and the king's sons and all who array themselves in foreign attire' (lit. 'strange clothing') (see Derrett, *LNT*, p. 127). *look at the guests*: an odd procedure, at first sight. The Targum on Zeph. 1^8 (see above) takes the word 'visit' in the weakened sense of 'inspect', equally applicable to a formal welcome of the guests and to an inspection of the military force with which they are identified on the 'holy war' view of the occasion. *wedding garment*: Mt calls it this in view of v. 1, but weddings were not treated differently in this respect from other festivities. 2 Ki. 10^{22} is sometimes cited, not very plausibly, in support of the view that each invited guest was provided with the appropriate garment, but Jeremias (*PJ*, p. 65) finds no evidence for such a custom in first century Palestine. The guest was expected to come in clean (preferably white) clothes; anything else (unless he had a valid excuse) would be an insult to his host (as in a similar parable attributed to R. Johanan ben Zakkai; see Jeremias, *PJ*, p. 188).

The motive for suggesting that the garment was provided was really a theological one, a wish to represent the righteousness with which the elect must be clothed as something 'imputed', not 'merited' (a Pauline thought not characteristic of Mt, who is very explicit, if also paradoxical, on the subject of reward). In fact the OT imagery of clothing and the language of reward go closely together (cp. Is. 61$^{8-10}$, Rev. 19^8, and see Linnemann, *Parables*, p. 169); and if for Mt himself the delinquent represents the Gentile convert, what is required of him is not a nominal adherence (cp. 7$^{21f.}$), but (as St Paul would have been the first to agree) to turn from his former way of life. The parable of R. Johanan (see above) is similarly concerned with repentance. *he was speechless:* i.e. he had no excuse to offer.

14. *many are called, but few are chosen:* (i.e. all are invited, but not all qualify for admission); an epigram doubtless originally independent of its context. The parallel often cited, 2 Esdr. 8^3, is not really close. For Mt the 'called' are those to whom the gospel preaching comes (vv. 3, 4, 8; cp. 13$^{18ff.}$), the 'chosen' those who actually enter the kingdom, who are by definition few (cp. 7$^{13f.}$). The gap between the two classes was a major problem for the apostolic Church.

22: 15–40 *The authority of Jesus vindicated:* three controversial answers: cp. Mk 12$^{13-34}$

For the way in which these illustrate standard rabbinic practice, cp. Daube, *NTRJ*, pp. 158ff. All are in Mk, and the first two are not significantly altered by Mt.

15–22 (1) The tribute money: cp. Mk 12$^{13-7}$

The evangelists present this as a trap question; a negative answer to it could be denounced as treasonable to Rome, while a straight affirmative would call in question God's sovereignty over his holy land and could thus be represented as compromising with the occupying power. If the questioners were in fact Pharisees (whose attitude to the Romans was, as a rule, by no means that of the followers of Judas the Galilean), their motive in asking must have been politics rather than theological controversy; the answer they got was in fact not far from their own position, and like them (or at any rate *ad hominem*), Jesus probably took a scriptural text as the starting-point for his ruling on a matter for which the Torah made no provision. Derrett (*LNT*, pp. 313ff.) takes up the suggestion of a number of Jewish scholars, that behind Jesus' answer lies Eccles. 8^2, in which the word 'king' could be (and in contemporary exegesis was) taken to refer, at different levels, both to the earthly ruler and to God. The ruling will then mean: obedience to Caesar in matters of civil government and administration (of which the law says nothing) is itself obedience to God; but where he has made his will known (primarily in the Torah) and particularly in any case of conflict between this and the demands of Caesar, God alone is to be obeyed. The suggestion of Dorothy L. Sayers (*The Man Born to be King*, p. 225; accepted by Bornkamm, *Jesus of Nazareth*, p. 123) that an analogy is intended between the image of Caesar on the coin, and the image of God in man, reaches a similar conclusion by a different route; money, and all thereby implied, may properly be paid in tax to the authority which issued it, but a man's whole self is owed to God.

For the historical background to the dispute, see E. Stauffer, *Christ and the Caesars* (ET London, 1954), pp. 112ff., and for the influence of Jesus' answer on early Christian attitudes to the state, see Rom. 13$^{1-7}$, 1 Pet. 2$^{13-7}$; also O. Cullmann, *The State in the NT* (ET London, 1957), pp. 51ff., T. M. Parker, *Christianity and the State* (London, 1955), pp. 18ff. That the first Christians were not more critical of the structures of contemporary society was unquestionably due to their imminent expectation of the end of the world; Nineham argues that this was in Jesus' mind also.

16. *Herodians*: taken over by Mt from Mk, probably without any clear understanding of who are meant; cp. on 16$^{1ff.}$. *regard the position of men*: lit. 'look at the face of men', a Semitic expression for impartiality. The literal meaning may be taken up in the question about the coin which follows.

17. *taxes*: the Gk word used is the equivalent of the Latin *census*, the poll-tax levied on all male inhabitants of Judaea, Samaria, and Idumaea from A.D. 6 (see Introduction, p. 26). A tax payable directly to Rome was in a quite different category, in Jewish eyes, from taxes paid to local rulers who might happen to be tributaries of the emperor.

19. *money for the tax*: a special silver *denarius* (see RSV mg) was issued for the payment of this tax. On a strict interpretation of the second commandment (Ex. 20^4) a coin bearing the head of a (possibly deified) emperor was an idol, but only a scrupulous minority of Jesus' contemporaries was prepared for the inconvenience of putting this into practice. His request indicates both his own readiness to handle such a coin, and his awareness that his questioners will have no difficulty in finding one (i.e. they cannot seriously mean to raise the issue of idolatry).

23–33 (2) The resurrection of the dead: cp. Mk 12$^{18-27}$

This question comes under the technical heading of *boruth* (vulgarity); i.e. it is a mocking question, designed to ridicule the beliefs of the rabbi questioned. Belief in resurrection was often a target for such questions (see Daube, *NTRJ*, pp. 159f.). The Pharisaic doctrine

184

of resurrection, with which Jesus here identifies himself, was more or less dominant in 1st century Judaism, but it was based on material from the extra-canonical writings, rather than on scripture; the Sadducees (see Introduction, p. 22), were conservative on biblical as well as on political matters, and rejected the idea of resurrection, as they did, e.g., that of angels (cp. Acts 23⁸) as unscriptural.

Jesus' reply falls under two heads:

(a) The doctrine of resurrection is not materialistic, and does not imply that the conditions of the future life will be merely continuous with those of life on earth (there is evidence that this was true of the rabbis also). From this premise it cannot be argued that the Torah by enjoining levirate marriage positively excludes resurrection, since the resurrection life has no place for marriage.

(b) The implications of the Torah, properly understood, positively demand resurrection, since God calls himself the God of the patriarchs who are no longer, in the earthly sense, living. The argument is *ad hominem* and rabbinic in form, and somewhat less than convincing to modern ears; the element of continuing truth in it is, as Loisy says, that 'God cannot have ceased to be the God of those who have served and loved him and been the recipients of his favour' (quoted by Nineham on Mk 12²⁶).

24. *Moses said:* Mk's reference is to Dt. 25⁵ᶠ·, but Mt has assimilated the wording to Gen. 38⁸ (the story of Tamar, ancestress of David and of Christ; cp. 1³). Judah's behaviour in that episode (supposedly narrated by Moses) was a breach of the later law revealed by God himself. The reader is meant to see the action of the religious authorities of the later Judah (Judaea) in referring to it as a witness against themselves.

The practice of levirate marriage, familiar from the Book of Ruth, is pre-biblical in origin; it had generally ceased before the first century B.C., but was not therefore banished from rabbinic arguments.

30. *angels:* a controversial point in view of the Sadducees' rejection of them.

32. Ex. 3⁶, the *ipsissima vox* of God (v. 31), as contrasted with Moses (v. 24).

34–40 (3) The greatest Commandment in the law: cp. Mk 12²⁸⁻³⁴

Mk relates this episode as a not unfriendly encounter between Jesus and a scribe; the latter is not identified as belonging to any particular party, and at the conclusion Jesus commends him. Mt on the contrary makes it the climax of three hostile questions put to Jesus; the interrogator is a spokesman for the Pharisees, and the purpose of the question is to 'tempt' Jesus, i.e. to trap him into an answer which could be used against him. For rabbinic Judaism all the precepts of the law were of equal weight and significance; there could be no question of greater and less. Jesus therefore declines to answer the question on its own assumptions; the texts he cites are not simply preferred above the rest, but seen as expressing the fundamental principle from which the law in all its detailed provisions derives. The substance of the answer is already in Mk and can be taken as a faithful reflection of the attitude of Jesus. For Mt it also sums up the sense in which Jesus' teaching is the final interpretation of the law (see introduction to the Sermon on the Mount, and cp. Barth, *TIM*, pp. 76ff.). It is thus appropriately placed at the climax of his dealings with the teachers of Judaism, immediately before his great denunciation of them, and as his final positive pronouncement on the subject of the law.

35. *a lawyer*: this word is uncharacteristic of Mt and has probably crept in through assimilation to Lk 10²⁵.

37. *You shall love . . . mind*: Dt. 6⁵. First century Judaism was at one with our Lord in its emphasis on this text, since it was embodied in the *Shema* recited daily by devout Jews (R. Akiba, tortured to death in A.D. 135 after the rebellion of Bar-Kokba, died with it on his lips).

The text cited differs from the independent version at Mk 12³⁰, without fully corresponding to the OT either at Dt. 6⁵ or at 2 Ki. 23²⁵. Possibly its form has been influenced by liturgical or catechetical use; see Stendahl, *School*, pp. 72ff.

39. *You shall love your neighbour as yourself*: Lev. 19¹⁸ (already cited at 19¹⁹). This text is found combined with the *Shema* also in the *Testaments of the XII Patriarchs* (*Test. Iss.* v. 2, vii. 6), but as it is certain that this Jewish work underwent Christian re-handling, its presence there does not rule out a dominical origin for the combination.

40. Mt's addition, and the key to his understanding of the pericope. *depend*: lit. 'hang', i.e. as a door on its hinges; a rabbinic image. *the law and the prophets*: Hummel points out how uncharacteristic this expression for the OT scriptures is of developed rabbinic Judaism, which preferred the tripartite division, law-prophets-writings. Mt's marked preference for the twofold summary (for which cp. Lk 16²⁹, 24²⁷, Jn 1⁴⁶, Acts 13¹⁵, 24¹⁴, 28²³) is significant for his theology. In the Sermon on the Mount he is concerned to uphold the true understanding of the law against those who subvert it in the name of prophecy (5¹⁷, 7¹⁵); the climax of his indictment of the Pharisees in the following chapter is their inveterate opposition to prophecy (23²⁹ᶠᶠ·).

22: 41–46 Conclusion: David's son is David's Lord: cp. Mk 12³⁵⁻⁷

Jesus has foiled three hostile questioners. Now he asks a question himself: How can David's Lord be David's son?, and with it has the last word. The substance of the passage is unaltered from Mk (on the question of its previous history see Nineham ad loc.); but the significance of its position at the climax of controversial activity in Jerusalem is enhanced by Mt's special concern in these chapters to present Jesus as the Son of David. Jesus has accepted the people's acclamation (21⁹; cp. 20³⁰ᶠ·), and by his actions fulfilled the Davidic type (21¹⁴⁻⁶). But he is not merely David *redivivus;* the Son of David (as already hinted in the parables, 21³⁷, 22²) is also Son of God (see Chap. 1). The Jews' inability to answer is for Mt an inability to accept Christ for what he really is.

44. Ps. 110¹ (universally, though incorrectly, attributed to David in Jesus' time; there is no reason why his human knowledge should be exempt from this limitation). The verse was a favourite proof-text of the exaltation of Christ in the apostolic Church (cp. 1 Cor. 15²⁵ᶠᶠ·, Heb. 1¹³, 10¹²ᶠ·, Rev. 3²¹). It is very possible that the whole passage had its origin in early Christian controversy arising out of this text.

23: 1–25: 46 *The Coming Judgement*

The immediate historical consequence of the rejection of Jesus by his people was the crucifixion, related in Chaps. 26–7. The long-term consequence (still within history) was the divine judgement on the people which rejected him. That is Mt's view of the significance of the destruction of Jerusalem in A.D. 70, and he conveys it by dividing his forecast of judgement to come into two phases: a judgement within history on the Jewish nation, and a final judgement of mankind which will come with the end of the world. In order to arrive at this construction he has expanded the relatively brief denunciation of the scribes at Mk 12³⁸⁻⁴⁰ with anti-Pharisaic material available to him in the tradition; and the omission of the episode of the widow's mite (Mk 12⁴¹⁻⁴) allows the 'apocalypse' from Mk 13 to follow immediately.

23: 1–39 I *The Judgement on Israel:* cp. Mk 12³⁷⁻⁴⁰, Lk 11³⁹⁻⁵²

The polemical tone of this chapter has tended to obscure the fact that, though it contains a blistering denunciation of the scribes and Pharisees, its final purpose is judgement rather than denunciation. As Hummel has written: 'In Mt's eyes God had already pronounced judgement. That was his justification for collecting everything from the tradition and experience of his church that could bear out the rightness of this judgement. Mt 23 is not only polemic but also interpretation of history'. (translated from *Auseinandersetzung* (see p. [xiv]), p. 89). The object of the judgement is Israel itself, symbolized by Jerusalem, the spiritual heart of the nation, but the guilty men who have brought it on her are the nation's spiritual guides, the scribes and Pharisees; so whereas the tone towards Jerusalem is reproachful (vv. 37–9), that towards the Pharisees is vituperative. They have failed as examples through their lack of integrity and humility (vv. 5–12); but they have failed also as interpreters of the law, through their preoccupation with its details to the neglect of its weightier matters (vv. 16–24), and above all through their unreceptiveness to prophetic insights (vv. 29ff.).

How far is this just, and how much of it goes back to Jesus? There is a certain ambivalence, so far as the records take us, about the relationship of Jesus to the Pharisees. On the one hand it is possible for P. Winter to claim that 'Jesus himself in his teaching stood closer to Pharisaism than to any other school of thought' (i.e. on those matters which distinguished Pharisees from other Jews) (*On the Trial of Jesus* (London, 1961), p. 120); and his opinion was clearly sought on questions of law. On the other hand he evidently fell foul of Pharisaic opinion through consorting with tax collectors and other outcast persons, through healing on the sabbath, and through declaring the forgiveness of men's sins; and the effects of these disputes are clearly discernible between the lines of his parables (see Jeremias, *PJ*, pp. 124ff.). However, the evidence of these suggests that what he criticized in the Pharisees was complacency and judgement of others (see especially the Pharisee and the tax collector, Lk 18[9–14], and the mote and the beam, 7[3–5]) rather than the insincerity and ostentation which figure so prominently in the collected anti-Pharisaic sayings of our present gospels. And the extreme bitterness of this chapter is out of character with what we can recover of the historical Jesus (though very much in line with the Johannine Christ; cp. Jn 8[39ff.]).

If then the voice that speaks here cannot be safely identified as that of Jesus of Nazareth, it is equally impossible to recognize in the portrait of the Pharisees that results the features of Mt's great contemporaries among the rabbis, such as Johanan b. Zakkai or Akiba; there is no room for greatness in it. Forty years of growing divergence followed by fifteen or so of bitter conflict leading to a point of no return have made genuine objectivity, let alone magnanimity, impossible on either side; and it is the way of controversy to magnify single episodes and localized shortcomings into standing and general grievances against the party held responsible. Yet, despite the distortions of fact, and the intemperance of the language (one has only to read the controversial writings of such outstanding Christians as Luther or Thomas More, to say nothing of the Fathers of the Church, to realize how recently religious controversy has come to be conducted with even elementary courtesy), there is a thread running through from Jesus himself to the situation of Mt's time and beyond. It was their zeal for the details of the law that blinded the Pharisees of Jesus' time to the prophetic and creative character of his infringements of it. Nobody who studies the later rabbinic writings can deny their continuing concern with *minutiae*, and this does not encourage us to expect any growth in openness to the claims of the prophetic. Yet is was only by appealing to the possibility of prophetic innovation that Christianity, in a Jewish setting, could hope to win a hearing. It is the failure of this appeal that Mt records and interprets in the light of the original rejection of Jesus.

23: 1–12 A. *The Introduction*

This section, which is an expansion of the short denunciation at Mk 12³⁸⁻⁴⁰, is addressed, like the parables discourse in Chap. 13, to the (uncommitted) crowds in the hearing of the disciples (contrast the Sermon on the Mount where it is the other way round). They are seen as the material from which the Church will be recruited (hence the instructions on discipleship, vv. 8–10). Jesus is addressing the future Church from a point at which it does not yet exist; already, from that point, he foresees the break with official Judaism which in fact only took place much later.

2–3. Jesus here apparently speaks with the voice of strict Jewish Christianity. No doubt this was the source from which Mt took the core of the saying; but from the fact of its inclusion it is often further inferred that he was writing for a church which had not yet broken completely free from the synagogue. This conclusion (which is in any case contradicted by 4^{23}, 9^{35}, 12^9, 13^{53}, etc.) is only necessary if one ignores the dramatic context of the passage. Jesus is saying—at a point before the parting of the ways—that the scribes and Pharisees are not impostors; their authority to expound the Torah has been a genuine authority, which, in so far as it is concerned with the word of God, still demands a hearing, but it is going to be forfeited on account of their unfaithfulness to its obligations. This is defined in the present context as a lack of integrity (in failing to practise what they preach, v. 4), and of humility (vv. 5–7; contrast the beatitudes on the meek and the pure in heart, $5^{5,8}$. Once again the righteousness of disciples is to surpass that of scribes and Pharisees); their shortcomings in the interpretation of the law itself are to be dealt with in the next section. *Moses' seat*: a reference to the interior of a synagogue, in which the rabbis and elders sat on a raised seat facing the congregation, which symbolized the teaching office exercised by them in succession to Moses. Cp. 5^1.

4. Mt uses this saying, which appears also at Lk 11^{46}, to modify the force of the instruction reproduced by him in v. 3 to do as the rabbis teach. Where the rabbis do not observe their own interpretation of the law, it cannot be treated as authoritative. This offers a basis for criticism of the oral 'tradition of the elders' (see on 15^2) which the original sense of v. 3 would have treated as sacrosanct.

5–7. The argument now shifts from the hypocrisy of the Pharisees to their ostentation; with v. 5, cp. 6^1. The basis of the passage is Mk $12^{38f.}$, but Manson (*SJ*, p. 230) argues that Mt is drawing on a parallel version of it. *they make their phylacteries broad*: a phylactery was a small leather box containing texts from the Torah, attached by a strap to the wearer's person (one on the head and one on the left arm). Broadening, if taken literally, can only refer to the strap, but this would not have given much scope for ostentation. However, the saying may really be concerned not with the objects themselves but with the length of time for which they were worn; wearing them was obligatory at the daily hours of morning and evening prayer, but the later rabbinic ideal was to wear them all day, and Mt may be attacking a movement in his own day to establish this. As the Heb. *tephillim* can mean both 'phylacteries' and 'prayers' (compare the history of the English word 'bead'), it has been argued (see Manson, loc. cit.) that Mt's version is a translation variant of Mk's *for a pretence make long prayers*; but he could equally well be interpreting Mk in the light of the Judaism he knew. *and their fringes long*: a similar problem arises. Mk has 'who like to go about in long robes', which attacks the scribes for wearing the voluminous outer garment which distinguished them from other people, not only at prayer time, when it was expected, but all the time. If Mt is offering, either from a different version or from his own knowledge, a more technical description of the practice objected to (which would suit his argument), the Gk word *kraspeda* is rightly translated *fringes* (implying the enlargement of the garment itself) rather than 'tassels' (i.e. those referred to at Nu. 15^{38}, Dt. 22^{12}).

being called rabbi: Mt's own comment on *salutations*, and his link with the following passage.

8–10. The three prohibitions in this section are all parallel and say substantially the same thing: the honorific titles affected by the scribes are not appropriate in a community of disciples. *rabbi:* the original meaning of this expression is 'one is great for you'. In Jesus' time it had not yet become a stereotyped form of address for teachers of the law (see Introduction, p. 30n.). Mt's form of the saying assumes this usage and challenges it, on the grounds that Christ is the authoritative interpreter of the law (5$^{2,17ff.}$), and all his followers are equally, and permanently, his disciples. *brethren:* the word is unexpected; 'disciples' would have been more natural. It may have been influenced by, or even displaced from, the following verse. *father:* This title, originally applied to the patriarchs Abraham, Isaac, and Jacob, came to be used, at any rate in retrospect, of a number of rabbis of the first and second centuries (see Manson, *SJ*, p. 232). It is here rejected as incompatible with the Christian emphasis on the unique Fatherhood of God, which derives from our Lord's use of *Abba* (see Jeremias, *PrJ*, pp. 11–65). *on earth . . . who is in heaven:* these appear to be explanatory additions by the evangelist, the latter very characteristic of him. Manson suggests that the original wording was: 'Call no one of your number "Father", for one is your Father'. This would improve the parallelism with the previous verse.

V. 10 seems to be a variant, for Greek-speaking Christians, of v. 8. *masters:* the Gk *kathēgētēs* is found only here in the NT, though cognate words are used by Josephus and Philo of the rabbis as interpreters of the law, which the parallel with v. 8 shows is the meaning here.

11–12. Mt here introduces sayings on the general theme of humility from traditional material available to him. With v. 11, cp. 20$^{26f.}$; with v. 12, Lk 14^{11}, 18^{14}.

23: 13–36 B. *The Seven Woes*

These are directed by Jesus at the scribes and Pharisees, but no change of audience is implied. They are denounced in the ears of the future Church. For Mt's literary model, cp. Is. 5$^{8-25}$, 10$^{1-4}$.

13. (1) Exclusion from the kingdom of heaven: cp. Lk 11^{52}

The most likely interpretation of this woe is that it reflects the working of the 'Test Benediction' (see Introduction, p. 29) which made it impossible for synagogue worshippers to be Christians as well.

16¹⁹ is probably to be seen as a Christian rejoinder to this (cp. Note C, p. 247).

(V. 14, printed in RSVmg, is omitted by the best authorities. It contains an additional woe based on Mk 12⁴⁷, but Mt has already used some of this material in his own way).

15. (2) Proselytizing activities

The bitterness expressed by Mt is that of a competitor. For the extent of Jewish proselytism in his time, see Hare, *JPC*, pp. 9ff., and the authorities there cited. *proselyte*: the technical expression for a convert who had undergone full initiation into Judaism, including circumcision. *twice as much a child of hell*: i.e. the zeal of the convert outstrips that of his instructor, a readily observable feature of conversion situations.

16–22. (3) Doubtful casuistry about swearing

The original form of this denunciation must surely date from the time when the temple was still standing, and may have been simply directed against dishonest casuistry (cp. 15³ᶠᶠ·); but Mt's indignation is clearly influenced by the rigorist Christian prohibition of all swearing (cp. 5³³⁻⁷).

Swearing by God (who is truth) guaranteed the truthfulness of the oath. But Jews of this period (and subsequently) were reluctant to name him. The usual way out of this dilemma was circumlocution, swearing by some object (heaven, the temple, the altar) commonly understood to stand for God; but it was possible by thorough equivocation to limit these to their strictly literal connotations (e.g. heaven= the sky, temple=the building) and so to evade the obligations of an oath sworn by them. Some rabbis denied the possibility of excluding God in this way; others who allowed it sought formulas that would eliminate it, such as the offering on the altar, or the gold of the temple.

The passage falls into seven closely-knit sections: (i) rabbinic ruling no. 1 (ii) refutation of it by a question (iii) rabbinic ruling no. 2 (iv) refutation of it by a question (v) counter-ruling to no. 2 (vi) counter-ruling to no. 1 (vii) ruling on a case not previously raised.

16. *blind guides*: see on 15¹⁴.

23–24 (4) Concern with trivialities: cp. Lk 11⁴²

The OT prescribed tithing only in respect of corn, wine and oil (Dt. 12¹⁷, 14²³). The scribal tradition extended it to herbs. Lk's version, which names only herbs which were never subject to tithing, seems to be reproaching the Pharisees with paying tithes which were not required of them, i.e. with a bogus piety; Mt's makes the charge one of preoccupation with minor obligations to the neglect of major ones. His retention of mint among the herbs mentioned is inconsistent with this, since it was never subject to tithing (whereas there is evidence that dill and cummin were); possibly he is conflating two versions of the saying, but he may simply have made a technical slip. *weightier*: not (in view of 11[30]) the more difficult matters, but the more important ones (in the sense of 22[36ff.]). *justice amd mercy and faith*: strongly reminiscent of Mic. 6[8], which itself stands in the context of a reproach to Israel. 'Faith' for a Jew was virtually equivalent to Micah's 'walk humbly with your God' (see Manson, *SJ*, p. 235). *straining . . . camel*: this remark has the ring of humorous exaggeration characteristic of our Lord's authentic sayings, but it is probably not in its original context; a rabbinic saying from the Talmud (*Shab.* 12a) 'he that kills a flea on the sabbath is as guilty as if he killed a camel' offers a clue to its original purpose. The gnat was regarded as unclean, and wine was therefore strained through a cloth before drinking.

25-26 (5) Priority given to external matters: cp. Lk 11[39-41]

The Pharisees' attention to the outside of the cup was based on the view that wine offered to God was holy and anyone coming in contact with it (through drops on the outside) became ceremonially impure. But the conventional addition of the *plate* (cp. 5[6] with Lk 6[21]) and the very strong language of v. 25b, as well as the sense of the following verse, make it clear that *cup* and *plate* are used figuratively of the scribes and Pharisees themselves, so that this woe is a return to the theme of hypocrisy.

27-28 (6) Whitewashed tombs: cp. Lk 11[44]

Palestinian graves were whitewashed annually, at passover time, to prevent accidental defilement of passers-by. Lk speaks of invisible graves, i.e. where the whitewashing has been neglected; this attacks the imperceptibly corrupting influence of Pharisaism. Mt may have adapted the passage to the theme of his two preceding verses—emphasis on the external; in his version the graves are whitewashed all right, but their outward beauty masks an inward rottenness.

29-33 (7) Persecution of the prophets: cp. Lk 11[47-8]

The scribes and Pharisees are here accused of failure to recognize prophets in their lifetime, for which they compensate by commemorating them after they have become part of the accepted tradition. Jeremias (see the summary in Hare, *JPC*, pp. 83f.) traces the practice of building memorial tombs to figures in Israel's past to the monument added by Herod the Great to the tomb of David. In that case it may well have been a controversial issue in the lifetime of Jesus himself. One motive for such constructions was certainly that of expiation for the sins of persecuting ancestors, and the ambivalence of this (were the builders identifying themselves with the prophets or with their ancestors?) was an easy target for the controversialist.

Mt sees in the scribal tradition, along with its preoccupation with matters of fixed law, a resistance to the element of creative renewal represented by prophecy in the tradition of Israel; it was this which, continuing the traditional hostility of Jerusalem to prophets, brought Jesus 'the prophet from Nazareth in Galilee' (21¹¹) to his death, and further prompted the rejection by Judaism of the mission of the Christian Church (cp. vv. 34ff., and 5¹²). *Fill up, then . . .:* the RSV rendering conceals a textual uncertainty. The imperative is the best attested reading, but the fact that v. 32 goes closely with v. 31, and in the original Gk is joined to it by the conjunction 'and', makes an indicative verb more likely. Both past (aorist) and future indicatives are found in the authorities; the former is better: 'Thus you witness against yourselves that you are the sons of those who murdered the prophets, and you have yourselves filled up the measure of your fathers'.

33. *brood of vipers:* cp. 3⁷, 12³⁴.

34–36 Conclusion: the judgement on Israel's representatives

The scribes and Pharisees are still addressed, but now in terms not of their past record but of their future response to the mission of the Church, which is seen as itself, through their foreseen rejection of it, inaugurating the judgement upon them. *prophets and wise men and scribes,* despite the echo of Jer. 7²⁵, must denote Christians. *scribes* are obviously distinct from those condemned with the Pharisees; they are also distinguished from *wise men,* the earlier designation of professional teachers of the law (see Introduction, p. 24), to whom some Christian counterpart could have arisen, though we lack other evidence of it. The convergence of the themes of wisdom and law in 11²⁵⁻³⁰ (with its model in Sir. 51) supports this interpretation. The fact that *scribes* appear in third place suggests, like 13⁵², the humbler role of transcribing texts or recording oral tradition. *prophets* have pride of place, as they usually do, after apostles, elsewhere in the NT (cp. 1 Cor. 12²⁸, Eph. 4¹¹); *Did.* x–xiii is evidence of the deference still paid to them at a period probably not far removed from that of Mt.

34. *some of whom you will kill and crucify:* on the treatment meted out to Christian missionaries see Hare, *JPC, passim,* and especially pp. 88ff. Since crucifixion was an exclusively Roman form of punishment, reserved for rebels against the empire, it is difficult to believe that Mt, even in the heat of indignation, would accuse the Pharisees of inflicting it on Christians. The verb is used causatively at Acts 2³⁶, 4¹⁰ of the Jewish instigation of Jesus' crucifixion by the Romans, but that concerns an actual case; we have no evidence of parallels. Only two minuscule MSS. actually omit the verb, but on internal grounds there is a strong case for its having been interpolated. *scourge in your*

synagogues: see on 10¹⁷. The wording implies (for Mt) the separation of Church and synagogue; cp. 4²³, 9³⁵, 12⁹, 13⁵⁴.

35. *innocent Abel:* rabbinic exegesis of Gen. 4¹⁰ represented Abel as a righteous man in the positive sense of the word. The NT reflects this; cp. Heb. 11⁴, 12²⁴, 1 Jn 3¹². However, the context, and Matthew's preoccupation with 'innocent blood' (cp. 27⁴·²⁴ᶠ·), are in favour of the RSV rendering. *Zechariah the son of Barachiah:* there appears to be confusion—or haggadic conflation—of two or three figures here: (i) Zechariah the prophet of the rebuilding of the temple, who was the son of Berechiah (Zech. 1¹·⁷) and comes near the end of the OT canon as Abel comes near the beginning. There is no tradition of his murder; but according to Manson (*SJ*, p. 104) later Jewish tradition was already identifying him with (ii) Zechariah the son of Jehoiada, murdered in the temple by the people (2 Chr. 24²⁰ᶠᶠ·), not really a prophet or a latter-day figure, but like Abel a type of innocent blood calling for vengeance, and the basis for a tradition of the martyred prophet as the type of the righteous sufferer; (iii) Zechariah the son of Baris (or Bariscaeus), murdered in the temple by Zealots, after a sham trial, shortly before the fall of Jerusalem (Jos., *BJ*, iv. 334ff.). A reference to him would be an anachronism on the lips of Jesus; if, however, the words attributed to him are really a threat of retribution on Israel or its temple, the tradition of the final case of innocent blood shed there may well have influenced the threat. Some scholars believe that the figure of the 'Teacher of Righteousness' of the Qumran sect has also influenced these words.

36. *come upon this generation:* the judgement which Israel's leaders and teachers have brought upon the nation will be executed within the lifetime of those addressed by Jesus. Mt clearly sees this as fulfilled in the events of A.D. 70, as the following section confirms, and the judgement of Israel therefore anticipates that of mankind as a whole

23: 37–39 C. *The Rejection of Jerusalem:* cp. Lk 13³⁴⁻⁵

Jesus' final words are addressed to the holy city itself. This moving lament marks the climax both of Mt's great denunciation and of the whole section beginning at Chap. 19 which contains Jerusalem's acclamation of its king and his cleansing of the temple. It is thus integral to its position in Mt (as it is not in Lk), and its oblique reminiscence of OT passages is characteristic of the specially solemn utterances of Jesus in this gospel (cp. 11²⁵⁻³⁰, 16¹⁸ᶠ·, 28¹⁸⁻²⁰). It convey's God's final abandonment of his people. Writing as he does after the destruction of Jerusalem and the failure of the Christian mission to Jews which continued beyond it into his own time, Mt sees both as 'concrete signs of the divine rejection which occurred at the time of the death of Jesus and the birth of the Church' (Hare, *JPC*, p. 155.

37. *killing the prophets and stoning those who are sent to you:* either the two halves are in synonymous parallelism and the whole reference is to the city's repeated rejection of the OT prophets, or, more probably, *those who are sent* is equivalent to 'apostles' in the technical sense (see on 10²), and the line draws a parallel between Jerusalem's treatment of OT prophets and its treatment of the spokesmen for Christianity. In that latter case Mt, or his source, may have in mind an episode such as the stoning of Stephen (Acts 7⁵⁴–8¹). *gathered your children:* the image is of a bird protecting her nestlings against attack by birds of prey, and may express either God's protecting presence in general (as in Ps. 91⁴, Dt. 32¹¹), or, more probably in this context, protection against impending judgement (for eagles as a symbol of this cp. 24²⁹).

38. *your house:* either the temple (as at 1 Ki. 9⁷), or the whole nation (as at Is. 5⁷). As the temple was the spiritual heart of the nation, and the rejection of the nation did involve, historically, the destruction of its temple, it is not necessary to distinguish sharply between the two. *and desolate:* omitted by some MSS. (perhaps by assimilation to Lk 13³⁵); if original, it may carry an allusion to Jer. 22⁵ᶠ·, which is actually addressed to the 'house' of the king of Judah as representing the nation.

39. *again:* Gk *ap' arti*, used again at 26²⁹·⁶⁴; in each case it expresses a decisive moment opening a new division of time (see next note). *Blessed . . . Lord:* this was Jerusalem's acclamation at the entry of Jesus as Messiah (21⁹); does its use here imply a last-minute repentance by Israel? The fact that the passage is a lament, and the exclusion of the 'sons of the kingdom' at 8¹², do not support this. Rather, as Hare puts it (*JPC*, p. 154), 'the abandonment is permanent. Henceforward the Messiah will no longer show tender concern for Israel; *ap' arti* Israel will only know him as judge'. That however applies to the nation. The conversion of individual Jews is clearly not outside the perspective of the gospel as a whole (see on the 'crowds' of 13², 23¹), and it would require a confession of faith in terms not far removed from the acclamation.

24: 1–25: 46 II *The Final Judgement:* cp. Mk 13

The fact that judgement has already been executed on the old Israel does not mean that its successor, the Church, can relax and forget about the prospect of judgement for itself. On the contrary, the backcloth to what God has already done for Israel in history is the judgement which he has prepared for the world as a whole, from which Christians will not be exempt. This is presented by Mt in the conventional form of an apocalypse.

Apocalypses, or advance disclosures of the last things, usually put into the mouth of one of the great figures of Israel's past (Enoch, Moses, Isaiah, Ezra, etc.) were a characteristic feature of one strain in late Jewish writing (see, e.g., D. S. Russell, *The Method and Message of Jewish Apocalyptic* (London, 1964); K. Koch, *The Rediscovery of Apocalyptic* (ET London, 1971); and the documents collected by R. H. Charles, *Apocrypha and Pseudepigrapha of the OT* (Oxford, 1913). Behind the often bizarre imagery in which the apocalyptists expressed themselves lay the conviction that since God is faithful to his people, the desperate plight in which they find themselves only makes his intervention on their behalf more certain. This involved the literary device of making the first stage of the prediction one that had already come about, with the implication that the rest is sure to follow and cannot be long delayed, whether this was taken as grounds for reassurance or for warning.

The most familiar of these compositions was that at Dan. 7–12, which owing to its privileged place within the OT Canon became the principal model for subsequent imitators, both Jewish and Christian (early Christianity shared the apocalyptic outlook, but took as its starting-point the resurrection of Jesus). Mk 13, which Mt had before him, puts an apocalypse into the mouth of our Lord, and a majority of scholars believe that this incorporates an earlier Jewish or Jewish–Christian apocalypse based on Daniel. (A comprehensive review of theories of the composition of the chapter is given by G. R. Beasley-Murray, *Jesus and the Future* [London, 1954]).

Mk's time-perspective was still short enough for him to see the recent persecution of his own church and the imminent (or recent) desecration and destruction of Jerusalem as part of the 'Messianic woes' inaugurated in the passion of Christ and shortly to culminate in his return. Mt's perspective has been stretched by the lapse of time and the failure of the earlier crises to usher in the last things, and he is therefore compelled to modify Mk in the following ways:

(a) There is now no correspondence between the events of the passion and those of the end (contrast Mk 13$^{35f.}$). For Mk the end is both 'here and now' and 'not yet'; for Mt it is only 'not yet'.

(b) The end is carefully distinguished from the destruction of the temple. The latter is no longer a part of the end, but an event in past history; its significance as the judgement on Israel has already been spelled out at 23$^{37-9}$. The apocalypse is not addressed to Jews. (On this see W. Marxsen, *The Evangelist Mark* (ET Nashville, 1969), pp. 198ff.)

(c) The church for which Mt wrote had apparently not known general persecution; its experience of martyrdom had been restricted to the treatment handed out to individual Christian missionaries (see Hare, *JPC*, pp. 96ff.). He therefore transferred the predictions of persecution which he found at Mk 13$^{9-13}$ to his section on the mission of the disciples, where they would be more appropriate; see 10$^{17-22}$.

(d) There is much greater emphasis on the period of waiting for the end, the danger of lukewarmness, and the need for vigilance—the theme of parables added by Mt at the end.

(e) The effects of the delay in the coming of Christ are counter-balanced by an intensified preoccupation with the thought of judgement to come (already raised in Chap. 13), which reaches its climax in the great canvas of the final assize at 25$^{31ff.}$.

The programme is built up as follows:
(1) Signs of the approaching end:
      (Warning against impostors: 24$^{4-5}$)
      World-wide disturbances: 24$^{6-8}$
      Hardship for Christians, and discouragement of many: 24$^{9-13}$
      Preaching to Gentiles throughout the world: 24^{14}
(2) Signs of the imminent end:
      The desolating sacrilege: 24^{15}
      Acute distress: 24$^{16-22}$
      (Warning against impostors: 24$^{23-8}$)

(3) The end:

Cosmic disturbances: 24²⁹

The sign of the Son of man: 24³⁰⁻¹

(4) Seven parables of warning:

certainty of fulfilment: the fig-tree: 24³²⁻⁵

suddenness: Noah's flood: 24³⁶⁻⁴¹

the need for wakefulness: three parables: 24⁴²⁻25¹³

the burglar in the night: 24⁴³⁻⁴

the good and bad slaves: 24⁴⁵⁻⁵¹

the ten maidens: 25¹⁻¹³

opportunities of making good: the talents: 25¹⁴⁻³⁰

service of Christ in his little ones: the great assize: 25³¹⁻⁴⁶

24: 1–3 The Setting

1. Jesus' departure from the temple has the same function as his entry into the house at 13³⁶; it marks off what is addressed to a mixed audience from what is reserved for disciples alone, and as at 13³⁶ it conveys a change not only of scene but of temporal perspective. Jesus has so far spoken to his own contemporaries about the historical future; he now speaks to Mt's contemporaries about the eschatological future.

2. *You see all these, do you not?:* better 'do you not see all this'. The Gk neuter plural, as Hummel points out, is an alteration of Mk and must refer, not, as Mk does, to the buildings, but to the content of the discourse so far, 'see' being used in a spiritual sense as at 13¹³⁻⁷. Thus this verse, like the preceding one, links the two halves of the discourse.

The tradition that Jesus had actually foretold the destruction of the temple may well be founded on fact; it seems to rest ultimately on the saying preserved in a garbled form at Mk 14⁵⁸ (par. Mt 26⁶¹) and independently at Jn 2¹⁹.

3. *Mount of Olives:* a reference, taken over from Mk, to Zech. 14⁴, which depicts the Lord as standing there on the final day, which this scene anticipates. *disciples:* in Mk these are the inner circle of four; in Mt there is no restriction, since they stand for contemporary Christians. *when will this be?:* the form in which the question is put in Mt makes it possible to separate the destruction of the temple, which is the starting-point of the apocalypse, from the end of the world. Mt by implication associates it with the troubles of his first phase. *sign:* see on v. 30. *coming:* Gk *parousia*, found in Mt alone of the evangelists,

and only in this chapter. Used in classical literature of the visit of a king to one of his remote dominions, it has by the later strands of the NT become a quasi-technical term for the return of Christ in the end-time. *close of the age* (Gk *sunteleia tou aiōnos*): Mt's characteristic expression for the final consummation (cp. 13$^{39f.,49}$, 28^{20})—possibly constructed by him from the phrase used in the parallel passage at Mk 13^4; though a Heb. equivalent is familiar from the DSS.

24: 4–14 First phase: signs of the approaching end: cp. Mk 13$^{5-8,13}$

6. *wars*: including for Mt the Jewish war, in which God's judgement on the Jewish nation was finally executed. *the end is not yet*: words taken over from Mk 13^7, but implying for Mt the prolongation of this first phase, in which his readers are presumed to be still living.

9. *Then they will deliver you up*: a residual summary of Mk 13$^{9-13}$, of which Mt has made fuller use at 10$^{17-22}$. The wording here suggests general unpopularity with occasional bloodshed rather than deliberate persecution; the persecutors must include Gentiles (*all nations*), without necessarily excluding Jews. It is not absolutely clear whether what is here predicted is for Mt's contemporaries a part of present experience, or of a genuinely eschatological future; but the details which follow seem to demand a 'present' interpretation for themselves and probably for the whole context.

10–12. These symptoms of discouragement are closely paralleled in the closing section of the Sermon on the Mount (7$^{13ff.}$) and in that of the parables discourse (13$^{36ff.}$), both of which are really addressed to Mt's contemporaries. For *fall away* (Gk *skandalizesthai*) cp. 13^{21} (also 18^6); for *false prophets* cp. 7^{15}; for *wickedness* (Gk *anomia*) cp. 7^{23}, 13^{41}. Barth (*TIM*, p. 75), sees a reference here, as at 7$^{15ff.}$, to an antinomian group.

12. *most men's love will grow cold*: Mt interprets the cooling of Christian devotion (love of God and love of neighbour as in 22$^{37-40}$) in his own time as a sign of the growing wickedness traditionally associated with the 'Messianic woes' in apocalyptic teaching. Cp., possibly, 6^{24}.

14. *this gospel of the kingdom*: expanded from Mk 13^{10}, but not transferred by Mt, with the rest of its Marcan context, to the original mission of the disciples, to which it would have been inappropriate. *as a testimony to all nations*: the response may be either positive (cp. 28^{19}) or negative (cp. v. 9 above). Since for Mt the mission to Israel is over (see Hare, *JPC*, pp. 164ff.) the *nations* are clearly the Gentiles, regarded individually rather than nationally (as at 28^{19}). The Gentile mission is now the Church's primary task and the principal reason that the *parousia* is delayed.

24: 15–28 Second phase: signs of the imminent end: cp. Mk 13$^{14-23}$

15. *desolating sacrilege . . . Daniel*: Dan. 11^{31}, 12^{11}

The original reference in Daniel is to the object set up on the altar in the temple at Jerusalem by Antiochus Epiphanes in 168 B.C. (1 Mc. 1⁵⁴), the climax of the actions which led to the Maccabean revolt. A similar attempt by the emperor Caligula in A.D. 40 to have his own statue set up in the temple, which nearly succeeded, may lie behind the Christian use of the text at Mk 13¹⁴, at any rate if Mk is using a source; his own use of it is too late for that and too obviously connected with the imminent (or recent) desecration of the temple by Titus and his armies. For Mt the text is scripture to be fulfilled, and his placing of it implies that so far it still remains unfulfilled. How he envisaged this fulfilment can only be guessed. His reference (explicit where Mk is deliberately obscure) to *the holy place* indicates that he continued to associate it with the temple site in Jerusalem. After the suppression of the Bar-Kokba rising (A.D. 135), the Romans did in fact erect a temple of Jupiter on the site; Mt, on the dating assumed for him in this commentary, cannot have known this, but speculation about such an eventuality could easily have been current in his day. He may also be using the prophecy to counter the expectation that the temple would eventually be restored; cp. on 21¹³, 28¹⁸⁻²⁰.

16–22. The suddenness and acuteness of the distress which follows is depicted by Mt in terms almost identical with Mk's.

20. *on a sabbath:* an insertion by Mt (or the tradition behind him). For Mt's own attitude to sabbath observance see on 12¹ᶠᶠ·. It would appear that the Christian community for which he wrote not only still kept the sabbath, but would not regard the emergency of the last time as dispensing from its observance. Heaven and earth have not yet passed away (cp. 5¹⁸), so the law remains in force.

21. cp. Dan. 12¹.

22. *those days . . . shortened:* see Dan. 12⁷ for the shortening of a week, (signifying a fixed space of time) to half a week (since if the tribulation ran to its full term, no human being would survive it). The *elect* are those destined to survive the trials and inherit the kingdom, the 'remnant' of Is. 7³, 10²¹.

26–27. Mt adds to Mk's warning of impostors at this stage a passage found also at Lk 17²³ᶠ·. Its meaning is that the *parousia* when it comes will be so unmistakable as to make any dependence on prophetic voices unnecessary.

28. A proverbial saying (cp. Job 39³⁰, and see Ehrhardt, *Framework of the NT Stories*, pp. 53ff.). The context would seem to demand 'vultures' rather than 'eagles', but despite RSVmg the Gk cannot mean this. The LXX translators nearly always rendered 'vulture' by 'eagle' possibly because the vulture was regarded as 'hateful to God and man'. In Roman times the association of the eagle with the standards of the Roman armies may also have made it a symbol of military destruction; cp. 2 Esdr. 11.

24: 29–31 Third phase: the end: cp. Mk 13²⁴⁻⁷

29. The cosmic disturbances which immediately precede the *parousia* are described by Mk, whom Mt follows closely, in language drawn from Is. 13¹⁰, 34⁴, and other prophetic passages.

30. *then will appear the sign of the Son of man in heaven*: Mt's addition, carrying several layers of meaning:

(a) *sign* gives a direct reply to v. 3, though, as we shall see, it answers the question 'when?' more explicitly than the question 'what?'.

(b) There may be a contrast intended between the delusive 'signs' performed by impostors (v. 24) and the unmistakable sign of the Son of man.

(c) The Gk word *sēmeion* is used in the LXX, in a number of prophetic texts, some of which Mt can be shown to have in mind here, to mean an 'ensign'—a signal mounted on a pole (as the brazen serpent was by Moses, Nu. 21⁸), usually on a hilltop as a rallying-point for those who see it. Thus Is. 13² connects the signal with the 'gathering' of scattered Israel, and Is. 18³, Jer. 51²⁷ link it with the trumpet for which Mt's primary source (quoted at v. 31, *a great trumpet*) is Is. 27¹³. This association of ensign with trumpet has persisted in Jewish liturgical usage; T. F. Glasson, who has collected the references noted here (*The Second Advent* (London, 1947), pp. 189ff.), quotes two instances from the *Jewish Daily Prayer Book* (ed. S. Singer, p. 48).

(d) Since however the 'sign' is to be seen in the sky (*in heaven*), it can only be, unlike the cross (cp. Jn 3¹⁴), an 'ensign' in a highly figurative sense. A 'sign in the sky' normally means a portent, e.g. in Rev. 12¹,³, 15¹. Cp. *Did.* xvi. 6 which has three signs, the first of which is 'a rift in the sky' (followed by the trumpet, as here, and then by the resurrection of the dead). This, however, could well be second-ary interpretation (cp. Mt 3¹⁶); Jerome's and Cyril of Jerusalem's understanding of it as the sign of the cross (perhaps influenced by the story of the emperor Constantine's conversion) certainly is.

Whatever the exact significance of the imagery, Mt clearly intended it to convey to his readers that both the visual and auditory signs of the Lord's coming would be too obvious to need interpretation. *and then all the tribes . . . mourn*: Zech. 12¹⁰ (added by Mt). *and they will see . . . glory*: Dan. 7¹³ (already in Mk). The composite quotation with its consonance between *will mourn* (*kopsontai*) and *will see* (*opsontai*) must either have already been in circulation or else have suggested itself to more than one writer, since it reappears at Rev. 1⁷; cp. Lindars, *NTA*, pp. 122–7.

31. The basic texts underlying this verse are Zech. 2⁶ and Dt. 30⁴ (both

already in Mk). For the *great trumpet* see (iii) above[1] and cp. also
1 Thess. 4[16].

The abruptness with which this prediction ends in Mk is softened
by Mt, who returns at the end of his parables to the tableau of Christ
the judge of all (25[31ff.]).

24: 32–25:46 Seven parables of warning

32–35 The inevitability of the end: (1) the fig-tree: cp. Mk 13[28–31]
Jeremias (*PJ*, pp. 119f.) thinks that, in its original context, the
fig-tree in leaf was a sign of the blessing of the coming kingdom (cp.
Joel 2[22]) rather than of the terrors which herald the approaching end,
as in both Mk and Mt. But either way the basic point remains
unaltered; the coming of the end can no more be halted when the
signs of it have been observed than can the coming of summer (under
Mediterranean conditions) once the fig-tree has been seen in leaf.
Vv. 34–5 make the point in plain language.

34. *this generation:* Writing when he does, Mt can hardly mean that some
of the original group of disciples will live to see the *parousia*. More
probably he sees the Church as the continuing company of Christ's
disciples, and interprets the words as a promise that it will survive
to the end (cp. 16[18]).

35. *my words:* a prophetic guarantee of the truth of his prophecy. But
Mt may also be contrasting the words of Jesus, which stand for ever,
with those of the Torah, which lasts only 'till heaven and earth pass
away', i.e. until the end of the present world order (cp. 5[18]).

36–41 The unexpectedness of the end: (2) Noah's flood: cp. Lk 17[26–30]
The point of v. 36 (=Mk 13[32]), which introduces this section, is
that while the nature of the end and the signs of its imminence are
revealed (by Jesus, the 'Son', in this apocalypse), its calendar date is
not. Therefore its actual coming will be totally unexpected.

36. *no one knows:* cp. Zech. 14[7]. *nor the Son:* i.e. as the agent of revelation.
The background of the saying in Mk is doubtless the Son of man in
Dan. 7[13f.], but Mt's understanding of the Son as receiving the
revelation of the Father must be seen in the light of 11[27] (which may
have developed out of the present passage). What the Father reveals
to the Son he reveals in order that it may be imparted to men. What
may not be imparted is not revealed.

The parable which follows is in verse form, and a fuller version,
containing a second strophe about the destruction of Sodom, is found
in Lk. Cp. 7[24ff.] for a flood as an image of the imminent end; this is the
basic meaning of the parable, but the emphasis here is on the un-
anticipated suddenness with which it comes. The same point is made
by the saying which follows in v. 41, which has a parallel (imperfect)
at Lk 17[34f.].

24: 42–25:13 The need for wakefulness: three parables

Mt, unlike Mk, separates out the theme of vigilance from that of the unexpectedness of the end. The injunction to keep awake at v. 42 (=Mk 13³⁵ᵃ) is repeated at 25¹³; this is *inclusio*, and indicates that the three parables bracketed together by these two verses are to be taken as illustrations of this theme, which their content anyhow demands.

43–44 (3) The thief in the night: cp. Lk 12³⁹ᶠ·

On this see Jeremias (*PJ*, pp. 48–51), who regards the original parable as a warning about the imminent end addressed by Jesus to his opponents. This was easily transmuted into a warning to luke-warm Christians (cp. 1 Thess. 5², 2 Pet. 3¹⁰), and because it was referred specifically to the *parousia*, allegorizing interpretation took the burglar, oddly as it seems to us, as the image of Christ himself (explicitly at Rev. 3³, 16¹⁵). The reference here to the *Son of man* is probably no less specific.

45–51 (4) The servant entrusted with supervision: cp. Lk 12⁴¹⁻⁶

The picture is of a trusted slave left in charge of a household in its owner's absence; it is clear that the parable speaks not of two slaves, but of two different ways in which one slave can discharge the responsibility laid upon him. The detail of the owner's long delay and sudden return would have fitted quite naturally into a general warning to Israel's leaders that the day of reckoning was near (Jeremias, *PJ*, p. 58), but a specific application of it to the return of Christ was, in the situation of the post-apostolic Church, inevitable.

45. *wise:* in the practical sense, not neglectful of the steps necessary for entering the kingdom; as in 7²⁴, and the following parable.

48. *that wicked servant:* the repetition of *that* from v. 46 makes clear that it is the same servant, though a different response.

51. *punish:* lit. 'cut him in pieces' (so mg)—a very severe punishment and, humanly speaking, an improbable one. It has been suggested that it rests on a mistranslation from the Aramaic; see Jeremias, *PJ*, p. 57 n. 31 for the details. *hypocrites:* if the meaning here is in line with the usage of the word elsewhere in Mt (e.g. 6²,⁵,¹⁶), it must convey that the unfaithful disciple will be no better off in the judgement than the unconverted Jew. *weep and gnash their teeth:* the transition from the master punishing the slave to the Judge of all consigning to hell is abrupt, and evidence of the evangelist's own hand; cp. 8¹², 13⁴²,⁵⁰, 22¹³, 25³⁰.

25: 1–13 (5) The ten maidens

The origins of this parable are greatly disputed; for a summary of the main positions see Linnemann, *Parables*, pp. 190ff. The basic possibilities are two: (a) an authentic parable of Jesus, later allegorized; (b) a parable of the delayed *parousia*, created by the later

Church and containing allegorical features from the start (Linnemann is exceptional in denying the presence of these). In this case the parable originated in the period at which the delay of the *parousia* had become a real problem, i.e. after A.D. 70, and it must therefore have reached Mt relatively unaltered. Possibly, as we have it, it is his own composition.

The stock objection to regarding it as a genuine parable based on real life—the alleged lack of parallels to the wedding customs implied —is well answered by Jeremias (*PJ*, pp. 171ff.). The rabbinic evidence is incomplete and the practice was extremely varied; while the crucial points of the reception of the bridegroom at the bride's house with lamps and the occasional delay of his arrival, which are not altogether absent from the Jewish tradition, have been strikingly confirmed by accounts of Palestinian weddings in modern times.

On the other hand the following features, at least, are probably the result of allegorization:

(a) the identification of the bridegroom with Christ himself is foreign to Jewish tradition, both in the OT and subsequently (cp. on 9¹⁵), and is first found in Christian use at 2 Cor. 11²; it can hardly have been used by Jesus.

(b) there is nothing in the text to suggest that the ten girls have a special function in relation to bride or bridegroom (though Jeremias cites a case in which the bride's attendants left her to go to meet the bridegroom). They simply act as representatives of the company, and their sex is as such irrelevant to this (in Lk 12³⁵, which is related in some way to this parable, it is disciples who are commanded to keep their lamps burning). Either Mt has made them feminine to balance the male servant in 24⁴⁵⁻⁵¹ (in which case this feature of the parable derives from its context in this gospel); or, as M. Meinertz has suggested, they stand corporately for the otherwise unmentioned bride, i.e. the Church (cp. Eph. 5²²ᶠᶠ·). In that case their allegorical meaning seems to conflict with their function in the story, though the fact that they are called *parthenoi* ('virgins') might not be unconnected with it (cp. 2 Cor. 11²).

(c) The detail that 'they all slumbered and slept' is very unlike the circumstances of a real wedding, whatever the hour, and since all the girls do it, no blame attaches to it in the story, but only to the negligence of those who failed to provide themselves with oil. Nor is it really required by Mt's use of the parable to illustrate the command to keep awake, since the previous parable has taken this in the broad sense of 'be prepared'. It seems that its function in the story is to set the scene for the great cry at midnight which awakens the sleepers (v. 6), the symbolic proclamation of the end of the world.

(d) Though the reply of the wise to the foolish is fully coherent with the story as a whole, the following parable shows that the thought of making wise use of the time allowed is present to Mt's mind. Christians are neither to depend on others for their fulfilment of God's demands, nor to defer their own efforts until too late.

1. *bridegroom:* a few MSS. add 'and the bride', but this is certainly secondary.

2. *wise:* cp. 24[45].

3–4. *lamps:* in the ancient world were small earthenware vessels with a spout through which the wick was drawn for lighting. Extra supplies of oil would be carried in small jugs.

11. *Lord, Lord:* cp. 7[21]—the cry of those who claimed discipleship in the last extremity and were rejected.

12. *I do not know you:* a formula used by a rabbi to forbid his disciple to approach him, equivalent to 'I will have nothing to do with you'.

25: 14–30 Opportunities of making good: (6) the talents: cp. Lk 19[11-27]

The point of this parable in its original form, like that of the labourers in the vineyard (19[30]–20[16]), seems to be the twist that it gives to accepted norms of economic practice. In real life the servant who has received too little capital is fully justified in refusing to take risks with it for which he would be accountable in case of failure. When a man's business is with God, however, no care with what has been entrusted to him, be that little or much, can be too great. See Derrett, *LNT*, pp. 17ff.

The original parable shows through for much of the time, as a comparison with Lk shows; but Mt has adapted it to his own pre-occupation with the delay of the *parousia*. He introduces it with the note of *a man going on a journey* (taken from Mk 13[34]), and his return is *after a long time* (v. 19). The lesson he uses it to convey is that the time before the *parousia* is not just for patient waiting, but for making the best possible use of God's gifts. The penalties for failure to do so are described not only in terms appropriate to the parable itself, but in those which belong to the final judgement.

14. *servants:* the Gk word means 'slaves', but the degree of responsibility assumed would imply that they were at least freedmen (cp. on 18[23]). The Aramaic equivalent is less explicit.

15. *talents:* see on 18[24].

21. *joy:* according to Jeremias (*PJ*, p. 60 n. 42), the Aramaic word can also mean 'feast', and this fits the context better.

24. *a hard man . . . winnow:* apparently a proverbial description of the capitalist who drives a hard bargain.

25. *I was afraid:* justifiably, since he would stand to make little profit with such an owner. *hid:* in rabbinic law burial was a security against theft. *you have what is yours:* a humorous Jewish disclaimer of responsibility.

26. *You knew:* the owner does not necessarily accept the servant's description of him, but retorts that, if true, it is more and not less reason for the servant to exert himself.
29. A saying originally independent of this context; cp. 13^{12} (=Mk 4^{25}).
30. The language, once again, is Mt's own; cp. 8^{12}, 22^{13} for the double description of the place of condemnation.

25: 31–46 Service of Christ in his little ones: (7) the great assize

The scene in which the whole forecast of the end culminates is really no parable at all, but a return to the depiction of Christ's coming and a vivid pictorial account of the judgement based on the biblical image of the shepherd separating sheep from goats (Ezek. 34^{17}). It is possible that, as J. A. T. Robinson has suggested (*Twelve NT Studies* [London, 1962], pp. 76ff.), this image formed a third with the separation of the wheat from the tares (13^{30}) and the sorting of good and bad fish (13^{48}); but it is no more than the starting-point of the scene presented here. Kilpatrick calls it 'a sermon which has passed into the evangelical content' (*Origins*, p. 97); this may possibly be true of the dialogue at the centre of it, but Robinson rightly draws attention to the Matthaean vocabulary of the frame in which it is set. As it stands we certainly owe the scene to Mt himself.

Who are under judgement? V. 32 says 'all the nations', but the actual judgement which follows is plainly of individual persons. In the light of this and of 24^{13}, 28^{19}, the reference must be not to nations as opposed to individuals, but to Gentiles as opposed to Jews (whose judgement as a people has already been pronounced at $23^{38f.}$). Gentiles who have not encountered Christ himself will be judged on the basis of their behaviour towards him in the persons of his disciples. That 'least' means these, and not suffering humanity in general (an edifying thought often read into the text), is borne out by the 'little ones' of $18^{6,10,14}$ (see commentary ad loc.), and above all by 10^{42} of which the whole scene is really an extended dramatization. It is the nearest that Mt, or the synoptic tradition generally, comes to the conception of the Church as the Body of Christ; though T. Preiss (*Life in Christ* [ET London, 1954], pp. 52ff.) is unlikely to be right in his contention that it was out of this passage, assumed to go back to Jesus himself, that the Pauline doctrine developed.

Does this interpretation imply the converse, that Gentiles who fail to serve Christ in his disciples pay the penalty of damnation? That would be to ignore the fact that the 'goats' are as surprised to be told that they have neglected Christ, as the 'sheep' are to be told that they have served him. The contrast is not between those Gentiles who show kindness to Christians, and those who do not, but between heathen who serve Christ without knowing him and Christians who know him without serving him, in the persons of their suffering fellow-Christians. The final warning is this addressed, like that of the Sermon on the Mount (7²¹⁻³) and the episode of the wedding-garment (22¹¹⁻⁴), to Christians who act as if their profession as such is a sufficient guarantee of salvation; and in particular to those who fail to recognize Christ in those fellow-members of whom they speak disparagingly as the 'least'; cp. introduction to Chap. 18, p. 159.

31. *Son of man:* as at 16²⁷ and 19²⁸, the figure of the glorified Jesus in the context of the final judgement (see Note B, p. 241). *angels:* for angels at the service of the Son of man (a characteristic Matthaean thought) cp. 13⁴¹,⁴⁹, 16²⁷, 24³¹, 26⁵³.

32. For Christ as judge of the world, cp. 2 Cor. 5¹⁰. *will be gathered all the nations:* this resumes 24³¹.

34. *King:* the direct use of this word on the lips of the earthly Jesus is unique and surprising, and the transition from *Son of man* awkward. But against the view that it has crept in from a source is Mt's fondness for parables introducing the figure of a king (cp. 18²³, 22¹,¹¹), and his preoccupation with the theme of Christ as king (cp. 2¹ᶠ·, 21⁵).

37. *the righteous:* i.e. those whom the judgement reveals to be such; cp. 13⁴³,⁴⁹. The context makes clear that the basis of the judgement is their actions and not membership of the Christian community.

40. *one of the least of these my brethren:* better 'one of these my brethren who are least'. Though the superlative form 'least' is not elsewhere used to denote disciples, its use in the saying preserved at 5¹⁹ seems to underlie the 'little ones' of 10⁴², 18⁶,¹⁰,¹⁴; *brethren* (see next note) confirms that the meaning is the same. *brethren:* Christian disciples are brothers to each other at 18¹⁵,²¹,³⁵, 23⁸ (cp. 5²³ᶠ·, etc.), and after the resurrection they are brothers of Christ (28¹⁰). The basis of this is (i) the Fatherhood of God (see on 6⁹); (ii) the saying at 12⁵⁰.

45. *one of the least of these:* see on v. 40.

46. *eternal punishment:* described as *fire* in v. 41, and this is to be understood in the light of 3¹², 13⁴². The thought is of irrevocable condemnation rather than of continuous torment, but this is less evidently true of the alternative images at v. 30.

4. REJECTION AND VINDICATION: THE PASSION AND THE RESURRECTION (CHAPTERS 26–28)

There are reasons for thinking that the passion narrative was the first part of the gospel tradition to be actually committed to writing. The present form of Mk's narrative has suggested to many scholars that it has been constructed round an earlier core (for reconstructions of this see V.

Taylor, *Mark* (London, 1952), pp. 653ff.; F. C. Grant, *The Earliest Gospel* (New York, 1943), pp. 175ff.). It is less easy to establish that the basic outline of the passion story was independently shaped into similar narratives in other Christian centres. Some scholars have held, though they have not demonstrated, that Lk's version alternates between Mk and another source which he often prefers. It is also arguable that Jn is wholly independent of the synoptic tradition, and a hypothesis of the stages of the development of the passion narrative on the basis of this possibility will be found in Jeremias, *EWJ*, p. 96. If there actually was a common outline of the passion story behind the local developments, it is likely that this would owe its origin to liturgical usage, more probably in connection with the annual observance of the Christian passover (also discussed by Jeremias [*EWJ*, pp. 122ff.]; cp. K. G. Kuhn in *SNT*, pp. 90ff) than with the weekly observance of the Lord's Supper, which has left a different mark on the gospel tradition (see on 26[26ff.] below).

Mt's passion narrative, however, shows no signs of the presence of a second version. Either the church for which he wrote had no separate tradition of the passion story, or it was so wholly superseded by the fuller version of Mk (presumably when the community became Greek-speaking) that it has disappeared without trace. What he gives is an edited and slightly enlarged version of Mk, and his additions and alterations can almost all be attributed to theological considerations. These can be analyzed as follows:

(a) Early Christian reflection on the crucifixion came to see it as the fulfilment of scripture and thus as part of the revealed and predestined will of God. This theme, already strongly present in Mk, is further developed by additional citations and allusions in Mt.

(b) The attitude of Jesus to the will of God thus revealed is one of obedient acceptance (see 26[12,18,42]). But the entirely voluntary character of this obedience means that, humanly speaking he is, as befits a king, in command of the situation at all times (see 26$^{17-9,53}$; and cp. Jn 10^{18}, 18$^{6-8}$ for the same motif in even higher relief).

(c) Judas' betrayal of Jesus is also in accordance with the scriptures, but this does not mitigate the enormity of what he does, nor diminish his responsibility for it; see 26$^{20-5}$ (especially v. 24, the key text), 27$^{3-10}$.

(d) In line with his general understanding of the rejection of Christ by his own people, Mt insists uncompromisingly on Jewish responsibility for Jesus' death (see 27$^{15-26}$). The accompanying references to the Romans seem designed less to exonerate them from guilt (as is the case in Mk and Lk) than to claim them as witnesses to his innocence, a function which they share with Judas (27^{3}) and even indirectly with the Jews themselves.

(e) Mt sees the passion as a literally earth-shaking event, and the supernatural phenomena which accompany it are described by him in vivid pictorial terms (see 27$^{51-4}$).

26: 1–5 *Introduction: The Priests' Plot:* cp. Mk 14$^{1-2}$

In place of Mk's matter-of-fact statement that the passover was near, Mt has a solemn announcement by Jesus himself of his approaching crucifixion. This follows immediately on his long prophecy of the last things, and it too is to be taken as a prophetic utterance. Only when he has thus given the word can the Jewish authorities begin to move, and their action is described in terms which recall Ps. 2^{2}—i.e. it too has been predetermined in scripture.

1. *all these sayings: all* (in this summary only) is emphatic. The whole teaching of Jesus contained in the five discourses is now concluded.
3. *Caiaphas:* Joseph Caiapha, high priest from A.D. 18–37; he had been appointed by Gratian, Pontius Pilate's predecessor as prefect of Judaea. Mk never names him; Mt supplies the name correctly from his own sources of information.
5. *Not during the feast . . . people:* taken over from Mk, who implies by it (i) that the Jewish authorities hoped to avoid doing away with Jesus at a time of maximum publicity; (ii) that this hope was frustrated in the event; (iii) that the consequence was indeed a 'disturbance'

(rather than *tumult*) of the people, but of an order that they could not foresee. There is thus heavy irony in the remark. Jeremias' suggestion (*EWJ*, p. 72) that the word *feast* should be translated 'festival crowd' is not really plausible in this context.

26: 6–13 *The Anointing at Bethany*: cp. Mk 14³⁻⁹, Jn 12¹⁻⁸, (Lk 7³⁶⁻⁵⁰)

Mk records at this point a story which originally circulated without any indication of time or place, and which presented our Lord as refusing to disallow an act of love done to himself in favour of an act of mercy ('alms') done to the poor. The climax of this form of the story is represented in Mt by v. 11 (or part of it). It owes its place in the passion narrative to the further thought that it supplied by anticipation a necessary omission in the hurried burial of Jesus. Mt takes this aspect of it more seriously than Mk; the women at 28¹ do not come to anoint the body as they do at Mk 16¹.

13. *this gospel*: altered by Mt from Mk's 'the gospel'. Whereas Mk thinks of the message of the preaching Church to the world, Mt, it would seem, is thinking specifically of the recitation of the passion story, presumably to the worshipping Church (see above).

26: 14–16 *Judas' Bargain*: cp. Mk 14¹⁰⁻¹

Mt's only real divergence from Mk is in naming the sum. Thirty silver shekels was the compensation fixed for the life of a slave in Ex. 21³², but this thought, if indeed it was present to Mt, came to him in association with Zech. 11¹², the significance of which will be disclosed at 27³⁻¹⁰. He offers no clue to Judas' motive.

26: 17–29 *The Last Supper*: cp. Mk 14¹⁷⁻³¹

17–19 (1) The preparation

Mk's version of this episode has a very close formal correspondence to that of the fetching of the colt in Mk 11¹⁻⁶ (=Mt 21¹⁻⁷). Mt's drastic reduction (similar to his re-handling of the miracle stories) has destroyed this parallelism. The prophetic sign disappears, and Jesus' instruction to the householder bears 'the clear stamp of a sovereign word of command' (Barth, *TIM*, p. 143).

Mt follows Mk, though with less emphasis, in depicting the Last Supper as an actual passover meal. This is not reconcilable with the position of Jn, who states that the crucifixion took place on the preparation day, Nisan 14, coinciding with the slaughter of the passover lambs (see Jn 18²⁸, 19¹⁴). It is easy to find theological motives for Jn's chronological preference (cp. Jn 19³⁶=Ex. 12⁴⁶), but this does not settle the problem, and Jeremias' vigorous defence of the Marcan chronology (*EWJ*, pp. 41–88) has not won general acceptance. It is possible that the Roman church, for which Mk was probably written, followed the Roman synagogues in a method of fixing the date of passover which differed from that in force at Jerusalem; if so, it is remarkable that the result should have been taken over without demur by a church as much nearer to Palestine as that for which Mt wrote.

If the Last Supper was not an actual passover meal, as Mk and Mt assert, what was it? The older suggestions of a *Kiddush* (preparatory celebration) or a *haburah* (fellowship) meal are disposed of by Jeremias (*EWJ*, pp. 26–31); the preparation for passover was a preliminary of the passover meal itself, and the technical description of a *haburah* does not fit the circle round Jesus. The only real possibilities are (i) that it was an anticipated passover celebration. There is evidence that some parties or sects within Palestinian Judaism used variant calendars (see, e.g. A. Jaubert, *La date de la Cène* [Paris, 1957]), but this would hardly have been countenanced within Jerusalem itself; if Jesus departed from the official practice, it could only be by a creative—and probably desperate—initiative of his own; (ii) that it was the last of the meals regularly shared by Jesus and the circle of his intimate associates; in which case it could hardly have failed to take some of its colour from the impending festival. The practical difference between these two views is not really very great.

18. *My time* (Gk. *kairos*): the moment appointed by God for the fulfilment of his will, which Jesus freely accepts.

20–25 (2) The prediction of betrayal

This passage illustrates the process by which an OT text used to interpret the passion story could develop into an actual episode in it. In Mk's version Jesus simply predicts that, in fulfilment of Ps. 41⁹, one of those who dip in the common bowl with him (i.e. enjoy the table-fellowship of his intimate circle) will betray him; the betrayer is nowhere identified by word or action. In Mt the text is beginning to be interpreted as a sign by which the traitor can be distinguished from the rest; the one who dipped in the bowl at the same time as the Master is the man. But the sign is not to be taken as exerting any compulsion or even pressure on Judas; he is still left with the responsibility for his own action (see on v. 24 below). The logical conclusion of the process is to be found in Jn 13²⁵⁻⁷, where Jesus actually hands a sop to Judas and sends him out with instructions to act quickly.

24. This verse, in which Mt follows Mk closely, is crucial to the evangelist's understanding of the role of Judas. What he did was both predetermined, since it was foretold in the scriptures, and at the same time his own free choice and the ground of his subsequent self-condemnation (see 27³ᶠᶠ·).

25. *Master* (Gk *rabbi*): the separate question of Judas is peculiar to Mt, and by its wording as well as its position signifies that he has already cut himself off from the number of the true disciples. In contrast with Mk (and in sharp contrast with Jn), Mt never allows the disciples to address Jesus as *rabbi* (in line with his rejection of the title for them at 23⁸). Judas' use of it here and at v. 49 reveals him as now identified with the reprobate old Israel to whom it properly belongs. *You have said so* (NEB 'the words are yours'): the lack of agreement among experts about the force of this expression (for the Jewish sources see Abrahams, *Studies in Pharisaism and the Gospels*, ii. 1–3, and cp. Barth, *TIM*, pp. 145, n. 1) and the fact that of the three places in which it is found in Mt (26²⁵·⁶⁴, 27¹¹) the first two are insertions by Mt himself, suggest that its meaning in this gospel is best settled on internal grounds. It is reasonable to assume that he intended an expression for which he shows such deliberate preference to mean the same in all three places. In each case the truthful answer to the question would be an affirmative, and in each case there are reasons (though not always the same reasons) for declining a full admission. The words would thus broadly correspond to a plea of not guilty in an English court of law, which need not signify an outright denial, but puts the burden of proof on the interrogator; cp. the conclusion of D. R. Catchpole, *NTS* xvii (1971), 213ff.; 'affirmative in content, and reluctant or circumlocutory in formulation' (p. 226). In the present case the effect of an affirmative answer would have been to exonerate Judas, since his betrayal of Jesus would then only be adherence to a course of action infallibly predicted by the Lord himself. The prediction is correct, but it is the voluntary action of Judas that will make it so.

26–29 (3) The institution of the Eucharist

The tradition of what Jesus had done at the Last Supper was naturally preserved and handed on in the context of the Christian community meals at which his actions were repeated. It therefore antedates the passion narratives in which it afterwards came to be incorporated, and 1 Cor. 11²³ᶠᶠ· reproduces the 'words of institution' independently of such a context. Two distinct forms of institution narrative can be distinguished in the tradition: that represented by St Paul (as cited) and, it would seem, independently by Lk 22¹⁹⁻²⁰ (assuming the longer form of this text; see RSVmg); and that found at Mk 14²²⁻⁵ and closely followed by Mt. Jeremias (*EWJ*, pp. 160ff.) argues that the Marcan version (though probably in its present form Roman) is closer to the Palestinian original than the Pauline–Lucan (probably produced by the Hellenistic and missionary Christian community at Antioch); the contrary view is maintained, e.g., by Bornkamm, *Early Christian Experience* (ET London, 1969,) pp. 134ff. The fact that Mt follows Mk so closely may have a bearing on this argument; it is easier to understand if the practice represented by Mk's version was so close to that of Palestine that a church with Palestinian roots could take it over without real violence to its own traditions. But it may mean no more than that the community for which Mt wrote had Mk ready to hand when it changed over from Aramaic to Greek.

Mt makes a few minor alterations to Mk in the interests of style and liturgical symmetry (see Jeremias, *EWJ*, pp. 111ff.), but his only material addition is the final clause of v. 28.

26. *as they were eating*: also in Mk. This probably means that in the churches for which Mk and Mt wrote, the eucharist was no longer an integral part of a meal, and their readers would need to be reminded that its institution took place in the context of one.

27. *drink of it, all of you*: comparison with Mk will show that a narrative detail has been turned by Mt into a dominical direction, for the sake of symmetry with the direction over the bread in v. 26.

28. *for many*: a semitism for 'all' (to which there is no exact equivalent in Hebrew or Aramaic). There may be a reference to Is. 53¹². *for the forgiveness of sins*: words added by Mt. Whereas Mk connects *covenant* with sacrificial blood (as at Ex. 24⁸), Mt's emphasis is on the new covenant of Jer. 31³¹ᶠᶠ. (especially v. 34). Note that in 31¹ᶠᶠ. the baptism of John is not said to be 'for the forgiveness of sins' as at Mk 1⁴; forgiveness is rooted in the person of Christ (cp. 1²¹) and in his sacrificial death. It is also possible that Mt's church emphasized the part played by the eucharist in the forgiveness of its members' sins, and even that it was preceded by mutual confession as at *Did.* xiv. 1.

29. Mk has added at this point a saying from another source, a 'vow of abstinence', found in a fuller form before the words of institution at Lk 22¹⁵⁻⁸. There are reasons for connecting the tradition which preserved this with the annual Christian passover observance; see Jeremias, *EWJ*, pp. 122f., 207ff. *again*: Gk *ap'arti*, followed by a negative as at 23³⁹ (contrast 26⁶⁴), introduces an extended period during which the thing anticipated will not happen. *new*: Mt's addition; cp. 9¹⁷ for the new wine of the kingdom. *my Father's kingdom*: substituted for Mk's 'kingdom of God'. Is the reference to the Messianic banquet, or to the eucharists of the Church? Almost certainly the former, since the latter would be part of the intermediate kingdom of Christ (cp.

13⁴¹) rather than of the final kingdom of the Father (cp. 13⁴³). Mt's usual 'kingdom of heaven' would have been ambiguous here (see Note A, pp. 235f.).

26: 30–56 *Gethsemane :* cp. Mk 14²⁶⁻⁵²

30–35 (1) The prediction of desertion and denial

Not only the treachery of Judas, but the weakness of the other disciples is known beforehand to the Marcan Christ; that of the ten is seen as the fulfilment of scripture, that of Peter is a case by itself, suggesting actual reminiscence. Mt makes little alteration to Mk here.

30. *Mount of Olives:* outside the city, but within 'Greater Jerusalem'; cp. Jeremias, *EWJ*, p. 75.

31. *I will strike . . . scattered:* a free version of part of Zech. 13⁷, slightly altered from Mk.

32. *I will go before you:* a continuation of the shepherd image (shepherds in the east lead their flocks from the front). For its interpretation see on 28⁷.

36–46 (2) The agony and prayer of Jesus

For the considerable but not insuperable difficulties in regarding this episode, with its deep implications for the humanity of Christ, as historical, see the balanced discussion in Nineham, *Mark*, ad loc. Mt preserves the substance and the spirit of Mk's narrative, but modifies it in the following ways: (i) Jesus explicitly expects the three disciples to 'watch with me', i.e. to share his hour of stress; this for Mt is inseparable from discipleship (cp. 16²⁴ᶠᶠ·, 20²²ᶠ·), whereas the Christ of Mk's passion story is left utterly alone; (ii) there is greater emphasis in Mt on the threefold pattern of prayer on one side and sleep on the other (corresponding to Peter's denial later on); (iii) a second version of Jesus' prayer of obedience has been constructed by Mt himself.

37. *the two sons of Zebedee:* this way of referring to James and John (contrast Mk 14³³) recalls 20²ᵒᶠᶠ·, in which they undertook to be able to share the cup of Jesus. He is now faced with the acceptance of the cup; their failure to enter into his testing time means that he has to accept it alone. *sorrowful and troubled:* the Gk words are stronger than this, expressing a combination of extreme pain and horror.

38. *My soul is very sorrowful:* Ps. 42⁶. *with me:* Mt's addition; see on v. 37.

39. *My Father:* found only here as a form of address by Jesus. Mt suppresses Mk's *Abba* (see on 6⁹), presumably because his Greek-speaking church (in marked contrast with those of the first Christian generation; cp. Rom. 8¹⁵, Gal. 4⁶) had become unfamiliar with it.

42. There is a progression from the prayer at v. 39 (taken from Mk) to that given here (Mt only); Jesus has now realized that the cup will

not pass from him, and steels himself to accept it. *thy will be done:* a direct quotation from the Lord's Prayer (6¹⁰).

44. Mk only implies a third spell of prayer; Mt is explicit about it.

45. *Are you still sleeping . . .?:* the words have often been taken as an imperative, but they are best understood as a question. *the hour is at hand:* i.e. of death; Mk, for whom it means that of arrest, says it has come.

46. *Rise, let us be going:* not to evade arrest but to meet it. The words may have been remembered independently, since they are reproduced in a superficially different context at Jn 14³¹.

47–56 (3) The arrest

Mt follows Mk closely, except that he records an intervention by Jesus on the subject of violent resistance (vv. 52–4). This is rejected on the grounds that (i) violence breeds violence, and it is the instigators who suffer most; (ii) God is able to look after his own, if their suffering is not his will; (iii) but the scriptures prove, on the contrary, that it is his will.

49. *Master* (Gk *rabbi*): see on v. 25. *kissed him:* the Gk word suggests a gesture of particular affection. There may be an echo of Prov. 21⁶, and thus irony in the following verse.

50. *Friend:* elsewhere used (20¹³, 22¹²) to rally an inferior who is clearly in the wrong. But it may also mean a 'table-companion' (cp. Derrett, *LNT*, p. 129, on 22¹²) and this will recall v. 23. *why are you here?:* the Gk *eph'ho parei* ('that for which you are here') is elliptical, and it is not easy to determine what has been suppressed. But since the words are added by Mt they are likely to reflect his usual motives in amending Mk's wording, and an imperative would be far more appropriate to his picture of Jesus fully in command of the situation than a question. The rendering 'do that for which you have come' (RSVmg) is thus much more likely than the text. Even the betrayer cannot proceed until he is permitted to do so.

52. *all who take the sword . . . sword:* there can be little doubt that these words express the true attitude of Jesus towards violence (cp. 5³⁸ᶠᶠ·). But Mt in putting them into his mouth at this point may have in mind the outcome of the Jewish war of A.D. 66–70, which was sparked off by a rebellion headed by *sicarii* (see Introduction, p. 26).

53. *Do you think that I cannot appeal . . . angels?:* Jesus can command any assistance he requires; his refusal to do so is the expression of his voluntary acceptance of his role. *twelve legions:* perhaps contrasted with the futility of resistance by twelve individuals against an armed band.

54. *how then should the scriptures be fulfilled . . . ?:* the passion is the consummation of what Jesus came to do (5¹⁷); but the fulfilment must be his free choice.

55. *robber:* the Gk word is that regularly used for an armed insurrectionist.

26⁵⁷–27² *The Jewish Trial*

26: 57–68 (1) Jesus before Caiaphas: cp. Mk 14⁵³⁻⁶⁵

The problem of the nature and historicity of these proceedings belongs really to a commentary on Mk rather than to one on Mt; but as it is too fundamental to pass over without comment, it is discussed separately in Note E, p. 252. Mt's alterations to Mk nowhere amount to a criticism of Mk's basic view of the trial, and indeed there are tendencies in Mk, particularly towards attaching the blame for the crucifixion to the Jewish people, which Mt carries further.

58. *to see the end:* Mt's addition, and probably ironical in view of 10²², 24¹³.

61. *I am able to destroy the temple of God:* Mk has 'I will destroy this temple made with hands'. Mt eliminates (i) the note of prophecy (since the temple was not to be destroyed for another forty years, and would then be destroyed for good); (ii) the contrast of 'made with hands'/'made without hands' (since the idea of a spiritual temple replacing the material one is foreign to him); (iii) the statement that the evidence was false. Note that there are two witnesses (cp. Dt. 19¹⁵). The claim attributed by them to Jesus would express not radical opposition to the temple, but Messianic authority over it. The high priest's next question in Mt is actually a demand for clarification of this. See D. R. Catchpole, art. cit. at v. 25.

63–64. Jesus' answer to the high priest in Mk 14⁶¹ᶠ· may be regarded as the Christological climax of his gospel, in which all the titles previously applied to Jesus are concentrated together. Mt subtly alters this answer to suggest a contrast between Jesus' Messianic role hitherto, and his transcendent role hereafter.

63. *I adjure you:* the high priest demands an answer on oath. This Jesus cannot give, as it conflicts with his own teaching at 5³³ (so Barth, *TIM*, pp. 144f.). *the Christ, the Son of God:* titles accepted by Jesus from Peter at 16¹⁶ᶠ, but the high priest asks the question too late; they are no longer expressive of his relationship to the old Israel. The people who have rejected Jesus as Messiah can now only encounter him as judge; cp. on 23³⁷⁻⁹.

64. *You have said so:* altered from Mk's 'I am'. See on v. 25. Though in Mt's eyes, as the reader knows, a truthful answer would be in the affirmative, a direct affirmative cannot be given, partly for the reasons stated in the previous notes, partly because Jesus is seen as in entire command of the situation and cannot be forced by the high priest's adjuration to condemn himself out of his own mouth. *But I tell you:* Mt's addition, expressing a contrast between the position attributed to Jesus in the high priest's question and that which will be his in the future. *hereafter:* Gk *ap' arti* (cp. 23³⁹, 26¹⁹) indicates the beginning of

a new significant period (from now on). It qualifies the two following expressions, the fulfilment of which therefore takes effect from the passion (and resurrection) of Christ. This is pictorially represented at 28[16ff.]. *seated at the right hand of Power*: Ps. 110[1]. *coming on the clouds of heaven*: Dan. 7[13] (of the Son of man coming to the Ancient of days). Whatever may be said of Mk's use of this expression, Mt's is in line with Daniel's, and the reference is not to the *parousia* (as *ap' arti* makes clear), but to the immediate glorification of the Son of man. The two images are parallel and express the same truth.

67. *spat in his face*: a specially gross insult to a Jew, but one foretold in scripture; see Is. 50[6].

68. *prophesy to us*: Mk says he was blindfolded first. Mt alters this game of blind man's buff to a simple challenge to identify strangers—possibly to avoid the suggestion of helplessness.

26: 69–75 (2) Peter's denial: cp. Mk 14[66–72]

Despite the scepticism of Bultmann, few episodes in the gospels can be as well attested as this. Doubtless it was preserved as at once a warning against apostasy, and an encouragement to Christians wavering under persecution, but no Christian community could have simply invented such a story about its leading apostle, and the alternative to this, since there would hardly have been witnesses to call on, is Peter's own reminiscence. Not only has it the ring of authenticity, but its setting in all four gospels (and details like the fire in Mk, Lk and Jn) strongly supports the view that there were nocturnal proceedings of some kind against Jesus in the high priest's house (cp. Note E, p. 256).

Mk sets the denial in deliberate counterpoint to the 'good confession' of Jesus in 14[62]. Mt retains the juxtaposition, but his emphasis is rather different. Jesus' answer in 26[64] is, as has been seen, not a direct admission, but a refusal to answer on oath; Peter, by contrast, denies with repeated oaths (see Barth., *TIM*, p. 145).

71. *another maid*: according to Mk the same one. *Jesus of Nazareth*: named a second time in Mt only.

72. *with an oath, 'I do not know the man'*: in Mk swearing and the denial of personal knowledge are confined to the third occasion. Mt emphasizes these details by repeating them.

27: 1–2 (3) Conclusion of the proceedings: cp. Mk 15[1]

Commentators on both Mk and Mt have mostly taken these verses to refer to a formal meeting of the Sanhedrin to try Jesus. The words *took counsel* do not mean this, and it is only the interruption of the narrative by the denial of Peter that has prevented readers from taking them as the final decision of the nocturnal proceedings. See

A. N. Sherwin-White, *Roman Society and Roman Law in the NT* (Oxford, 1962), pp. 44f.

27: 3–10 *Digression: the End of Judas*

This, the largest of Mt's insertions into Mk's passion narrative, has only the loosest connexion with its narrative context. Its starting-point is the Sanhedrin's condemnation of Jesus; but the chief priests who figure in it are in fact otherwise occupied at this point, in securing his condemnation by Pilate.

There are two versions of the tradition with which Mt is working, his own and that preserved at Acts 1[15ff.], and two basic elements in it: (i) a conviction that the traitor must have come to a bad end (possibly he was known to have done so, but the existence of two divergent accounts of what that end was suggests that the true facts had been forgotten); (ii) the existence in or near Jerusalem of a piece of land named *Akeldama* ('Bloodacre') which local Christian tradition connected with the money received by Judas. Mt has worked this up into a piece of Christian *haggadah* by the use of a number of texts which he sees as fulfilled by it; these are so freely cited that there is no full agreement as to which they are. Zech. 11[12f.] (part of a prophecy which was heavily drawn on in the interpretation of the passion) is clearly basic; for reasons for the attribution of the whole to Jeremiah see the notes. And for explanations of the way the texts are handled see Kilpatrick, *Origins*, pp. 44–6; Stendahl, *School*, 120ff.; Lindars, *NTA*, pp. 116ff.; Gundry, *Use*, pp. 122ff.

3. *thirty pieces of silver:* Zech. 11[12]—already referred to at 26[15] and the starting-point of the whole passage.

4. *innocent blood:* Jer. 19[4] (see on v. 8 below for the associations of 19[6]), 26[15]. The latter speaks of the murder of the prophet as something which will bring innocent blood on the city and its inhabitants—which Mt certainly sees as a consequence of the death of Jesus (see on vv. 24f.). Judas himself is witness to Jesus' innocence. *what is that to us?:* expiation of sin is the priests' business. But they cannot expiate for this sin, for they are themselves implicated in it. Judas must bear the full responsibility. The 'innocent blood' betrayed by him will be shed for the forgiveness of sins (26[28]), but not yet.

5. *hanged himself:* see Acts 1[18] for another account. Mt's may be influenced by the fate of Ahithophel, who conspired against David (2 Sam. 17[23]).

6. *treasury:* the main crux of the passage. The Heb. of Zech. 11[13] (followed by RV) has 'cast it to the potter', which is very obscure and probably corrupt; see RSV which has corrected it from the Syriac to 'cast it into the treasury'. Mt's text is easiest understood on the assumption that he is familiar with both readings (or at any rate two interpretations) and has made them the basis for a complicated piece of exegesis which brings in other texts. Possibly the thought is: if you read 'treasury' the scripture is not strictly fulfilled, since the money was blood money and could not be put in it. But if you read 'potter' it can be seen as fulfilled with the help of passages from Jeremiah which contain the word.

Mt's word for 'treasury', *korbanan*, is elsewhere used to mean 'gift' (cp. Mk 7[11], which Mt, perhaps significantly, does not reproduce in his parallel, 15[5]). But this could include money for the temple or its sacrifices. There is an analogue to Mt's use of it in Jos., *BJ*, ii. 175.

7. *potter's field:* Jer. 32[6ff.] relates the purchase of a field but mentions no potter (though 32[14] refers to an 'earthenware vessel'); Jer. 18[1-6] and 19[1ff.] mention a potter but no field. Mt seems to have conflated the two, using one or both of the potter passages to make the connexion with Zech. 11[13], and 32[6ff.] to bring in the money transaction and the field. Obscure as this is, it is probably safer to accept Mt's own indication that he has Jeremiah in mind than to reject it, as many scholars do, from sheer incomprehension of his association of ideas. *to bury strangers in:* presumably the remembered use of the piece of ground about which the tradition grew up. It has been suggested that its real name was *Akeldamak* ('field of sleep').

8. *called the Field of Blood:* a possible reminiscence of Jer. 19[6].

9. *Jeremiah:* what follows is actually Zech. 11[13], except for the word *field*, which, as has been seen, probably recalls Jer. 32[6,9]. Gundry (*Use*, p. 125 n. 3) gives a full list of explanations offered for the discrepancy. But the ascription of a composite quotation to a single prophet is not unique (cp. Mk 1[2]), and if it is accepted that the whole context is full of allusions to Jeremiah, this is the most natural explanation, especially in view of Mt's preoccupation with him as the prophet of the destruction of Jerusalem (cp. on 16[14]).

10. *as the Lord directed me:* Lindars (*NTA*, p. 121) finds here a verbal echo of Ex. 9[12] as the final item in Mt's involved piece of *midrash*.

27: 11–26 *The Roman Trial:* cp. Mk 15[1-14]

Though Mt here rejoins Mk, there is a continuity in theme from the Judas passage; Judas has testified to Jesus' innocence; his testimony is now repeated by Pilate and his wife, and the Jews take full responsibility for his death.

11. *King of the Jews:* neither here nor in Mk is it explained how Pilate arrived at this question. *You have said so:* cp. 26²⁵,⁶⁴, though here Mt is following Mk. Evidently, from the evangelist's point of view, the answer is yes; and, equally, a straight affirmative would be an admission of guilt in Roman eyes.

12. *he made no answer:* a fulfilment of Is. 53⁷.

15–23 The release of Barabbas and the condemnation of Jesus

There is (a) a historical problem behind this incident as Mt found it in Mk, and (b) a textual problem in his own version.

(a) Apart from a single hint in the Mishnah (*Pesahim*, viii. 6; Danby, p. 147), there is no external evidence to corroborate a custom of releasing a prisoner at passover time, and to do so while a trial was pending or after sentence had been passed would not have been within the prefect's competence. If there is some truth in the story, in which the evangelists are only interested as evidence of Jesus' innocence and of Jewish responsibility (or Roman non-responsibility) for his crucifixion (see Note E, p. 255), it must have been seriously misunderstood in the course of transmission. P. Winter (*On the Trial of Jesus*, p. 99) conjectures that it arose out of a confusion about the identity of the prisoner; and there have been other suggestions.

(b) One small family of MSS., and some versions, have preserved the reading 'Jesus Barabbas' (RSVmg), which was known to Origen. It is quite certainly the correct reading, since the whole tendency of the early Church was to suppress cases of a person other than Christ bearing the name Jesus, and for a scribe to amend his copy in the opposite direction would have been unthinkable. But the reading has survived only in the text of Mt; there is no evidence for it in the parallel passage in Mk. Many scholars believe that it was there originally and that Mt derived it from Mk, but it is difficult on that view to understand why the reading was preserved only in Mt, which was much more read in the early Church and correspondingly more liable to undergo emendation.

Mt in any case intensifies the formal correspondence between Barabbas and Christ. In his version Barabbas is no longer a guerrilla implicated in bloodshed (so Mk 15⁷), but simply a 'notable prisoner' (v. 16, RV; RSV's *notorious* has a pejorative connotation which the Gk lacks). Pilate asks if he is to release 'Jesus Barabbas or Jesus called Christ', and this parallelism runs right through the passage. The claims of the two prisoners are evenly weighted—even their names are the same; the only thing that is allowed to distinguish them is that one of them is 'called Christ', and it is this claim which the Jews are explicitly invited to accept or reject.

16. *Barabbas*: either 'son of Abba' (see Abrahams, *Studies in Pharisaism and the Gospels*, ii. 201ff. for parallels), or 'son of Rabban' (suggested by Winter, *On the Trial of Jesus*, p. 95). But it could have been taken as meaning 'son of the Father', and if Mt was aware of this irony it would be a further point in which the details concerning Barabbas are allowed to double those concerning Jesus Christ.

19. The intervention of Pilate's wife is peculiar to Mt, and the motif of her dream a characteristic one for him (cp. Chaps. 1-2). The apocryphal *Gospel of Nicodemus* calls her Claudia Procula, thus displaying a biographical concern foreign to Mt, who is only interested in her as a witness to Jesus' innocence.

20. *persuaded*: toned down from Mk's 'stirred up'. Mt does not allow his crowd to act in a state of diminished responsibility.

22. *Let him be crucified*: a correction of Mk's 'crucify him', with the implication that the Jews are themselves passing sentence.

24-25. Another addition by Mt. For Pilate's disclaimer cp. 2 Sam. 3^{28}; for handwashing as a symbol of it, Dt. 21^{6-9} (the irony of this allusion is that Pilate follows a ritual designed to dissociate Israel itself from the consequences of blood-guilt); also Ps. 26^6, 73^{13}. By it the prefect officially acknowledges the innocence of his prisoner, and at the same time declines to be held personally responsible for his death. The people respond by accepting full responsibility for themselves and for their children; cp. Jer. 26^{15}. *and on our children*: Mt seems to have regarded the destruction of Jerusalem as the execution of judgement on Israel for its rejection of Christ (see on 23^{37-9}). Those who suffered then were the *children* of Jesus' contemporaries.

It is this passage that was used by Christians down the centuries to fix the guilt for the crucifixion of Christ on the Jewish people. Mt has much to answer for; but it is only fair to add that he was not thinking of Jews by race (he was probably one himself, and the church he was writing for would certainly have contained them), and that, so far from expecting it to be visited on infinite generations of Jews, he saw the events of A.D. 70 as a definitive judgement.

27: 27-31 *The Crowning with Thorns*: cp. Mk 15^{16-20}

Mk sees in this incident both the fulfilment of scripture (Is. 50^6, $53^{3,5}$) and the irony of the 'King of the Jews' being only acclaimed, and that in mockery, by representatives of the Romans (the climax of this is in the *titulus* affixed to his cross). It is possible that the details reflect a regular ritual farce with a mock king (for evidence of this in the ancient world, and its limitations, see Nineham, ad loc.).

Mt by his wording and introduction of a mock sceptre emphasizes the second motif. Lindars (*NTA*, pp. 70f.) suggests a deliberate reminiscence of Zech. 6[11f.], the crowning of Joshua (=Jesus) the high priest (called 'the Branch'; cp. on 2[23]). Note that the crowning here is done, though in mockery, by Gentiles, and that Zech. 6[15] foreshadows an Israel to which Gentiles will be admitted.

28. *scarlet robe:* the *chlamys*, worn both by generals and kings; Mt is clearly thinking of the latter.
29. *crown:* probably not an instrument of torture, as it is represented in the tradition of Christian art, but a radial crown of the sort worn by contemporary rulers as depicted on coins of the period, and possibly connected with the cult of the sun.
30. *reed:* in Mt's version, Jesus is struck with his own mock-sceptre—perhaps symbolic of his royal command of the situation in which he suffers.

27: 32–44 *The Crucifixion:* cp. Mk 15[21–32]
Mt's additions to Mk are mostly to do with the mocking. The most significant is the insertion of the words *if you are the Son of God* (v. 40), which take the reader back to the temptation narrative in 4[1ff.]. The invitation to come down from the cross is for Mt, with his heightened Christology, not a taunt but a temptation, and the Jews in making it have identified themselves with the party of Satan.

32. *carry his cross:* what the condemned man had to carry was the cross-bar, the upright being already in position at the place of execution.
34. *wine . . . mingled with gall:* for Mk the offering of 'myrrhed wine' is a friendly act (see Prov. 31[6–7]), and the refusal of it perhaps a fulfilment of the vow of abstinence at the Last Supper. For Mt the offering of wine with gall is the action of Jesus' enemies (fulfilling Ps. 69[21]), with which he will have nothing to do.
35. This well-attested right of soldiers charged with an execution is seen as a fulfilment of Ps. 22[18].
36. *kept watch:* Mt's addition, the point of which becomes clearer at v. 54. It also anticipates the watch at the tomb (v. 66).
37. The *titulus* was a normal feature of crucifixion; Mt's insertion of the name of the prisoner, missing in Mk, is probably right, though his place of origin would probably have been included too; cp. Jn 19[19].
38. *robbers:* i.e. guerrillas; cp. on 26[55]. *right . . . left:* cp. 20[23].

43. *He trusts . . . desires him:* Mt's insertion from Ps. 22⁸, where the psalm-
ist speaks as the representative of Israel and the words are found on
the lips of his persecutors. Mt puts them into the mouths of the Jewish
bystanders, now the enemies of the true Israel. *he said, 'I am the Son of
God':* probably a reference to Wis. 2¹³, the context of which is the
conspiracy of the ungodly against the righteous man. (Wis. 2¹⁸ is
virtually the same as Ps. 22⁸).

27: 45–50 *The Death of Jesus:* cp. Mk 15³³⁻⁷

At the heart of this section lies the cry from the cross (v. 46
=Ps. 22¹), recorded by Mk and Mt only. The MSS. of both
gospels offer at this point a bewildering variety of readings
(inevitable for Greek-speaking copyists reproducing Semitic
words; see Stendahl, *School*, pp. 83ff.); but the consensus of
scholars is that Mk reproduces it in Aramaic. Mt at least
partly in Hebrew. The most obvious reason for the change is
that the form *Eloi* (Mk) evidently could not be confused by
the bystanders with the name of Elijah. Mt's *Eli* is the only
undisputed Hebraism in his version, and he need not have
gone to independent tradition for it; familiarity with the
Hebrew Bible, and an awareness of the linguistic difficulties of
Mk's version, would sufficiently explain the correction.

For the interpretation of the cry, and on the question of its
historicity, see Nineham, *Mark*, ad loc. The facts that for Mk
it is the climax of the total isolation of Jesus, and that Lk and
Jn suppress it, are against its having been originally understood, not as a cry of despair, but as the confident use of a
psalm which, taken as a whole, is not despairing. And if the
words do in fact express that sense of abandonment which on
the face of it they convey (and which is psychologically altogether likely), then the overwhelming probability is that they
were remembered, and not the work of subsequent devout
reflection.

45. A fulfilment of Amos 6⁹. Mk (15²⁵) has already noted that the
crucifixion was carried out at the third hour (9 a.m.). Probably all his
indications of time, which correspond to the division of the Roman
day, are artificial.

47. *Elijah:* popularly supposed to intervene, like a patron saint, on
behalf of people in distress. The misunderstanding, if historical, is

likely to have been deliberate. Mt may see in it a case of reprobate Israel perverting the inspired words of its own scriptures.

48. *vinegar*: usually understood as the soldiers' *posca* (a mixture of egg and vinegar). The evangelists are only interested in it as fulfilment of Ps. 69²¹, and it is possible that they have run together an act of kindness on the part of the executioners and the final mockery of the spectators (see Nineham, *Mark*, ad loc.).

50. *yielded up his spirit* (lit. 'the spirit'): the wording is unique in the synoptic gospels and half anticipates Jn 19³⁰. It may simply express the voluntariness of Jesus' death. But the use of *spirit* to denote a component of a human being is foreign to Mt. Conceivably it means the Holy Spirit, implying that the mission of the Servant of the Lord, for which Jesus was invested with the Spirit (cp. 12¹⁸⁻²¹), is now accomplished.

27: 51–54 *The Aftermath*: cp. Mk 15³⁸⁻⁹

In Mk the tearing of the curtain of the temple (to be understood theologically as a symbolic expression of the free access to God now open to all) and the centurion's confession of faith (the first to be made by a Gentile) are both consequences of the death of Jesus. In Mt the former is treated as a portent, to which others are added, and it is the impression made by these which elicits the confession of faith, here made by the whole execution party. The representatives of the Gentile world are witnesses of the death of the Son of God and its earth-shaking character, as they were of the signs which accompanied his marvellous birth (2¹⁻¹⁰).

51. *curtain*: for this gospel, probably that which hung before the sanctuary of the temple (which would be an omen of its future destruction), rather than the inner veil covering the entrance to the holy of holies (which would imply its present desecration), the more probable meaning in Mk. Josephus records a number of portents which were said to have heralded the destruction of the temple, including the automatic opening of one of the sanctuary doors (*BJ*, vi. 293ff.; cp. Montefiore, *Josephus and the NT*, pp. 18ff.). Mt may reflect in an obscure way the influence of these traditions; their influence on the apocryphal *Gospel of the Nazaraeans* (see *NTAp i*, p. 139) was more direct.

52. *the saints who had fallen asleep*: i.e. the holy men of the old covenant, who were popularly expected to rise and share in the reign of the Messiah. Mt may be implying some doctrine of the descent of Christ

into the place of departed spirits, as at 1 Pet. 3^{19}. Cp. also Ezek. 37$^{1-14}$.

53. *after his resurrection*: to emphasize that Christ himself is the first-fruits. The anticipation here is made in order to secure the balance between the Jewish past, and the Gentile future.

54. *this was*: perhaps ironical in view of the next chapter. Mt intensifies the confession of faith by altering Mk's 'this man'. *the son of God*: this rendering (as against 'a son of God' [RSVmg, the earlier version of the text, and NEB]) is certainly right. The evangelists were not concerned with what the words (assuming them to have been actually spoken) might have meant to a Roman officer, but solely with their witness to what they themselves believed about Jesus Christ.

27: 55–56 *The Women*: cp. Mk 15$^{40-1}$

There has been no previous reference, either in Mk or Mt, to women accompanying the group that followed Jesus from Galilee to Jerusalem. Their introduction here is (i) an indication (perhaps reliable) of eyewitness testimony, (ii) possibly a fulfilment, in the matter of distance, of Ps. 69^8, 88^{18}; (iii) a preparation for their part in the resurrection story.

56. *mother . . . sons of Zebedee*: Mt's indentification of Mk's Salome; cp. 20^{20}.

27: 57–61 *The Burial*: cp. Mk 15$^{42-7}$

This is really the first item in the resurrection story, rather than the final one in the passion, since the discovery of the tomb empty presupposes a prior identification of it. The historical problems which this raises are discussed by Nineham, *Mark*, ad loc. Mk's version represents the burial as the work of a well-disposed Jew. Mt, besides simplifying the account, makes him a disciple; by this stage, in his view, there is no middle way between identification with the old Israel, and identification with the disciples of Jesus.

57. *a rich man*: Mt makes explicit a reference to Is. 53^9 which is probably implied already in Mk (so Nineham, ad loc.). *a disciple*: Mk says he was 'expecting the kingdom of God', which need not imply a crypto-disciple. Mt has his own reasons (see above) for taking it in that sense. Cp. Jn 19^{38} which explains the discipleship as secret 'for fear of the Jews'.

58. Mt suppresses Pilate's surprise that Jesus was already dead—implausible if the death was attended by an earthquake.

59. *shroud:* Mt also omits the detail that Joseph bought this, as difficult to reconcile with the legal requirements of the feast.
60. *new tomb:* in the nature of things the tomb would not have been used before, but motives of reverence and the theological understanding of the resurrection as a new beginning both add emphasis to the detail; cp. Jn 19[41].

27: 62–66 *The Guard*

This, Mt's own contribution to the story of the burial, is the first half of an episode completed at 28[11–5]. Apologetic motives, and not altogether creditable ones, underlie it. Presumably Jewish propaganda met the Christian account of the empty tomb with the claim that the disciples had stolen the body, and Christian counter-propaganda then explained this as a story that the guards at the tomb were bribed to put about. It may be compared with the apologetic element in Chaps. 1–2.

62. *after the day of Preparation:* i.e. on the Saturday.
63. *Sir:* Gk *Kyrie*, which in this gospel expresses Lordship and is used only for Jesus, for God himself, or for figures in the parables which stand for one or other of them. The Jewish authorities have now no lord but Caesar's representative. Cp. Jn 19[15]. *After three days:* as predicted (but to disciples, not unbelievers) in 16[21], 17[23], 20[19].
64. *his disciples:* now objects of fear.
65. *You have a guard:* RSVmg 'Take a guard' is more probable. 28[14] clearly envisages that the soldiers are Roman.

28: 1–15 *The Resurrection:* cp. Mk 16[1–8]

The earliest Christian preaching of the resurrection, if 1 Cor. 15[3ff.] is typical, looked for confirmation to the appearances of the risen Christ, rather than to a tradition of his tomb having been found empty. The latter is first found in Mk, i.e. thirty years or more after the event, and scholars remain divided as to whether it has nevertheless a genuine historical foundation, or offers a symbolic and pictorial account of what resurrection was anyhow held to involve. H. von Campenhausen, *Tradition and Life in the Early Church* (ET London, 1968), pp. 42ff., and C. F. Evans, *The Resurrection and the NT* (London, 1970), may be taken as respectively representative of the two positions.

The discovery of the empty tomb is, however, the kernel of the resurrection story in all four gospels. Lk and Jn both amplify it with accounts of post-resurrection appearances which seem to embody independent oral tradition (see Dodd, *More NT Studies*, pp. 102ff.), though in a form clearly shaped by theological interpretation. Is the same also true of Mt? A comparison with Mk suggests, on the contrary, that there is nothing in Mt's narrative (save the late legend of the bribe to the guards, vv. 11–15) which could not have derived from reflection on Mk.

The characteristic features of Mk's narrative are: (i) when shorn of the spurious 'longer ending' (Mk 16⁹⁻²⁰ in RSVmg [RSVCE text]), it ends so abruptly that scholars still dispute whether what we have is the whole gospel or the real ending has been lost (see Nineham, *Mark*, pp. 439ff., for the arguments on either side); (ii) it confines itself to the discovery of the empty tomb, without reporting any appearance of the risen Christ; (iii) there is, however, a hint of more to come in the words of Jesus 'I will go before you into Galilee', quoted back to the women by the young man in 16⁷. This has been variously taken to mean: (a) the prospect of an actual meeting (the majority view); (b) the designation of Galilee as the place of the *parousia* (E. Lohmeyer); (c) a promise to lead the disciples into 'Galilee of the Gentiles', i.e. the Gentile world (C. F. Evans). Do these features sufficiently account for what we find in Mt? (i) Many scholars have assumed that Mt is working from a more 'complete' version of Mk and that this explains the enlargement of his account. There is nothing that compels this conclusion, and a good deal to suggest the opposite. The language of the final commission is characteristically Matthaean, and if this and vv. 11–5 are excluded from consideration, the material that remains is too thin and too colourless to have stood on its own. (ii) Mt does add two resurrection appearances, but the first of these is his own correction of the story of the frightened withdrawal of the women in Mk 16⁸, and the second is so stylized and un-circumstantial that it is pointless to look for a historical tradition behind it; (iii) All of the three suggested interpretations of Mk 16⁷ appear to have contributed to the build-up of the final scene in Mt: (a) the disciples proceed to Galilee to keep a rendezvous (v. 16); (b) what they see there is, in Evans' phrase, a 'stupendous Christophany', which, though not the *parousia*, anticipates a number of its features; (c) its climax is the command to make disciples of all nations (v. 19), a task in which the Lord will be with them (v. 20).

Thus, while there is some evidence for a 'Galilean' tradition of resurrection appearances (where else would the appearance to five hundred, 1 Cor. 15⁶, have been possible?) against the exclusively 'Jerusalem' tradition associated with Lk (and Jn 20), Mt makes no material addition to it. The contribution of his gospel is not to the evidences of the resurrection, but to the theological understanding of it, and it is concentrated in the commission at vv. 18–20 which is at once the narrative and the Christological climax of the whole book.

1. *after the sabbath:* the Gk means 'late on the sabbath', but it is clear from what follows, and from Mk, that early morning is meant. Mt evidently begins his days, in Roman style, at sunrise. *to see the sepulchre:* since it is sealed and under guard, this is all that they can do; anointing, the purpose of their visit in Mk, is out of the question (it would in any case be too late to prevent corruption). Cp. on 26⁶ᶠᶠ·.

2–4. Mt's addition. Like the death of Jesus (see 27⁵¹⁻⁴), the resurrection is followed, rather than accompanied, by supernatural portents. *His appearance:* this, and the effect on the guards, is described in language reminiscent of Dan. 10⁶ᶠ·.

5. The *angel* of the earthquake is now identified with the mysterious 'young man' of Mk 16⁵.

7. *he is going before you to Galilee:* a reference back to the words of Jesus at 26³². 'Go before' can mean (i) 'go ahead of' (and await), (ii) 'go at the head of', like a Palestinian shepherd with his flock. V. 16 suggests that Mt's surface meaning is (i), but the promise of v. 20 indicates that (ii) is also present to his mind. For 'Galilee of the Gentiles' cp. 4¹⁵.

8–9. Mk says that they fled and told nobody, 'for they were afraid'. Mt takes this as an inappropriate response to the good news that they have received, and substitutes his own version. Campenhausen (op. cit., p. 62) points to the duplication of the angel's charge at v. 7 as evidence that Mt is reproducing an alternative and indeed more original form of the tradition. But Mt tends in these chapters to duplicate details which Mk spells out only once (e.g. the prayer in Gethsemane, $26^{36ff.}$, and Peter's denial, $26^{67ff.}$), as well as to modify Mk's extreme reticence here about the marvellous.

10. *my brethren:* in view of 12^{50}, 23^8, 25^{40}, this must mean the disciples (cp. v. 7) rather than Jesus' natural kin.

11–15. See on 27^{62-6}.

14. The inherent improbability of the chief priests having influence of this sort with the Roman authorities in respect of the activities of the latter's own troops betrays the late origin of the story, at a time when the real position of the Sadducees had been forgotten.

28: 16–20 *Christophany and Final Commission*

If Mk was really meant to end at 16^8, a possible explanation of the abruptness is that his final item could only be the *parousia*, imminently expected but still in the future. This could have a bearing on the interpretation of Mt's final scene. Here as elsewhere (cp. especially his alterations at 26^{64}) Mt shifts the emphasis from the future return to the present exaltation of Christ (the earliest Christian thinking did not distinguish sharply between the resurrection and the exaltation; the idea of the ascension as a separate stage is peculiar to Lk–Acts). The curtain is drawn aside (as it will be at the *parousia*), but what it reveals is the risen and glorified Christ of present Christian experience, who has been showing through here and there in the earlier part of the gospel (e.g. 11^{25-30}, $14^{28ff.}$, $16^{18f.}$, and the healing miracles generally); a figure of majesty, invested with the attributes of the Son of man in Dan. 7^{14}, but still an object of faith (v. 17) and, though exalted to the throne of God, still present with his disciples in their work of evangelizing the nations, the means by which his kingly rule is to be realized on earth. (See further, Bornkamm in J. M. Robinson (ed.), *The Future of our Religious Past*, pp. 203–29.)

B. R. Molina's interesting suggestion (*NTS*, xvii (1970), pp. 87ff.) that Mt's literary model for the final commission is 2 Chr. 36^{23}, the proclamation of Cyrus of Persia to Jews in exile, may seem at first sight far-fetched; but it is supported not only by the fact that Mt has already begun his gospel as it is now suggested that he ends it, with material from the corresponding part of Chronicles (see on 1^{1}ff., and Introduction, p. 14), but by Is. 45^1, which addresses Cyrus as 'my anointed' (i.e. Messiah, Christ). Cyrus (i) claims to have received world dominion from God; (ii) sends the people he addresses on a journey (in their case to rebuild the temple); (iii) invokes the helping presence of God to be with them on it. Mt's substitution of the mission to the nations for the restored temple, so that the mission itself became the *locus* of the divine presence, may be directed at fellow-Christians or Jewish controversial opponents who still looked forward to the latter; but in any case it is central to his theology of the Church and its mission (and not foreign to the Cyrus–typology; cp. Is. 45^2).

The vocabulary of the commission is thoroughly characteristic of Mt himself. The only exception to this is the command to baptize in the name of the Trinity, which in addition breaks up the regular rhythmical pattern which can be detected in the rest of the passage. For this reason it is necessary to take seriously the fact, first pointed out by F. C. Conybeare in 1901, that the citations of these verses made by Eusebius of Caesarea prior to the Council of Nicaea (A.D. 325) have, instead of the command to baptize, only the words 'in my name'. The resultant text is as follows:

> To me has been given *all* authority
> In heaven and on earth;
> Go therefore and make disciples of *all* nations
> In my name,
> Teaching them to observe *all* things
> That I have commanded you;
> And lo, I am with you *all* the days
> Till the consummation of the age.

The readily recognizable verse-structure of this, with its recurrent emphasis on the word *all*, amounts to a strong internal argument for the originality of the shorter text, despite the unanimity of the surviving MSS. in favour of the longer. The alteration would have had to be made very early for the MS.

tradition to carry no trace of it—possibly before the general dissemination of the gospel (? from Antioch) to the rest of the Christian world. If Mt was in fact written in south-western Syria (see Introduction, p. 32), Caesarea is as likely a place as any for an uninterpolated copy to have survived. (See H. B. Green in *Studia Evangelica*, IV (ed. F. L. Cross, 1968), pp. 64ff.).

16. *mountain to which Jesus had directed them:* there has been no previous indication of this direction. But the passage which prefigures the Gentile mission at 15²⁹⁻³¹ makes a mountain in Galilee its symbolic starting-point, and this may be what Mt is referring to. Cp. also the mountain from which Jesus is shown (and promised) the kingdoms of the world, 4⁸.

17. *some doubted:* i.e. this revelation of the risen Christ, for all its sublimity, still demands an act of faith from the disciple—in contrast with the *parousia*, which will leave no room for doubt. As at 14³¹, the resolution of the doubt comes with the assurance that Jesus is 'with' them (v. 20).

18–19. The words *All authority . . . given to me* and *all nations* are taken from Dan. 7¹⁴, where they express the dominion of the Son of man. Their use here confirms that Jesus' assumption of this role (cp. 26⁶⁴) is effective from the decisive moment of his resurrection (see Note B, p. 241). *make disciples:* a Matthaean word (cp. 13⁵³, 27⁵⁷), with a rabbinic background which must not be lost sight of. As the Eusebian reading 'in my name' and the following verse both make clear, Christian missionaries are to make their converts disciples of the one authoritative Teacher (cp. 23⁸,¹⁰). *all nations:* cp. on 24¹⁴. It is by individual conversions of Gentiles that the *nations* are to be given to the Son of man. *baptizing . . . Holy Spirit:* see above. Early Christian baptism was unquestionably 'into the name of the Lord Jesus' (see Acts 2³⁸, 8¹⁶, 10⁴⁸, 19⁵; I Cor. 1¹³ff., 6¹¹), expressed not by a formula spoken by the baptizer, but by the candidate's own profession of faith (cp. I Cor. 12³, Rom. 10⁹, etc.). The instruction to baptize in the name of the Trinity at *Did.* vii. 1 (it is not necessary to assume dependence on Mt) reads more like a liturgical formula pronounced by the baptizer, and it is known that Syrian baptismal practice emphasized the importance of this at a much earlier date than the rest of Christendom. (Baptism at Rome was Trinitarian by the time of Justin Martyr (c. A.D. 150; cp. *First Apology*, lx.), but the evidence of Hippolytus (*Ap. Trad.* xxi.; ed. Dix, pp. 36f.) some sixty years later makes clear that this is still to be referred to the threefold profession of faith made by the candidate in the water.) Whether the command to baptize in Mt is integral to the text or a very early interpolation, it must in any case represent baptismal practice in Syria about the turn of the first century; the *Didache* is probably to be taken as corroborating this.

20. *observe:* used of the commandments of the law at 19[17] and of the teaching of the rabbis interpreting them at 23[3]. The commandments of the earthly Jesus (note the past tense) are to be observed as the definitive interpretation of the law; see on 5[19]. *I am with you always:* a clear echo of the meaning of *Emmanuel* (1[23]), and cp. 18[20]. Mt does not think of an absentee Christ such as is suggested by some passages of Acts; the risen Christ is continually present with his disciples. At the same time he apparently has no explicit thought of the Holy Spirit as accomplishing this presence, such as in characteristic both of Paul and Jn (see especially Jn 14[16ff.], 16[7ff.].). The experiential reality which the Spirit language expresses is nevertheless present to his mind. *the close of the age* (NEB 'the end of time'): Mt's characteristic expression for the end of the world (for which see on 24[3]) furnishes the appropriate note on which to end his gospel.

NOTE A. THE KINGDOM OF HEAVEN[1]

It is generally agreed that there is no distinction between the expression 'kingdom of God' used elsewhere in the NT and 'kingdom of (the) heaven(s)' (*malkuth shamayim*), which Mt in all but four instances prefers. 'Heaven' is here simply a reverential circumlocution for 'God', common in later Judaism and quite possibly used by Jesus himself, while 'kingdom' signifies neither an area of territorial jurisdiction (from which in the case of God no place can be excluded) nor an abstract social ideal, but the dynamic exercise of kingly power; it is shorthand for 'God rules'.

The idea of God as king has its roots deep in Hebrew religious history: first as king of his chosen people, then as king of the surrounding nations also; next as king of the created order (this is one implication of the 'enthronement' festival in which, as many scholars hold, the king of Israel represented

[1]On the whole subject see N. Perrin, *The Kingdom of God in the Teaching of Jesus* (London, 1963); R. Schnackenburg, *God's Rule and Kingdom* (ET London, 1963); G. E. Ladd, *Jesus and the Kingdom* (London, 1966).

Yahweh); and finally, when Israel seemed at the mercy of its conquerors, as the king who would intervene to establish his rule among those who still rejected it. This final understanding was developed in apocalyptic, and it is from this phase that the expression 'kingdom of God' derives; but it would for all that have meant different things to different parties. Sectarians like the Qumran community looked forward to the intervention of God on their behalf without any action on their part to precipitate it; the advocates of direct action against the Romans held that God's rule would be established by their own force of arms. Pharisaic teaching in the years after A.D. 70 settled into a conception of the rule of God as (i) an eternal fact ('thy kingdom is an everlasting kingdom': Ps. 145^{13}); (ii) partially realized on earth in the obedience of Israel, from Abraham onwards, to the commandments of the one God (as contrasted with the polytheism of the surrounding nations); (iii) acknowledged by the individual by his taking upon him the observance of the law as the 'yoke of the kingdom', and in his daily recitation of the *Shema* (see on 22^{37}); (iv) not to be fully revealed until the Messianic 'age to come', when God's sovereignty would be recognized by all the nations. This final stage would be brought about by the act of God himself, but some rabbis taught that its coming could be hastened by repentance or by meritorious action on the part of Israel.

This position has been too thoroughly purged of apocalyptic to be a safe guide to the teaching of the Pharisees contemporary with Jesus, but it may well be of significance for the study of Mt; cp. the petition added to gloss 'thy kingdom come' in Mt's version of the Lord's Prayer (6^{10}).

What then was distinctive about Jesus' own understanding of the kingdom? First, its absolute centrality to his message; every other aspect of his teaching must be understood in relation to it. Since the work of Weiss and of Schweitzer at the beginning of this century this has been beyond dispute.

Secondly, Jesus thought of the kingdom, as did the Pharisees and the Qumran covenanters, as something transcendent, not to be fully realized in this-worldly conditions (hence a lack of interest in setting the situation of the world, including his own people, to rights; see on 5^{38-42}, $22^{15ff.}$), and yet he saw it as very near indeed. Just how near has continued to be a matter of debate. Weiss and Schweitzer held that though Jesus expected the kingdom he proclaimed to come very shortly, it still lay wholly in the future for him; C. H. Dodd at one time seemed to be saying[2] that he thought of its presence as already realized in his own proclamation of it. The truth, it is now widely agreed, lies somewhere between these two extremes. That the main thrust of Jesus' view of the kingdom is still future, however imminent, is shown by the petition 'thy kingdom come', by his repeated use of the image of a supper (i.e. the Messianic banquet) in connection with it, by the promises of future fulfilment or reward contained in the Beatitudes and elsewhere, and the obverse of these in the warnings to the unrepentant contained in many of the parables.[3] But at certain points the coming kingdom is seen as already present by anticipation, always in connection with Jesus' own mission. It is thus that we have to interpret his anticipations of the Messianic banquet to which he invited tax-collectors and other outcasts (see commentary on $11^{16ff.}$, $22^{1ff.}$, and cp. 9^{15}), his declarations of God's forgiveness of the sinner *now* (see on $9^{1ff.}$), those parables (somewhat mis-leadingly called 'parables of growth') which find the kingdom present in its small beginnings as well as in its abundant final fulfilment (see on $13^{3ff.,31-3}$), his claim that something greater than Jonah or Solomon is here ($12^{41f.}$), and above all, the declaration that in his exorcisms the kingdom of God is presently at work (12^{28}), and involved in conflict (cp. 11^{12}).

Thirdly, as the thought of its imminence shows, the kingdom is not something to be achieved gradually by human effort, but brought about by God, i.e. it is gift or grace, to be bestowed on those who cannot earn it but desperately need it; this is vividly expressed in the parables of Lk 15 which repre-

[2]Especially in *Parables of the Kingdom* (1935).
[3]See Jeremias, *PJ*, pp. 160ff.

sent God as actively seeking the lost, and it was acted out in the priority among the hearers of his message accorded to those whom devout Jewish society rejected. But at the same time it is also demand; it comes to men in the form 'follow me' (i.e. be my disciple, accept and learn all I have to say), and they drop everything and follow Jesus (cp. 4^{18-22}, 9^9).

Between the teaching of Jesus and the writers of the NT lies the experience of his death and resurrection, and the birth and expansion of the Church. Some transmuting of his view of the kingdom in the light of the new situation was therefore only to be expected. This holds good for the evangelists as for the rest; though they have preserved from the tradition the authentic sayings which are the only clue to what Jesus actually taught, these are found alongside other material (like gold in an ore deposit), and organized by each evangelist in a way that reveals his personal viewpoint. How far then does Mt's idea of the kingdom represent a modification of that of Jesus?

(a) As for Jesus, so for Mt—more than for any other evangelist—the theme of the kingdom is central to the whole gospel message.

(b) Mt retains the original range of the expression, covering both the present and the eschatological future. In his parables chapter, some form of the introductory formula 'the kingdom of heaven is like' is used indiscriminately to introduce parables which represent the kingdom as the subject of current secret growth ($13^{24,31,33}$), as the object of present search ($13^{44, 45}$), and as synonymous with the end-time (13^{47}, which is in line with the usage outside that chapter; cp. 18^{23}, 20^1, 22^2, 25^1).

He has introduced, however, the sub-concept of the kingdom of the Son of man, which occupies the period between the resurrection (see 28^{18}) and the final judgement (see 13^{41}, 16^{28}), and which is not to be restricted to the Church (see on 13^{38}), though it belongs to the same division of time; it is by the missionary activity of the Church that its effective sway is extended. This is contrasted with the kingdom of the Father, the final eschatological reign (13^{43}). But it is not contrasted with the kingdom of heaven; rather it is the mode in which that kingdom is presently at work. (For the Pauline parallel to it, see Introduction, p. 35).

Mt's comprehensive understanding of the kingdom means that he finds no difficulty in including those sayings in which Jesus spoke of it with present reference (e.g. 11^{12}, 12^{28}). Nevertheless, of the sayings in Mt which refer to the kingdom, the greater part envisage it as something to be attained in the eschatological future. The bulk of these speak of 'entering' it (5^{20}, 7^{21}, 18^3, 19^{23-4}, 21^{31}, 23^{13}; implicitly also 7^{13}, 8^{11}, 16^{19}); 25^{34} of 'inheriting' it (cp. $5^{3,10}$). 18^3 confirms that there is a concealed future reference in the expression 'greatest in the kingdom of heaven' in $18^{1,4}$ (cp. 19^{14}), and this presumably holds good for the converse at 5^{19}, 11^{11}. Since of all these sayings only 18^3 and $19^{23f.}$ come from Mk, few have other synoptic parallels, and a number show signs of having been formulated by Mt or by sources very close to him, they argue a distinct preference on the part of Mt himself for the idea of 'entering' the kingdom—a spatial image which suggests that he was unconsciously influenced by the literal meaning of his preferred circumlocution for the 'rule of God'.

(c) Most of these latter sayings have a strong ethical emphasis; they speak of the quality of life that admits a man to the final kingdom. It is not too much to say that for Mt (ethical) righteousness and the kingdom are correlatives (see on 5^6, 6^{33}). This is not to say that men can hasten the coming of the kingdom by their actions (except by preaching the gospel to the nations; see 24^{14}). Nor does it mean that the thought of grace is absent from this gospel; Mt's warnings against judgement of others ($7^{1ff.}$), his concern for the 'little ones' and their forgiveness (Ch. 18), and the prominence he gives to the parable of the labourers in the vineyard ($20^{1ff.}$) are sufficient to disprove that. But because he wrote for an established community, in which the gospel could too easily be presented as (in Bonhoeffer's phrase) 'cheap grace', he found it necessary to emphasize that the experience of grace does not remove the reality of judgement, and therefore it is the aspect of demand that is uppermost in his teaching.

NOTE B. THE SON OF MAN

The expression 'Son of man' is relatively common in the gospels, and is reproduced without comment by the evangelists; it is, however, never found except on the lips of Jesus. In Greek it is simply a barbarism; it seems to be a literal translation of the Aramaic *bar nash(a)* (=Heb. *ben adam*), an example of the Semitic idiom which speaks, e.g., of an enlightened person as a 'son of light', and similarly of a human figure as a 'son of man'. 'A man' (or 'the man' in the case of *bar nasha*) would convey the meaning quite adequately. But the literal sense of the expression matters less than the associations, both general and biblical, which it might have had for a first century Palestinian Jew. It could have conveyed any of the following:

(a) (in Palestinian Aramaic usage) a circumlocution for the speaker. The evidence for this has recently been reviewed by Vermes[1], who concludes that the words can be equivalent to 'I' (especially in contexts where the speaker is referring to his own 'humiliation, danger or death', or where an attitude of humility would be appropriate). Jeremias[2], who denies this, admits that they can be used indirectly as we use 'one'.

(b) (as in the book of Ezekiel, exclusively) a designation for a prophet (but here only when addressed by God).

(c) (as in Ps. 8, which is linked with the creation narrative of Gen. 1), 'man' in the sense of inclusive or representative humanity, with his special preeminence in the created order. It is not a long step from this to the pre-existent 'heavenly

[1] In Black, *AA*[3], Appendix E, pp. 310ff.
[2] *NT Theology i*, p. 261.

man' of much current religious speculation, both Jewish and non-Jewish.[3]

(d) (as in the later chapters of the book of Daniel) a semi-divine figure who will appear before God in the end-time to receive authority over men (see Dan. $7^{13f.}$). This too appears to be connected with the 'heavenly man' myth, though the allegorical interpretation in Daniel makes the figure stand for 'the people of the saints of the most High' (Dan. 7^{27}). The corporate reference in any case disappears in the later apocalyptic writings which speak of the Son of man, IV Ezra (=RSV 2 Esdras) 13, and the *Similitudes of Enoch* (*I Enoch* xxxvii–lxxi).

No single one of these uses will accommodate all the instances of 'Son of man' in the synoptic gospels. They fall into three distinct groups. For one of these, as for Daniel, the Son of man is a future figure, destined to appear in the end-time. A second uses the expression in a present sense, of the person of Jesus in the context of his ministry. The third, which is confined to the gospel of Mk and its parallels in Mt and Lk, uses it in contexts in which the passion and resurrection of Jesus are predicted by him in terms so specific that it is virtually impossible not to conclude that they have been framed after the event. These are clearly referred to the person of Jesus; what is in doubt is whether they also contribute something fresh to the content of the expression 'Son of man'.[4]

Did Jesus himself actually use the expression? This is probably the most heavily debated single question in the whole of NT scholarship, and it cannot be pretended that agreement is in sight. The majority of scholars, especially German-speaking ones, start from the position that the 'apocalyptic' use of the expression was so dominant and its influence so pervasive in first century Palestine that it was really impossible

[3] On this see F. H. Borsch, *The Son of Man in Myth and History* (London, 1967).

[4] As is maintained by M. D. Hooker, *The Son of Man in Mark* (London, 1967).

for a speaker to mean anything else by it. From this assumption three alternative conclusions can follow:

(a) Jesus both used the expression of himself (which accounts for the 'present' usage) and understood it in the apocalyptic sense (which accounts for the 'future' usage); i.e. he saw himself as the Danielic (or Enochic) Son of man.[5]

The main difficulty in this is the psychological one of a prophet presuming to identify himself with a transcendent figure in biblical and apocalyptic imagery. John Knox goes so far as to write: 'A sane person, not to say a good person, just could not think of himself in such a way'.[6] It is of course hard at our present distance to lay down with absolute certainty just what was or was not psychologically possible for a first century Jew; but the burden of proof rests nevertheless with those who maintain that Jesus could have thought thus of himself.

(b) Jesus used the expression, and understood it in the apocalyptic sense; but he used it of a figure distinct from himself. It follows from this that the 'present' instances of it are all creations of the later Church, dating from a time when the 'Son of man' of the genuine sayings had been identified with the risen and glorified Jesus.

This view commands widespread support.[7] But it puts a lot of weight on the saying at Mk 8^{38}=Lk12^8 (par. Mt 10^{33}), in which Jesus appears to distinguish between himself in the days of his ministry ('whoever is ashamed of me . . .') and the Son of man in the end-time ('of him shall the Son of man be ashamed . . .'). N. Perrin[8], however, has argued persuasively that the original form of Lk 12^{8a} had the future passive ('shall be acknowledged', i.e. 'God will acknowledge') as 12^{8b} still has, and that the saying in its original form therefore contained no reference to the Son of man. If the main-

---

[5] So Jeremias, op. cit., pp. 264ff.; C. Colpe in *TDNT*, viii. 400ff.
[6] *The Death of Christ* (Fontana edn., London, 1967), p. 53.
[7] See especially H. E. Tödt, *Son of Man in the Synoptic Tradition*; also A. J. B. Higgins, *Jesus and the Son of Man* (London, 1964).
[8] *Rediscovering the Teaching of Jesus*, pp. 188–91.

prop of this position is thus removed, no other text tells decisively in its favour.

(c) Jesus used 'Son of man' neither of himself nor of anyone distinct from himself.

This rather drastic solution is usually the consequence of first assuming that no non-apocalyptic use of the words is plausible for first century Palestine, and then concluding, for other reasons,[9] that no 'future' instance of them in the mouth of Jesus can be genuine. The question that it fails to answer is: why, if Jesus himself did not use the expression, is it never found in the gospels (and only once in the rest of the NT: Acts 7[56]) except on his lips?

Since none of these answers is really satisfactory, it is reasonable to challenge the assumption from which they start. As the 'Son of man' figure is found in only two of the many surviving documents of post-biblical apocalyptic, and of these the *Similitudes of Enoch* is notoriously difficult to date with confidence (especially as it is not among the portions of *Enoch* discovered at Qumran), or to pronounce free from Christian interpolation, is it so certain that 'Son of man' would necessarily have had an unmistakably apocalyptic ring for a first century Palestinian? The evidence collected by Vermes (see (a), p. 237) is most apposite and telling at this point. It allows us to entertain the possibility that Jesus used the expression without meaning anything explicitly theological by it; that he really had this roundabout way of speaking of himself, for reasons (perhaps connected with his prophetic vocation, perhaps just deliberately enigmatic) which we cannot now fully penetrate, and that after his death it was remembered by his disciples and reinterpreted by them, with the help of the OT scriptures, in the light of their conviction of his resurrection. On this view some (not all) of the 'present' instances of the expression could be authentic, e.g. Mt 11[19] (=Lk 7[34]; see commentary for Perrin's

[9]As does, e.g., P. Vielhauer, who regards the 'Son of man' concept as incompatible with Jesus' teaching on the kingdom; see Tödt, pp. 329ff., Borsch, pp. 27ff.

arguments in its favour), 8^{20} (=Lk 9^{58}), and perhaps the 'riddle' ('the Son of man will be delivered to men') which Jeremias[10] thinks lies behind Mk 9^{31}. The apocalyptic 'future' instances will represent the mainstream of post-resurrection reinterpretation; an alternative line, emphasizing the 'heavenly man', has led to the usage of the fourth gospel and may underlie the alusions to Ps. 8 at 1 Cor. $15^{25ff.}$ and Heb. 1.

Mt belongs to the mainstream. His use of the expression, and in particular the fact that he sometimes substitutes 'I' for it where it stood in his sources, and occasionally vice versa, shows that he always intends it to be understood of Jesus personally (as was probably already the case with Mk); this means that he had no difficulty in taking over all the instances of it that he found in his sources, including the Marcan predictions of the passion. But it is his alterations of these, and more especially those parts of the gospel which seem to be his own composition, which indicate most clearly how he understood it. Its meaning for him may be summarized as follows:

(a) Even in the days of his earthly ministry the title conveys a special dignity for Jesus. Mt's alterations to Mk at 12^{32} (probably) and 16^{13} carefully distinguish the Son of man from 'men', and so have the effect of distancing him from ordinary humanity.

(b) Mt's addition to Mk at 26^{64} indicates that the enthronement of the Son of man will take effect 'from now', i.e. when the passion is complete, and the final commission of 28^{18-20} reveals Jesus as invested with the attributes of the Son of man (as at Dan. 7^{14}) from his resurrection (cp. 16^{28}). $13^{37ff.}$ speaks of the Son of man as active in his kingdom before the final judgement (v. 37) as well as at it (vv. 41–3).

(c) The full majesty and sovereignty of the Son of man will nevertheless only be revealed to the world at large at the *parousia*, when, surrounded by angels and with his disciples for co-assessors, he will act as the Father's vicegerent in the judgement (see 13^{41-3}, 16^{27}, 19^{28}, $24^{30f.}$, $25^{31ff.}$).

[10]op. cit., pp. 281f.

NOTE C. ST. PETER IN EARLY CHRISTIAN TRADITION AND IN THE GOSPEL OF MATTHEW

It is widely supposed, in view of the 'Petrine supplements' to the earlier synoptic tradition which Mt contains, and of $16^{13ff.}$ in particular, that the evangelist had a special interest in the figure of St. Peter and his authority in the Church. In order to determine whether this really is so, it is necessary first to ask what, apart from this gospel, can be established about Peter in the early tradition.

(a) If the existence of an inner circle of twelve round Jesus is accepted as historical (and there are good grounds for this; see on 10^2), it is necessary to take account of the fact that Simon 'called Peter' stands at the head of all the lists of their names. There are strong reasons for accepting the tradition that Simon received the name (more strictly nickname) Peter (*kēpha*, 'rock') from Jesus himself. Not only is the linguistic gackground of the word-play unquestionably Aramaic (see on 16^{18}), but the conferring of a new name was an action with prophetic overtones (cp. Is. 7^3, 8^3), and according to Mk 3^{17}, James and John were nicknamed by him also. The meaning of the name Peter certainly suggests a leading position in the group.

Since the early tradition had little interest in chronology, there is no agreement between the gospels about the point in the ministry at which the naming occurred. Jn associates it with Simon's original call, and Mk and Lk with the appointment of the twelve; Mt alone makes a connection between it and the acknowledgement of Jesus' Messiahship attributed to Peter by all four evangelists, and this is clearly artificial.

(b) According to our oldest record, the early fragment of resurrection preaching quoted by St. Paul at 1 Cor. $15^{3ff.}$, Peter was the recipient of the first resurrection appearance (cp. also Lk 24^{34}).

(c) The significance of the name already borne by him during the ministry of Jesus, and his privileged position with regard to the Easter message, together make it probable that Acts is correct in depicting Peter as the original leader of the Christian community in Jerusalem.

(d) At some stage James, the Lord's brother, assumed sole charge of the Jerusalem church, and Peter seems to have undertaken responsibility for the Christian mission to Jews of the Dispersion. Which of these developments was cause and which effect, and to what extent they involved conflict within the Church, we have no clear means of telling; but in any case Peter is found practising an itinerant ministry which took him to the Mediterranean coast (Acts 10), to Antioch (Gal. 2[11]), possibly to Corinth (1 Cor. 1[12]), and ultimately to Rome.

(e) Though he was neither the apostolic founder of the church at Rome, nor its first bishop (the evidence seems to suggest that the Roman church was not in fact monepiscopal until some way into the second century),[1] there is no need to doubt that Peter, like Paul, found his way there, and that both died there as martyrs, probably in the Neronian persecution of A.D. 64. The veneration of the two apostles as the greatest of Rome's local martyrs is certainly early, and was in ancient times undisputed; the recent excavations under the Basilica of St. Peter have disclosed fragments of a monument of some dignity, dating from the middle of the second century, near the site of Nero's circus, though the arguments for connecting this with a first century burial have less than demonstrative weight.[2]

Acts clearly regards Rome as having superseded Jerusalem as the geographical centre of the Christian world, though it characteristically sees this as symbolized by the person of Paul rather than Peter. Other NT writings do not appear to share this attitude (Jn 21[18-23] may even tacitly contradict it), and there are no internal indications of it in Mt, though

---

[1] See Telfer, *Office of a Bishop*, pp. 55–63, 89–93.
[2] See J. M. C. Toynbee and J. B. Ward Perkins, *The Shrine of St Peter and the Vatican Excavations* (London, 1956).

16$^{18f.}$ was much later to become a key text in the argument for the Roman primacy.

What the evidence so far suggests is an original pre-eminence of Peter which was afterwards somewhat diminished in the course of the expansion of the Church, and only much later, and posthumously, recovered in association with the Roman See. Since for Mt, at the time when he wrote, there was as yet no question of the latter, what kind of significance could Peter have had for the church for which the gospel was written? Partly historical, in that his role as leader of the twelve could hardly be forgotten; partly perhaps traditional, in that Mt appears to write from the standpoint of Greek-speaking Jewish Christianity, and it was this sector of the early Church to which Peter had particularly ministered, and which would thus have looked back on him as a revered teacher. (It is even possible that the Christians of this area were exercised by the problems created by the death of the original apostles; though we cannot tell if any idea of 'succession' was envisaged, let alone in what terms.) But partly also contemporary, since in this gospel the disciples commonly stand for the Christians of the evangelist's own day. Peter is introduced as the representative of these, both as the archetypal disciple whose faith is the pattern of that demanded of all (cp. 14$^{28ff.}$), and as their spokesman (cp. 15^{15}, 16^{16}, 17^{24}, 18^{21}). There is as yet no explicit indication that the latter role has developed into a ministry *to* the Church, such as was already being exercised in Syria, not long after the gospel was written, by the monarchical bishop.

If then we are looking for a possible original 'life-situation' for the saying at 16$^{18f.}$, there is a wide range of possibilities to choose from. Among the answers suggested[3] have been the following:

(a) Though the context in which it is now found has been artificially created for it by Mt, it is nevertheless an authentic saying of the historical Jesus.

[3]There is a valuable summary of these by B. Rigaux in *Concilium*, vii. 3 (1967), 78ff.

The objection to this is not primarily the linguistic problem of finding a convincing Aramaic equivalent for 'church', which is not insuperable (see commentary ad loc.), but rather the absence of the idea of a continuing new community from the solidly attested sayings of Jesus, and the difficulty of making room for this, in whatever sense, in a gospel message so concentrated on the imminence of the coming kingdom. Cullmann[4] attempts to get round it by situating the saying at the Last Supper, where the institution of the eucharist clearly envisages some sort of continuation of the band of Jesus' disciples. This cannot be dismissed as impossible, unless the institution narrative in any recognizable form is rejected with it, but it can hardly be called a straightforward or natural solution to the problem. It means either that Peter received his name on this occasion (which is rather late on for a nickname which stuck to him universally), or that originally it conveyed something different from the meaning given to it in this saying (which *ex hypothesi* cannot be earlier than the Last Supper). And the text does not assort well with others whose association with the occasion may well be thought better founded, such as the prediction of Peter's denial.

(b) The saying comes not from the historical ministry of Jesus, but from the risen Christ, and is to be connected with the post-resurrection appearance to Peter.

If this were the case, the saying could not in the nature of things be a transcript from Peter's actual experience, but only a subsequent account of it at one or more removes. And that would put it in the category of Christian reflection on the call and role of Peter, rather than in that of promises uttered by the historical Christ, i.e., (c) rather than (a).

(c) The saying was created by the prophetic activity of the early Church, either in connection with controversy about the position of Peter during his lifetime, or with the problems raised for the Christian community by his death.

[4]*Peter*, pp. 182ff. (this book is the fullest treatment of its subject in English, but it is somewhat unrepresentative of the German-speaking scholarship from which it derives).

This again is not impossible, but does not throw much light on the background of the text, since we lack evidence for the situations postulated.

(d) There remains the possibility that the saying had no previous currency independently of Mt's gospel, but arose out of reflection on the context in Mk, and on the meaning of the name Peter in the light of OT texts with which it has associations; in other words, that it is *midrash*. A number of features both of the saying and its context support this:

(i) Even if the verse 16^{18} is taken by itself, it contains two separate references to Is. 28: the corner-stone of Is. 28^{16}, and the forces of Sheol (Hades) which threaten it at Is. $28^{15,17,18}$. Its background is thus not a motif from the common stock of biblical imagery, but a specific passage of scripture.

(ii) We know that this is an area of the OT which Mt has already drawn upon. 11^{25} (another midrashic passage) seems to take Is. 29^{14} as its starting-point, and Is. 29^{13} is quoted at 15^{8f}. The process is continued with the reference to Is. 22^{22} in 16^{19}. Isaiah seems in fact to have been Mt's special quarry for texts prefiguring the supersession of the old Israel by the Church, as Jeremiah was for prophecies of the judgement on Jerusalem.

(iii) Mt has not only inserted 16^{17-9} into a context in Mk, but has at the same time significantly altered that context. The dispute about the loaves in Mk 8^{11-21} is turned into a warning against the 'teaching of the Pharisees and Sadducees', and this is emphasized by the omission of the healing of the blind man of Bethsaida (Mk 8^{22-6}; cp. Mt's omission of the story of the widow's mite, Mk 12^{41-4}, which similarly interrupts his train of thought; see p. 186). As modified by Mt, the context of the saying at 16^{17-9} is reminiscent of the denunciation of the rulers of Israel at Is. 28^{14ff}.

See also commentary on 16^{23} for the way Mt has introduced into this context the early Christian association of the elect cornerstone of Is. 28^{16} with the stone of stumbling of Is. 8^{14}.

(iv) To regard 16^{18f} as *midrash* is not to deny it a real life-situation; in the nature of things it is likely to be the result of 'applied' rather than 'pure' exegesis (see Introduction, p. 12). The situation implied by Mt's modified context is the conflict between the Christian Church and neo-Pharisaic Judaism. The language used of the Church in this text clearly shows that it is regarded as having taken the place of the temple; this means both that the latter has been destroyed, and that the synagogue is not its rightful successor. Now it is striking that in Is. 28^{15} the rulers of Israel are said to have 'made a covenant with death, and with Sheol . . . an agreement', which has enabled them so far to avoid the 'overwhelming scourge'. This would have been very applicable to the escape of R. Johanan ben Zakkai from Jerusalem during the siege, and the terms obtained by him from the Roman authorities which ensured the continuation of organized Judaism in Palestine (see Introduction, p. 28). It may even throw light on the puzzling association of 'Pharisees and Sadducees' at 16^{1,5,11} (cp. 3^7 where they are accused of attempting to 'flee from the wrath to come'); we do not know if any Sadducees survived to make common cause with R. Johanan, but in any case the Pharisees who followed him were adopting the traditional Sadducaic policy of collaboration with the Romans. By implication, the leaders of the new Judaism are charged with having evaded the judgement that is their due, and assured that they will not escape it for long; the Christian Church alone is to survive into the age to come.

Verse 19 with its keys and its promise about binding and loosing reflects a further stage in the conflict. 23^{13} accuses the Pharisees of shutting up the kingdom of heaven, neither entering themselves nor allowing others to do so. This looks like a reference to the 'Test Benediction' (see Introduction, p. 29) which prayed for the exclusion of Christians from the age to come and became in effect a sentence of excommunication for them. Verse 19 represents the Christian reply: it is now the Church, not the synagogue, which has power to admit to the kingdom or to exclude from it.

There is thus no feature of these verses (apart from the

saying incorporated at v. 19b) that cannot be accounted for in terms of Mt's known methods of biblical exegesis. The process was not necessarily completed in a single stage; indeed, we have seen that there are at least two layers in the text as we have it. Nor is it implied that reflection on the meaning of Peter's name began no earlier than the circle round Mt, only that 16[18f.] is its end-product, not its starting point. But the conclusion, if valid, does mean that Mt's apparent interest in the figure of Peter is not really directed to his person, or his office, but to the Church for which, as the archetypal man of faith, he stands.

NOTE D. JESUS AND MARRIAGE[1]

The teaching of Jesus on marriage must be understood against the attitudes of its Jewish background. For these, *adultery* can only be committed by a woman against her husband, or by a man against the husband of the woman he has seduced; it cannot be committed by a husband against his wife. *Divorce* is not a decree awarded by a court, but action taken by a husband against his wife, within the limits laid down by the Torah at Dt. 24[1ff.] (for the dispute between the rabbis Shammai and Hillel (first century B.C.) over the scope of this, see commentary on 19[3ff.]). The purpose of the certificates of divorce was to protect the wife against a charge of adultery in the event of her remarriage.

The basis of Jesus' teaching lies in his appeal to the creation texts recorded at Mk 10[1ff.]. Though the question with which Mk introduces this can hardly be original (see Nineham ad loc.), the background to his answer is clearly the Shammai–Hillel dispute, and in it he dissociates himself from both. The

[1]On the whole subject see F. W. Beare, *The Earliest Records of Jesus* (London, 1964), pp. 191–3; G. D. Kilpatrick in *The Church and the Law of Nullity of Marriage* (London, 1955), Appendix 7, pp. 61ff.; Derrett, *LNT*, pp. 363ff.; J. Dupont, *Mariage et divorce dans l'évangile* (Bruges, 1959); A. Isaksson, *Marriage and Ministry in the New Temple* (Lund, 1965).

permission of Dt. 24^1 must be read in the light of the purpose of the original creation. The oneness of man and woman in marriage is something inherent in humanity as created by God; no man (i.e. husband) has the right to undo this.

It is just possible that the specific application which follows came not from Jesus but from the early Church, but the balance of probability is on the other side. We have seen that it was normal practice for a Jewish teacher to follow up a controversial answer addressed to opponents with a private elucidation of it delivered privately to disciples (see p. 130 above); and 1 Cor. 7 shows that a specific practical application of the new teaching on divorce was being taught, with appeal to dominical authority, even in Gentile churches from an early date. At the same time the form of it given at Mk 10$^{10ff.}$ can hardly be the original one, since it assumes the possibility of a wife divorcing her husband, provided for in Roman law but not, formally speaking^2, in Jewish. The alternative version at Mt 5^{32} more faithfully reflects the Jewish background which the original saying, if authentic, must have had. The position is here stated in terms of adultery by the wife, and her action in remarrying is, despite the hardness of the case and the certificate of divorce, firmly characterized as this. But the responsibility for the situation is placed squarely on the shoulders of the husband who sent her away; he is really the guilty party. This has the same fresh and revolutionary character as the principle it is applying; it does not explicitly challenge the assumptions of Jesus' audience about the contemporary institution of marriage, but its final effect is quietly to stand them on their head. The method is the same as in many of the dominical parables.

The most difficult feature of the version at Mt 5^{32} is the exceptive clause 'except on the ground of unchastity (*porneia*)'. For the possible meanings of *porneia* see commentary ad loc.; it is difficult to exclude adultery from them in the light of the grave view of it taken by the Torah and of the fact

^{2}On the means of redress open to Jewish wives, see Derrett, *LNT*, pp. 381–3.

that not long after the time of Christ, Jewish husbands were compelled to divorce unfaithful wives,[3] and this may have begun earlier than the period from which we have evidence. Can the clause be regarded as an integral part of the original saying? The answer to this will depend both on the view taken of its meaning and on the extent to which Jesus is regarded as an innovator capable of taking an independent line against the Judaism of his day.

(a) It is possible that, as C. R. Fielding[4] maintains, the exception is no exception at all, but a mere truism: a woman who is already an adulteress cannot be made one by the action of her husband. On this view there is no thought of a special ground for divorce, and so no conflict between the thought here attributed to Jesus, and the independence of his position on marriage. But qualifications of this sort are the mark of the legislator rather than of the prophetic voice.

(b) On the other hand, J. Dupont[5] argues strongly that the legal phrasing of the exception shows that it has been formulated in the light of Dt. 24[1]; in that case it must safeguard the Jewish husband's presumed obligation to divorce an unfaithful wife. It is rather improbable that Jesus himself, having depreciated the binding force of Dt. 24[1] in the light of the Genesis creation texts, then proceeded to readmit it by the back door; and if the *pericope adulterae* preserved at Jn 7[53]–8[11] authentically represents his real attitude, he is unlikely to have shared the general Jewish view that a wife's adultery self-evidently destroys the unity of the marriage. It is, however, only too likely that early Palestinian Christianity was less than ready to follow so radical a lead, especially if Jesus' position on divorce, as on the sabbath, was less explicitly and more enigmatically stated than our present gospel accounts make it look.

On either interpretation, therefore, the exceptive clause

[3] See Nineham, *Mark*, pp. 261f. (citing C. G. Montefiore).
[4] In Beare, pp. 192f.
[5] op. cit. pp. 86f.

is likely to have been the product of early Christian casuistry (see below) in a Jewish–Christian setting.

What, on the basis of these sayings, can be established about the attitude of Jesus to divorce?

(a) He reaffirmed the lifelong character of the marriage bond, in the order of creation, over against the implications of existing legal provisions for its termination.

(b) He condemned any initiative taken by a spouse (in a Jewish situation, the husband) to break up his marriage.

(c) Originally by implication only (as at Mt 5³², but later formulations make it explicit; see Mk 10¹¹ par., Lk 16¹⁸) he treated man and woman as on an equal footing in the marriage, both in the obligation to fidelity and in the right to a lasting relationship.

How did this revolutionary teaching fare in the new situation of the apostolic Church?

(i) St. Paul in 1 Cor. 7 strictly maintains the Lord's prohibition of divorce (vv. 10–11), but allows converts with unbelieving partners who are not prepared to accept the new situation to abandon their marriages (vv. 12–6; that this carried with it the right to remarry is not expressly stated). Paul is going on the principle that the strictness of the Christian rule can be applied only to the marriage of Christians fully understood as such; and his ruling may perhaps be seen as the germ of the later nullity principle, which looks for such defects in the original contract of marriage as would render it void *ab initio*. It is along these lines that the tradition of western Catholicism has sought relief in hard cases from the rule of absolute indissolubility.

(ii) Mt 5³² possibly and 19³ff. certainly allow an exception to the rule of indissolubility in the case of adultery by the wife. There is widespread agreement that this did not come from Jesus himself, but represents a relapse into the assumptions of surrounding Judaism. Nor, as has been shown in the commentary on 19³ff., are there any decisive grounds for thinking that it has been dictated by concern for special cases—unless the deeply-rooted Jewish feeling about conjugal infidelity, which would make it impossible to continue with a marriage, falls into this category. But pastoral considerations have certainly figured in the subsequent use of this text, both in the Christian east from patristic times, and in the reformed Churches; and in both traditions the application has gone rather beyond the case of a wife's adultery.

It is not for a commentary on the gospel text to suggest lines of further development. But it is proper to point out that the texts which have determined the Christian doctrine of marriage have come down to us from a period when marriage was more of a guaranteed institution of society, and less of a demanding personal relationship than it has become in modern times. The contemporary application of them must take into account the greater weight now laid upon the aspect of personal relationship, and be ready to ask in specific cases whether the essential conditions for this ever existed, or whether, if they did, they have irretrievably broken down. Both the directions taken by earlier Christian casuistry from NT times are thus patient of further extension.

NOTE E. THE TRIAL OF JESUS

The fixed point in the evidence about Jesus' death is that he died by crucifixion, which was a Roman penalty, and therefore his effective trial and condemnation was that before Pilate. All discussion of the problem must start from here. But at the same time all the gospel records agree that he was handed over to the Romans by the Jewish authorities after proceedings of their own. In Jn these are confined to an informal examination by Annas, the father-in-law of the high priest. Mk, followed by Mt, treats them as a formal trial, and Lk does not contradict this, though he suppresses the irregular feature of a trial in the middle of the night.[1]

[1]That Lk's version is based on independent source-material is argued or assumed by several contributors to E. Bammel (ed.), *The Trial of Jesus* (London, 1970).

On the basis of this evidence, three positions are possible:

(a) There was a Jewish trial and sentence before Jesus was handed over to the Romans.[2]

(b) There was no formal trial, but it was nevertheless the Jewish authorities who handed him over.[3]

(c) The initiative in apprehending Jesus was taken by the Romans themselves, and the shifting of responsibility for it, to the Jews which we find in the gospel accounts, was done from apologetic or polemical motives.[4]

(a) rests on the Marcan account of the trial, and this is challenged on two counts, (i) the competence of the Jewish authorities in Roman times to carry out a capital sentence awarded by their own courts, and (ii) the possibility of convening a formal meeting of the Sanhedrin in the middle of the night.

(i) Mk represents the verdict of the Sanhedrin as one of condemnation for blasphemy (though neither the saying attributed to Jesus at Mk 14[57], nor his reply to the high priest's question at 14[62] in fact amounts to blasphemy as defined in the OT or later Jewish writings (see Danby, *Mishnah*, p. 392),[5] and the authenticity of the latter saying and the original context of the former are both highly disputable). This would have carried in Jewish law the penalty of death by stoning, whereas Jesus died by crucifixion. Jn 18[31] explains the action of the Jewish authorities in referring the case to the Romans on the grounds of their own inability to inflict capital punishment; the correctness of this was challenged by J. Juster and H. Lietzmann on the basis of a number of instances including Stephen (Acts 7[57ff.]) and James the Lord's brother (Jos., *Ant.*

[2] The best defence of this is by J. Blinzler, *The Trial of Jesus* (ET Cork, 1959).
[3] This is the view of Sherwin-White, *Roman Society and Roman Law in the NT.*
[4] This is the general position of Winter, *On the Trial of Jesus.*
[5] On this, and on Jewish capital jurisdiction, see G. D. Kilpatrick, *The Trial of Jesus* (Oxford, 1953).

xx. 200 ff.), and the well-known inscription discovered in the temple area which threatened Gentile trespassers with summary execution. None of these can be regarded as conclusive for judicial procedure as opposed to lynch law, and the strictness with which the imperial power elsewhere kept capital jurisdiction in its own hands (to avoid the judicial elimination of its local supporters) is a very strong argument against its having made an exception for so unsettled a region as Judaea.[6]

There can be no absolute certainty either way. But even if it could be established that the Jewish authorities had capital jurisdiction at the time, this would not rule out the possibility that they chose not to use it in this instance. For the religious leaders of a community to invoke the *de facto* secular power as a convenient means of doing away with a figure whose popularity made it dangerous for them to proceed against him directly would hardly be without historical parallel. What would be unnecessary and indeed most unlikely on this view is that they went to the trouble of a formal trial of their own first. There are other grounds for finding this improbable.

(ii) A formal trial by the Sanhedrin in the middle of the night would have been highly irregular, difficult to mount at short notice, and in the special circumstances of the passover festival almost certainly impossible (the determined arguments of Jeremias[7] to the contrary have not met with wide acceptance). The combination of Mk's view of the proceedings and Mk's chronology of the passion (see commentary, p. 211) is thus very difficult to defend. The combination of Jn's account of them and Jn's chronology is on the other hand quite plausible, and helps to explain why the Jewish authorities were in such a hurry. For if the execution of the prisoner was to be got over before the beginning of the feast, it would have been necessary to catch the governor early, before his morning's work was finished (usually by around 10 a.m.). If the case against Jesus was to be prepared in time, the morning would

[6] So Sherwin-White, pp. 35–9.
[7] *EWJ*, pp. 41ff.

have been much too late to start work on it; hence the necessity for a nocturnal interrogation.[8]

The Johannine account is thus, in its outline at least, both coherent in itself and consistent with the general trend of the evidence (including, it would seem, the original core of the Marcan passion narrative).[9] The radical alternative, that the Romans acted on their own initiative without being put up to it by the Jewish authorities, is not so much a conclusion from positive evidence as an inference from the indubitable fact that the gospels progressively shift the responsibility for Jesus' death away from the Romans and on to the Jews. But the latter process is by no means to be dismissed as straightforward anti-Jewish propaganda. The matter which called most urgently for an explanation from Christians in the Roman world was the fact that their master had died the death of a rebel against the imperial authority. Yet to establish his innocence was hardly less embarrassing to them, since this on the face of it would imply a serious miscarriage of Roman justice. The story of Pilate's vacillations, and the overriding of his scruples by the Jewish mob, which is true neither to the probabilities of the judicial situation nor to Pilate's known character, is probably best understood as a way out of this dilemma. It is only in the final stage represented by Mt and Jn that there are clear dogmatic motives for emphasizing Jewish guilt. But the fact that the evangelists stepped up the responsibility of the Jewish authorities for what had happened is hardly sufficient to establish that they had none to start with. If the Romans suspected Jesus of being a subversive, this either means that he was one (which the most crucial pieces of evidence do not bear out; see on 5^{38ff}, 22^{15ff}), or that they were given reasons for thinking that he was—by whom? Either by their own intelligence over-reacting to episodes like the cleansing of the temple and to the prominence of the idea of the kingdom in his teaching, or by some section of Jewish opinion that had an

[8]So Sherwin-White, pp. 44–6. This tells against the Lucan account also.
[9]See Taylor, *Mark*, pp. 659, 661.

interest in getting rid of him, as the Sadducees, to whom his action in the temple was a direct challenge, certainly had, and possibly the Pharisees also (see introduction to Chap. 23). It is very doubtful whether the Romans would have risked eliminating a charismatic and popular figure in Jerusalem on the eve of the great feast without at least the connivance of the priestly authorities; indeed that either party acted unilaterally throughout is far from likely. The question outstanding is which of them initiated the action taken against Jesus.

In an area where the possibilities are as evenly balanced as this, a single piece of evidence may be enough to tip the scale. Peter's denial is placed by all four gospel accounts at night by a fire[10] in the courtyard of the high priest's house. It hardly owes these details to the composer of the original passion narrative, since it is broadly agreed that the story was originally independent of the latter, and only subsequently incorporated in it; they must therefore be regarded as integral to the episode itself. If the story is true, it confirms that there were nocturnal proceedings of some kind against Jesus in the high priest's house;[11] if these are rejected, it would seem that Peter's denial must be rejected with them, and that, as we have noted (see on 26[69ff.]), carries the further implication that the early Church invented a highly discreditable story about its leading apostle. The improbability of this is strongly in favour of an initiative from the Jewish rather than the Roman authorities.

---

[10]Mt's omission of this single detail is not significant.
[11]So Sherwin-White, pp. 45f.

INDEX

261

vows, 145, 213

wealth, dangers of, 32, 69, 76, 92f., 167, 171f.
Weiss, J., 233f.
Westcott and Hort, 178
Williams, C. S. C., 54
Wilson, R. McL., 120
Windisch, H., 73
Wink, W., 62, 139
Winter, P., 187, 220f., 253n
wisdom, 40, 79, 118, 120, 193

women, in the genealogy of Christ, 52f.; in the new order, 100; witnesses of the death and resurrection of Jesus, 225, 227-9

yetzer, 78
yoke, 122, 175f.

Zealots, 25f., 194
Zebedee, sons of, 174, 214, 225, 242
Zechariah, 75, 194, 218f.